PENGUIN

ANCIENT RHETORIC
FROM ARISTOTLE TO PHILOSTRATUS

THOMAS HABINEK is Professor of Classics at the University of Southern California. He has published extensively on Roman literature and culture, Greek and Roman rhetoric, and the afterlife of classical thought. His books include *The Politics of Latin Literature* (1998), *The World of Roman Song* (2005), *Ancient Rhetoric and Oratory* (2005), and *Cicero: On Living and Dying Well* (2011).

Ancient Rhetoric

From Aristotle to Philostratus

Translated and Edited by
THOMAS HABINEK

PENGUIN BOOKS

PENGUIN CLASSICS

UK | USA | Canada | Ireland | Australia
India | New Zealand | South Africa

Penguin Books is part of the Penguin Random House group of companies
whose addresses can be found at global.penguinrandomhouse.com.

This edition first published in Penguin Classics 2017

007

Translation and editorial material © Thomas Habinek, 2017
All rights reserved

The moral right of the editor has been asserted

Set in 10.25/12.25 pt Sabon
Typeset by Jouve (UK), Milton Keynes
Printed in Great Britain by Clays Ltd, Elcograf S.p.A.

ISBN: 978–0–141–39264–6

Contents

Chronology

427 BCE Gorgias arrives in Athens and inaugurates formal instruction in rhetoric

340–335 Aristotle, *Rhetoric*

91 Dramatic date of Cicero, *On the Orator*

86 Roman conquest of Athens, relocation of many Greek intellectuals to Rome

80s Anonymous, *Rhetoric to Herennius*

84 Cicero, *On Invention*

55 Cicero, *On the Orator*

46 Cicero, *Brutus*

44 Assassination of Julius Caesar in Rome

27 Conventional date for commencement of the Roman Principate under Augustus Caesar

30s CE Seneca the Elder, *Suasoriae* and *Controversiae*

71 Emperor Vespasian establishes first endowed chair of rhetoric at Rome, recognizing importance of rhetorical instruction throughout the Roman Empire

95 Quintilian, *Oratorical Instruction*

230s Philostratus, *Lives of the Sophists*

354 Libanius appointed to chair of rhetoric in Antioch; rhetoric continues to be taught to pagan and Christian students alike

Introduction

Classical rhetoric is one of the earliest and best-attested versions of what is today sometimes referred to as media studies. Although the ancient rhetoricians were chiefly concerned with the production and analysis of public oratory, whether in the courtroom, in the legislature or on ceremonial occasions, the techniques they developed were considered applicable to virtually all communicative systems, including the visual and plastic arts, music, writing and scientific discourse. According to the two most influential definitions from antiquity, rhetoric was either the art of finding in any given context the most effective means of persuasion or the art of speaking well, with 'well' implying the moral, logical, pragmatic and aesthetic aspects of communication. Rhetoric considered – and fostered – the interplay between artist, audience and message in specific contexts.

Rhetoric came into being as a technical discourse due to the high value placed on oral communication, persuasion and deliberation in the emerging city-states of the ancient Mediterranean world. New frameworks for collective decision-making, as well as the substitution of formal legal procedures for violent conflict resolution, required participants who could clearly articulate issues for others and move members of an audience to decisive action, even when their individual or family well-being was not at stake. In addition, the expansion of political and cultural communities beyond kinship networks, and the persistence of such communities over time, required the articulation of unifying ideals and cultural memories through formal procedures of praise, blame and recollection, responsibility for which gradually passed from priests and poets to orators and statesmen.

The earliest teachers of rhetoric built their instructional system on the successful strategies of communication they encountered in the practice of speakers and writers in their midst. In turn, the training they provided generated certain expectations among the informed members of political, judicial and ceremonial audiences. The teachers of rhetoric thus created a kind of feedback loop whereby the more effectively they taught, the greater the need for their continued instruction. As a result, the production of guidebooks for students of rhetoric took on something of a life of its own, starting (probably) in the late fifth century BCE and continuing through and beyond the end of classical antiquity. No two handbooks of rhetoric contained exactly the same set of guidelines, as writers sought to differentiate themselves from their rivals and predecessors without straying too far from standard topics and approaches.

The present volume attempts to recreate an idealized version of classical rhetoric through direct quotation of the leading ancient authors on the subject without giving pride of place to any one text or approach. Treatises translated here include works originally written in Greek as well as Latin, dating from the fourth century BCE to the third century CE. The reader will note occasional differences in definitions of terms or handling of topics between one author and another. Inclusion of such variation is intentional, as it conveys a sense of the fluid and sometimes controversial nature of rhetorical instruction. The works presented here also vary in historical context and in the type of oratory they refer to, from the deliberative speeches of the Athenian democracy, to the judicial orations that played a key role in the political and legal system of the Roman Republic, to the display speeches of the so-called sophists who travelled from city to city during the heyday of the Roman Empire. The adaptability of classical rhetoric to changing political and social circumstances in the ancient world anticipates its continued revival and reuse in the centuries after the end of antiquity.

The selections translated in this volume are organized not in chronological order of composition, but according to the logic of instruction that characterized ancient training in rhetoric: first, an exhortation to the study of the field, followed by a set of possible definitions; an overview of the system; and separate sections on what came to be the five canonical tasks of the orator (invention, arrangement, style, memory and delivery). At this point, the ancient model is set aside, and three additional sections address aspects of classical rhetoric that cut across the ancient divisions but have proven to be of interest to subsequent students. These include a brief section on the underlying model of human cognition that informs a great deal of rhetorical teaching, especially on the part of Roman authors; a lengthier section on the theory and practice of ornamentation, or the reworking of the raw material of language to make it more impressive (a subject of great interest to theorists of other arts besides public speaking); and a set of readings that illustrate the lived experience of the ancient orator – from childhood education, through a career in the forum and beyond. Indeed, one of the most compelling reasons for studying classical rhetoric is the insight it provides into the daily lives and social interactions of the educated citizens of ancient communities. Although at times it must have seemed like an austere or forbidding subject, rhetoric was the lifeblood of ancient politics, law and administration, a shared discourse that enabled communication across boundaries of ethnicity, status and ideology. The rhetoricians and orators presented in this volume include political outsiders who rose to high office, distinguished professors and anonymous schoolteachers, natives of mainland Greece and Italy as well as Gaul (modern France), Spain, Asia Minor (modern Turkey) and Rhodes. A larger volume could easily have included material from North Africa, Syria and Britain.

Of the treatises that are excerpted at length in this volume, the earliest in date is Aristotle's *Rhetoric*. Aristotle (384–322 BCE) was an important Greek philosopher, the student and successor of Plato and founder of a programme of scientific research and instruction that encompassed biology, physics, zoology and meteorology, as well as politics, psychology, ethics, logic and literature. He was born in Stagira, in northern Greece, relocated to and spent much of his life in Athens, which was the centre of Greek intellectual activity, but was eventually recruited to the court of Macedon by King Philip to serve as mentor to his son, the future Alexander the Great. Although his political writings treat the achievements of the Athenian democracy respectfully, they have a consistently conservative tone and show a preference for orderly leadership on the part of the propertied sectors of society. Returning to Athens after Alexander succeeded to the Macedonian throne and embarked on his career of conquest, Aristotle resumed teaching and research there, only to depart suddenly, shortly after the untimely death of his patron.

The *Rhetoric* of Aristotle is a three-volume treatise, which Aristotle regarded as an extension of his work on politics. Like all surviving works of Aristotle, it seems to consist of detailed notes assembled by the philosopher himself or his students for use within expert circles. It lacks stylistic polish and contains numerous digressions, corrections-in-stride and internal summaries. It treats some issues in great detail and passes over others with barely a mention. Despite its analytical form, it contains many decidedly evaluative pronouncements. For all that, it is an invaluable work for two reasons. First, it introduces clear and distinct terminology for various aspects of rhetoric, such as *ethos*, *pathos* and *logos* (persuasion via character, emotion and reasoning, respectively), enthymeme (formal argument concerning probable truths) and the typology of speeches as judicial (pertaining to trials), deliberative (arguments for or against a course of action) or epideictic (speeches of praise and blame). Second, it places special emphasis on deliberative oratory, in other words the speeches made in assemblies or other political gatherings concerning public policy. Aristotle thus takes for granted the political value of free yet orderly deliberation aimed at persuading a decision-making body of the advantages of one or another course of action. He seeks to establish a framework for reasoned debate in which all participants inform themselves about the issue under discussion.

Next in order historically is the anonymous Latin treatise called the *Rhetoric to Herennius*. Probably composed in the 80s BCE for a burgeoning audience of politically ambitious Roman and Italian youths, the treatise seems to hew closely to the form and style of Hellenistic Greek manuals. It is both more concise and more detailed than Aristotle in its coverage of the mechanics of speech-making and the preparatory exercises to be undertaken by the student of rhetoric. If Aristotle provides a systematic overview of the discipline of rhetoric, the author of the treatise to Herennius shows how to put it into practice on a step-by-step basis, providing numerous examples along the way. In this volume, the *Rhetoric to Herennius* is used as the primary source for instruction in the identification of issues, for a long list of figures of thought and figures of speech that contribute to the enrichment of a speaker's style and for one of the memory-systems used to help orators deliver speeches with a minimum of prompting.

The numerous examples contained in the treatise, most of which were composed by the author for instructional purposes, with many alluding to episodes in Roman history of the generation just preceding his, give an insider's view both of the day-to-day types of cases and personalities one might encounter in Roman public life and of the effective use of rhetorical speech at moments of high controversy and crisis. The author seems at least mildly sympathetic to the political programme of the reform wing of the Roman elite, figures like the brothers Gracchi and Saturninus, who sought the empowerment of the popular assemblies (at the expense of the senate) and repeatedly proposed land reform as a solution to Roman Italy's acute economic and demographic problems. Indeed, the use of rhetoric by newcomers and reformists at Rome partly accounts for the low regard in which teachers of rhetoric were viewed, at least during some periods of Roman history.

Apart from their political significance, the examples provided by the anonymous author also provide rare access to a Roman listener's or reader's likely reaction to various devices found in Latin literature, whether poetry or prose. By telling his students the goals they can achieve by using, for example, metaphor or rhetorical question or unusual word order, the author is also helping the modern reader understand how Romans might have reacted to their use by others. The ease with which this author, like others who appear in this volume, moves between examples from prose and examples from poetry gives a sense of the ways in which rhetoric informed literary composition of every sort.

The composition of the *Rhetoric to Herennius* probably took place during the young adulthood of the most famous of all Roman orators, Marcus Tullius Cicero (106–43 BCE). In addition to his many speeches, which earned him fame and political power during his lifetime, Cicero composed philosophical dialogues, letters, epic poetry (mostly lost) and several treatises on rhetoric, including a technical handbook, *On Invention* (which he says he wrote while a young man), a more reflective dialogue, *On the Orator*, and a memoir of famous Roman orators called *Brutus* (after its dedicatee), all of which are featured in this volume. Cicero was born in the small town of Arpinum to a family that was locally prominent but had few significant connections in Rome. His early success as a courtroom pleader propelled him up the political ladder and he attained the highest magistracy, that of consul, in 63 BCE, at the youngest age legally allowable. As was customary for ex-consuls, Cicero remained actively involved in political, legal and cultural affairs at Rome, until the rise of the First Triumvirate, an informal power-sharing arrangement between Pompey, Julius Caesar and Crassus starting in 59 BCE, led to his temporary withdrawal from politics and the forum. During this period he maintained a public profile in part by writing treatises, including the magisterial work *On the Orator*, which considered the significance of rhetoric and oratory to the smooth functioning of the Roman Republic and explored the cultural and moral obligations of public speakers. Cicero soon returned to public life, only to retreat again during the dictatorship of Julius Caesar (48–44 BCE), once again remaining engaged with Roman affairs by writing philosophical and rhetorical treatises, including the *Brutus* (46 BCE), which integrates a narrative history of Roman oratory into an elegiac lament over its prospects under dictatorship. Cicero's final return to public life after the assassination of Julius Caesar included a series of speeches aimed at Caesar's successor, Mark Antony, which led to his execution by Antony's soldiers in 43 BCE.

In the present volume, a selection from Cicero's work *On Invention* serves to introduce principles of rhetorical disposition or arrangement. This is one of the most straightforward branches of rhetoric, since it involves breaking a speech down into its component parts and adopting the gestures, language and persuasive techniques appropriate to each. *On the Orator* is the source for three sections of this volume: Why Study Rhetoric?, Rhetoric and Cognition and Rhetorical Ornament. The work as a whole purports to record a conversation held among leading Romans in 91 BCE, shortly before the Roman world was convulsed by a series of civil conflicts, political assassinations and proscriptions that claimed the lives of a number of the figures represented in the dialogue. Cicero's presentation of his characters' commitment to the cohesive power of eloquence gains emotional force from his readers' awareness of the consequences that follow on the collapse of institutions that guarantee reasoned deliberation.

The primary speaker in Cicero's *On the Orator* is Crassus, who argues for the unity of wisdom and eloquence and presents the ideal orator as a kind of culture hero who deploys all the diverse knowledge available in Roman society of the time. In contrast, Antonius expresses scepticism about the importance of technical training in rhetoric and the ability of any human being to master the curriculum advanced by Crassus. Their discussion, which draws in a number of interlocutors, is less a sharp debate than a shared deliberation in which each prompts the other to refine, restate or further develop his position. The participants enact, in the context of a friendly discussion, the very principles of rhetorical discourse they jointly develop. Both main speakers draw heavily on the learning embedded in Greek rhetorical handbooks, but present it gracefully, and without the sometimes hectoring tone found in textbooks. Crassus' discussion of ornament, in particular, integrates a detailed discussion of rhetorical devices and prose rhythms into a call for a refined or polished approach to life as well as language. It is perhaps no wonder that the discovery of the full manuscript of *On the Orator* (*De Oratore*) in Italy in 1421 was treated as a watershed event by European humanists, who interpreted the treatise as advancing both a theory of artistic style and a model of civilized discourse.

From *Brutus* we derive Cicero's retrospective account of his own developing career as an orator, and in particular his rivalry with the slightly older orator Hortensius, who had died a few years before the composition of the treatise. As in *On the Orator*, Cicero tries to show how political, temperamental and stylistic differences can mask an underlying shared commitment to the principle of ethically responsible communication. The treatise also presents a genealogy of rhetorical achievement, with each generation learning from its predecessors and providing inspiration and examples for its successors. In Cicero's account, rhetoric becomes not just a tool for addressing pressing contemporary issues, but also an honourable way of life to be passed down from one generation to the next, as he now seeks to pass the torch to Brutus.

Despite the political rupture at the end of the republic that Cicero feared would leave eloquence bereft, his own achievements as orator, statesman and writer served as inspiration and point of reference in the schools of rhetoric that proliferated under the Roman Empire. His political choices were debated, his fate lamented, his style held up for inspection and, generally speaking, admiration. Among his most ardent admirers was the first tenant of an endowed chair of rhetoric at Rome, Marcus Fabius Quintilianus, i.e. Quintilian (*c.*35–100 CE). Quintilian's life is not as well documented as that of Cicero, but he seems to have had a successful career as an orator and an instructor prior to the composition of his magnum opus, *Oratorical Instruction*. Aimed chiefly at his fellow instructors, Quintilian's treatise describes the formation and career of an orator from infancy to retirement. Naturally he covers much of the same ground as Aristotle, the author of the *Rhetoric to Herennius* and Cicero, but he adds to their treatment a rich discussion of what actually happened in the rhetorical classroom and in the law-courts based on personal experience and observation. Quintilian understands the ideal orator to be a kind of Roman sage (*Romanus sapiens*), that is, a person who combines deep knowledge and wisdom with an ability to speak well and effectively in a variety of situations. Reading his treatise helps the modern reader to see how and why rhetoric was the favoured form of education among the elite and upwardly mobile sectors of the Roman citizenry. He can be respected as one of the first and most eloquent proponents of the view that a liberal arts education prepares the student not just for a career, but also for full participation in civic and cultural life, and, in Quintilian's view, for full realization of one's highest potential as a human being.

In recognition of the distinctive contributions of Quintilian's treatise, the selections drawn from it here include his discussion of the multiple possible definitions of rhetoric, his account of the exercises used to prepare young boys for rhetorical training, his rejection of the memory-system proposed in the *Rhetoric to Herennius* and numerous anecdotes (some quite humorous) about misguided attempts to summon listeners' emotions, or bizarre uses of gestures and vocal effects. While several of the other treatises illustrate the intersection of public oratory and political ideology, Quintilian puts us in the shoes of the anxious orator trying to make his case in the presence of rivals, judges and critics. He also provides ample evidence of the continuing vitality of rhetoric and oratory under the Roman emperors. Although politically charged public trials of the sort that characterized the career of Cicero had largely come to an end, and debate in the senate was to varying degrees constrained by the presence of the emperor or his agents, the day-to-day activities of trying cases and discussing policy continued, providing outlets for rhetorical talent and training. In addition, the type of education described by Quintilian seems likely to have been beneficial to Roman officials at various levels of administration, since it taught students how to consider opposing perspectives, evaluate evidence and develop and analyse arguments. For all of his emphasis on the practice of speech-making, Quintilian shares the understanding of rhetoric as a type of intellectual formation that characterizes the approach of Aristotle and Cicero as well.

The final treatise drawn upon in this volume is the collection of *Lives of the Sophists* by Lucius Flavius Philostratus (*c.*170–*c.*250 CE). Philostratus was a Greek intellectual who seems to have achieved some prominence in the imperial court at Rome, possibly as part of the circle around the empress Julia Domna. His account of famous travelling intellectuals, called sophists, from the fifth century BCE down to his own lifetime, serves as a kind of justification for his own intellectual status, in addition to commemorating the achievements of a group of men who often served as ambassadors of Greek communities to one another, and eventually to Rome. Although there has been much debate, in antiquity and among modern scholars, over the precise meaning of the term 'sophist', the individuals described by Philostratus share a common ability to speak fluently and intelligently before large audiences on a wide array of topics, often with little or no time for preparation. Sophists of the sort described by Philostratus didn't replace the practitioners in the law-courts or political assemblies – and indeed they frequently participated in such activities as well – but their biographies illustrate the use of oratory as a form of display and even entertainment. While the speeches they delivered in praise of one city or another or offering advice to figures from the distant historical past may seem of little value in a strictly practical sense, they served to foster both local and cosmopolitan identities in the multi-ethnic context of the Roman Empire. Indeed among the most striking stories told of the sophists are those in which they are said to delight even listeners who could not understand what they were saying. With the sophists, rhetoric seemed to have found a way to liberate language from meaning.

In line with Cicero's insistence that the serious orator needed a broad understanding of a wide range of issues and disciplines, classical rhetoric as a field, viewed synoptically, can be seen to encompass not just language, literature and other communicative systems, but also politics, psychology, law, history, aesthetics and child development. In at least one glaring respect, however, it was not the universalizing discourse it purported to be: rhetoric and oratory in the ancient world were almost exclusively the reserve of men. None of the rhetoricians presented here or cited within these texts are female, and references to female orators are few and far between in the ancient record. This is perhaps more puzzling than it might seem, since we do hear of female participation in philosophical training and female attendance at literary recitations, and the work of a small but significant number of female poets either survives or is explicitly mentioned by ancient sources. Girls also had access to elementary instruction in language and literature, in at least some contexts.

The exclusion of women from the world of the rhetoricians, which corresponds to their exclusion from political office and legal practice, may be due in part to the implicit understanding throughout much of antiquity that political and legal speech is a privilege granted in exchange for men's availability to serve in the military. Rhetoric is often paired with military achievement as a contributor to a society's well-being, as in the opening of Cicero's treatise *On the Orator*; and the terminology used to describe courtroom procedures, in both Greek and Latin, echoes the language of aggressive physical confrontation. Indeed, it is precisely during the periods when upper-class men were freed from military obligations that rhetoric was put to uses that had little to do with the day-to-day management of civic affairs. To some extent, the quest for glory on the battlefield had been replaced by the competition for prizes in the school of declamation.

A final issue that has plagued the history of rhetoric is its alleged competition with philosophy for pre-eminence among the disciplines. Initially the quarrel between rhetoric and philosophy was a professional dispute as to who would inherit the traditional role of poets and priests as educators of succeeding generations. The discussion between the philosopher Socrates and rhetorician Gorgias in Plato's *Gorgias* can be read as an attempt to negotiate the boundaries between the two fields (or, as Quintilian would have it, an assertion of the value of *true* rhetoric).

In time, however, it became clear that philosophy and rhetoric were, by and large, dealing with fundamentally different models of human thought and communication. Whereas philosophers like Plato emphasized the autonomous thinker's observation and use of external reality to arrive at abstract truths and decontextualized knowledge, rhetoricians generally understood human thought to be embodied (hence the emphasis on emotions, gesture, delivery) and interactive or distributed (hence the significance of writing and memory-systems, as well as the deep respect for knowledge attained through shared discussion and deliberation). To be sure, there were forays from one camp into the other. For example, Aristotle, in his philosophical rhetoric, seeks to strip rhetoric of some of its embodied and interactive tendencies and to attribute special significance to rhetorical arguments or enthymemes that are, in his view, to be modelled on logical syllogisms. Moving in the opposite direction, the Stoic philosophers, with their account of the continuity of brain, body and environment and of the physicality of all actions, including thinking, perceiving and speaking, provided a philosophical foundation for the teachings of rhetoricians like Cicero's speaker Crassus in *On the Orator*, or Quintilian, who, in *Oratorical Instruction*, explicitly derives his definition of rhetoric from the Stoics. Although the approach to thought as internalized and autonomous has tended to dominate academic discussion at least since the Enlightenment, many cognitive scientists have begun to return to an understanding of cognition as variously embodied, externalized and distributed. Whether such a shift in our understanding of cognition will lead to a revival of interest in rhetoric remains to be seen.

In the meantime we can appreciate classical rhetoric for its historical significance, its political idealism, its insights concerning human motivation and its precise analysis of techniques of persuasion that continue to be valid. The selections that follow have been chosen to illustrate all of these aspects of ancient rhetoric, in both theory and practice, and, hopefully, to provide a foundation for the continuing use of classical rhetoric today.

Further Reading

For an introduction to the social significance of classical rhetoric and oratory, see Thomas Habinek, *Ancient Rhetoric and Oratory* (Malden, MA: Blackwell, 2005). Laurent Pernot, *Rhetoric in Antiquity*, trans. W. E. Higgins (Washington, DC: The Catholic University of America Press, 2005), provides a historical narrative of the key moments in the development of rhetorical theory and practice. Indispensable for studying the use of rhetorical techniques in ancient and later literature is Heinrich Lausberg, *Handbook of Literary Rhetoric*, trans. D. E. Orton and R. D. Anderson (Leiden: Brill, 1998). Lausberg also helps the reader find his or her way through the competing yet overlapping systems of terminology adopted by different rhetoricians. Essays touching on many of the topics treated in this volume can be found in the *Oxford Handbook of Rhetorical Studies*, ed. Michael MacDonald (Oxford: Oxford University Press, 2017).

Translations of the major ancient treatises on rhetoric, with facing Greek and Latin texts, can be found among the volumes of the Loeb Classical Library, published by Harvard University Press. Numerous studies of Aristotle, Cicero and Philostratus are available, including George Kennedy (trans. and ed.), *Aristotle on Rhetoric: A Theory of Civic Discourse* (Oxford: Oxford University Press, 2007); Elaine Fantham, *The Roman World of Cicero's De Oratore* (Oxford: Oxford University Press, 2004); Maud Gleason, *Making Men: Sophists and Self-Presentation in Ancient Rome* (Princeton: Princeton University Press, 1995); and *Philostratus* (Greek Culture in the Roman World), ed. Ewen Bowie and Jaś Elsner (Cambridge: Cambridge University Press, 2009).

English-language scholarship on the *Rhetoric to Herennius* and on Quintilian is less well developed, apart from the volumes in the Loeb Classical Library. Ancient declamation is the subject of an important work by Erik Gunderson, *Declamation, Paternity, and Roman Identity: Authority and the Rhetorical Self* (Cambridge: Cambridge University Press, 2003). The political value of ancient rhetoric is the subject of Josiah Ober, *Mass and Elite in Democratic Athens: Rhetoric, Ideology, and the Power of the People* (Princeton: Princeton University Press, 1989). W. M. Bloomer, *The School of Rome: Latin Studies and the Origins of Liberal Education* (Berkeley and Los Angeles: University of California Press, 2011) considers the educational function of rhetorical training in and beyond antiquity, while Raffaella Cribiore, *Gymnastics of the Mind: Greek Education in Hellenistic and Roman Egypt* (Princeton: Princeton University Press, 2005) examines papyrological and other evidence for rhetorical training in Egypt under the Greeks and Romans.

ANCIENT RHETORIC
FROM ARISTOTLE TO
PHILOSTRATUS

WHY STUDY RHETORIC?

It was common for treatises on technical subjects to begin with a description of the benefits to be acquired from careful study of the subsequent material. In the opening pages of his dialogue On the Orator, *the great Roman orator Cicero interweaves a justification for the study of rhetoric with reflections on the current state of affairs at Rome. In his view, rhetoric provides a generalized framework for rational deliberation and conflict resolution that is as useful to the well-being of a society as military prowess. He, along with the primary speaker in the dialogue, Crassus, insists on the comprehensive nature of the challenge facing the orator, and thus on the breadth of education required of him. For Cicero, as for Crassus, philosophy is but one manifestation of the human capacity for rational thought and communication, and thus a component of rhetorical education rather than a replacement for it. Like the fictionalized speakers in his dialogue, Cicero voices respect for the technical expertise of Greek teachers of rhetoric, but suggests that just as Roman power has eclipsed Greek, so Roman eloquence should surpass the standard set by Greek. He seeks to redirect the Roman drive for glory to cultural as opposed to military or narrowly political achievements.*

Cicero
On the Orator
1.1–23, 30–34, 45–54, 64–5

Whenever I reflect on the past, brother Quintus,[1] it seems to me that the men who enjoyed political office and renown for achievement during the heyday of the republic were truly blessed, inasmuch as they could maintain as a course of life either risk-free engagement in affairs or dignified retirement. That's how it was when I decided that it would be appropriate – and meet with general approval – for me to begin to relax and to turn my attention to our shared intellectual interests, once the infinite labour of the courts and the demands of political life had come to a standstill, thanks to my stepping down from office and the advance of age. But the gravity of public affairs as well as the variability of my personal situation betrayed my hopes and plans. The very place[2] that seemed as though it would be most peaceful and tranquil became the site of the greatest heaps of trouble and the most violent disturbances. Although we desired and prayed for the benefits of peace, no opportunity arose for jointly practising and honouring the arts to which we had been devoted from boyhood.

For the present upheaval had begun already when we were young, and during my consulship[3] I plunged into a struggle that would decide everything, and all of my time since then I have spent in keeping the waves that flooded in against me from destroying the community as a whole. Nevertheless, despite my difficult circumstances and the constraints on my time, I will commit myself to our studies, and whatever leisure the duplicity of enemies, the legal troubles of friends and the affairs of state will allow, I will dedicate first and foremost to writing. I won't fail you, my brother, whether you urge or ask, for no one has a greater claim on my obedience or my affection.

My aim is to bring to life a set of memories that has never been recounted in sufficient detail but can satisfy your request to learn what the most celebrated and eloquent men believed concerning every aspect of eloquence. As you have often told me, the teachings available to our young people in Latin handbooks are sketchy and underdeveloped, not at all up to date or suited to the practice I've developed in my many orations; and so you would like me to publish something more polished and complete. What's more, you often disagree with me in our discussions of rhetoric, because I insist that eloquence is dependent on highly developed artistic training, while you think it derives from something other than careful instruction and is instead to be identified with a kind of inborn genius supplemented by experience.

For my part, whenever I look for role models of great talent and distinction, I find myself wondering why there are more who are worthy of admiration in every field of endeavour other than eloquence. Wherever you direct your attention, you will see numerous men who excel in each type of art, even the most demanding.

Who wouldn't rank the general ahead of the orator when measuring the utility or the prestige of prominent men's practical knowledge? Who could deny that from our city alone it's possible to present an almost infinite number of outstanding military leaders, but hardly any who excel at public speaking? In our own day there are many who are capable of ruling and guiding the republic, thanks to their good sense and practical wisdom; in the generations of our parents and ancestors even more such men existed. But for long stretches of time, no good orators, and scarcely a decent one per generation, are to be found. And should someone happen to suggest that rhetoric is better compared with disciplines treated in recondite handbooks and various types of writing than with the glorious feats of a general or the shrewd advice of a good senator, let him stop and consider just who and how many excelled in those other disciplines. He'll quickly acknowledge the relative paucity of orators past and present.

Surely you're aware that the most erudite thinkers consider philosophy, as the Greeks call it, to be creator or parent of all the honourable arts. It's difficult to list all the men of great knowledge and great diversity of approach who have either developed individual topics of philosophical inquiry or covered everything they could in their pursuit of knowledge and methodical discussions. Who isn't familiar with the puzzling topics and diverse subtle methods that occupy the mathematicians? Has anyone devoted himself to music or to the literary studies professed by so-called grammatici[4] without grasping the all-but infinite force and power of those disciplines? I think it would be fair to insist that of all the liberal arts and sciences, poetry and oratory have the smallest number of distinguished practitioners. And of this group, in which true excellence is extremely rare, if you examine the combined lists of Romans and Greeks, far fewer orators than good poets will be found.

This situation is even more remarkable in that the other disciplines have hidden, esoteric sources, whereas rhetoric derives entirely from common experience and concerns the human capacity for verbal communication. In all other arts, excellence requires a departure from the knowledge and sentiment of non-experts; in oratory, however, the greatest vice is to disdain conventional language and ordinary feelings. What's more, it's not possible to claim that there are more students of the other arts and sciences, or that they are motivated by greater pleasure or higher hopes or the prospect of more generous rewards. To pass over Greece, which has always asserted its leadership in eloquence, and in particular Athens, which discovered all the principles through which the power of speech has been discovered and perfected, in this city of ours, no pursuit has ever flourished as vigorously as the pursuit of eloquence.

After our universal empire had been established and the regularity of peace had secured opportunities for leisure, no ambitious young man failed to devote himself entirely to public speaking. At first, being ignorant of the whole discipline, thinking there was no point in practice and nothing artistic to be learned, they accomplished as much as they could through native wit and imagination. Later, when they had listened to Greek orators, become familiar with their writings and employed Greek instructors, our predecessors burned with eagerness to learn.

The grandeur and complexity of the subject excited them, as did the numerous types of cases to which it could be applied, so that whatever type of instruction each pursued was supplemented with frequent practice, which is more valuable than the precepts of any teacher. There were then, as now, extraordinary rewards set forth for this endeavour, in influence, wealth and political advancement. The inborn talent of our people, as we can infer from numerous examples, surpassed by far that of every other nation. All of which being the case, who wouldn't be surprised to discover that so few orators are recorded in tradition, regardless of the era or political situation?

Truly, rhetoric is a greater subject than people are inclined to believe, having been assembled out of a greater number of arts and disciplines. What other reason can one give for the huge number of students, the extraordinary supply of teachers, the outstanding talents of practitioners, the infinite variety of cases and the generous rewards assigned to eloquence except the unbelievable grandeur and difficulty of the subject?

For there must be secure knowledge of countless matters, without which the flow of words is empty and ridiculous; and language disciplined by both the choice and the arrangement of words; and every emotion that nature has assigned to human beings must be understood thoroughly, because the force and method of rhetoric are necessarily directed at settling or exciting the minds of the audience; and there must be a certain charm and wit and erudition as suits a free person and both speed and brevity in responding and attacking joined with urbanity and grace. All of prior history, especially compelling examples, must be kept in mind; nor can knowledge of law and civil procedure be neglected.

Must I really go on to speak about delivery? It must be tempered by movement of the body, gesture, facial expression, tone and variety of enunciation. Its magnitude is evident even from the less serious art of actors and the stage: although everyone strives for moderation of face and voice and movement, just think how few there are and have been whom we can bear to watch without irritation. And what of memory, the treasure house of everything? Without it as guardian, everything discovered or invented by the speaker, no matter how outstanding, will come to nothing.

And so, let us cease to pursue an explanation for the paucity of good speakers, now that we understand that eloquence depends upon a universe of attainments, each of which it would be a major effort to recount in detail. Instead, let us encourage our children and everyone else whose glory and dignity are dear to us to embrace the greatness of the subject, trusting that they can acquire what they seek if not through the precepts, teachers and exercises that everyone employs, then certainly through other means.

In my opinion, no one deserves the title of orator unless he has attained knowledge of all topics and disciplines. Oratory must arise and proceed from understanding of the matter at hand. Unless the orator knows his subject, he gives an empty and childish speech. To be sure, I won't place such a heavy burden, least of all on our orators, who are greatly involved in the life of the city, that I forbid them from being ignorant of anything at all. Still, the power of the orator and his profession of eloquence would seem to require that he speak fully and formally about every topic placed before him.

No doubt this challenge seems immense, even infinite, to most people. I also recognize that intelligent and knowledgeable Greeks, including some with abundant opportunity for study, have divvied up the art of speaking and, rather than elaborating every aspect, have isolated the type of speaking practised in court and in deliberations and reserved it alone for the orator. In these books of mine I won't cover more than what has been assigned to this category after careful inquiry and much discussion, according to the consensus of the leading authorities. I'll be seeking not a list of specific precepts based on our training in early boyhood, but the teachings I believe were presented by our most eloquent predecessors, and in a manner befitting their high status. Which isn't to say that I look down on the work of Greek writers and teachers. Still, such instruction is readily available to all and can't be presented more ornately or expressed more precisely in a translation of mine. You will forgive me, then, dear brother, for granting more authority to those considered eloquent by Romans than to Greeks.

Cicero then explains the setting and context for the dialogue to follow, placing it in 91 BCE at the Tusculan estate of the former consul Lucius Licinius Crassus. He specifies the other main characters, including Marcus Antonius, Quintus Mucius Scaevola and Quintus Lutatius Catulus, all former consuls, Catulus' half brother Gaius Julius Caesar Strabo Vopiscus, and two rising politicians of a younger generation, Gaius Aurelius Cotta and Publius Sulpicius Rufus. The alert Roman reader of Cicero's day would have understood that the year 91 BCE represented an uneasy kind of calm before the storm of civil disorder that would soon break out. Crassus would die later that year, and four of the other interlocutors would perish not long thereafter in political violence. Here at Tusculum, however, the speakers take time to engage in a vigorous but friendly discussion of the nature and function of oratory, and the best means for attaining eloquence.

[Crassus][5] began by noting that Sulpicius and Cotta seemed deserving of praise rather than advice because they had already achieved a competency in public speaking unequalled by their peers and comparable to that of their elders.

'There's nothing more remarkable,' he said, 'than to be able, by speaking, to retain the attention of assemblies, entice men's minds, and direct their wills in whatever direction you wish. This one activity has always flourished and always been pre-eminent among every free population and especially in calm and peaceful societies.

'For what is more remarkable than the ability of one man, either alone or with a very few others, to exercise effectively a natural capacity given by nature to all? What is more appealing to ear and mind than a speech enriched with wise opinions and impressive language? What so powerful or impressive as the ability of a single man to affect the emotions of the people, the scruples of the judges, the sober deliberation of the senate, all by means of a speech? What so kingly, so befitting a free person, so generous as bringing aid to suppliants, reviving the afflicted, securing an acquittal, freeing from danger, preserving the rights of citizens? And what so essential as to possess the weapons with which to protect yourself or safely accuse others or when injured attain revenge! But you needn't always be thinking about the forum, the benches, the speakers' platform or the senate-house. What could be more enjoyable while at leisure or more appropriate for a cultured person than conversation that is witty and not at all unpolished? After all, our greatest advantage over wild animals is our ability to converse among ourselves and to express our thoughts in speech.

'Who then would not rightly marvel at this ability and consider it especially worth developing in order to surpass other human beings as much as human beings surpass beasts? To come at last to the most important point, what else could have gathered scattered people into a single locale or led them from a wild and rugged way of living to our present state of civilization or supplied settled communities with laws, courts and rights?

'And so as not to pursue further the almost innumerable advantages, I will sum up briefly: it is my conviction that the guidance and wisdom of the ideal orator is the basis not only of his own dignity but also of the well-being of the great majority of private citizens and of the state as a whole.'

Scaevola responds to Crassus, arguing that the latter has granted too much power to eloquence and made the task of the orator greater than it really is. He implicitly differentiates eloquence from wisdom and points to instances in which excellent speakers have persuaded others to engage in misguided or immoral actions. But Crassus is not convinced.

To which Crassus replied:

'I am well aware, Scaevola,[6] that the Greeks routinely discuss and debate such matters. For I heard the most distinguished men, when as quaestor I had come to Athens from Macedonia, while the Academy was at its best, as people often said, when Charmadas and Clitomachus and Aeschines were in charge.[7] There was also a certain Metrodorus, who along with the others had diligently attended the lectures of Carneades, a man, it was said, who was the most keen and expansive speaker; Mnesarchus as well, who had studied with that Panaetius of yours, was in his prime; so too Diodorus, student of the Peripatetic Critolaus.[8] And there were many other princes and nobles of philosophy who sought as if with a single voice to drive the orator from governance, to deny that he had any learning or knowledge of important matters and to banish him to lawcourts and unimportant assemblies as if to a mill.

'But I didn't agree with them or with Plato, who invented such arguments and was himself by far the most serious and eloquent speaker. I read his *Gorgias*[9] very carefully with Charmadas while I was in Athens and was especially surprised that in making fun of orators Plato himself appeared to be an orator of the best sort. For controversy over a word has long tormented Greeks, who are fonder of dispute than of truth.

'Why, even if the term "orator" is restricted to one who has the ability to speak resourcefully in the courts or before the people or in the senate, it's still necessary to attribute a great deal to such a person. He can't handle such responsibilities capably without a great deal of experience in public affairs of every sort, without knowledge of regulations, customs and law, and without understanding the nature and habits of human beings. But if he knows these things, without which he cannot provide even basic guidance in legal cases, what, really, will he be lacking with respect to knowledge of the greatest matters? And even if you limit the orator's power simply to speaking in an orderly, polished and expansive manner, I still want to know who can accomplish even this without the very knowledge that you refuse to grant him? For there is no real virtue in speaking unless the speaker knows of what he speaks.

'And so, if the natural scientist Democritus[10] spoke in a

polished manner, as is reported and seems likely to me, his subject matter was that of a natural scientist, the polish of his
language that of an orator; and if Plato spoke exceptionally
well, as I acknowledge, about matters far removed from public
controversies; if Aristotle also, if Theophrastus,[11] if Carneades
on the topics of their disputations were eloquent and appealing
and polished, let's accept that the matters they discussed belong
to other disciplines, but their language is part of this discipline
alone which we are now discussing and investigating.

'For we also see how it is possible to discuss the same topics
in a dry and feeble manner, as for example Chrysippus,[12] who
was said to have been a most keen disputant and not in this
respect inadequate for philosophy, but lacked eloquence, which
would have been obtained from a different art. What then
is the difference or how will you distinguish the richness of
speech of those I have named from the weakness of the others,
who do not make use of such variety and elegance of speaking?
There is exactly one thing that the good speakers bring as
theirs and theirs alone: language that is ordered, graceful and
marked by a certain artistry and polish. Yet this style of speaking, if the underlying matter is not perceived and understood
by the orator, is of no value at all and subjects him to universal
derision. For what is so preposterous as the empty sound of
excellent and highly polished language if it lacks substance and
knowledge? Therefore, whatever the idea, from whatever discipline, of whatever sort, the orator, as if pleading the case of
a client, will speak of it in a better and more graceful fashion
than the person who invented or developed it.

'Now, if someone claims that certain topics and issues are the
special concern of orators and that their knowledge is limited to
the courts, I will readily admit that our way of speaking is more
consistently exercised in such affairs; still, these affairs include
much that the instructors, called rhetoricians, neither teach nor
understand. Who is unaware that the orator's greatest power is
to incite the minds of men whether to anger or hatred or sorrow
and to recall them from these same emotions to gentleness
and pity? None of which he can accomplish in a speech unless
he has a thorough understanding of human nature, of the full

range of human culture and of the ways and means of fostering or transforming human beliefs.

'And this whole area of inquiry may seem appropriate for philosophers, nor will the orator ever object on my account. But once he concedes understanding of some matters to philosophers, for them alone to develop at length, let him claim for himself their treatment in speech, granting that such treatment is nothing without the philosophers' knowledge. For this is the special possession of the orator, as I have already often insisted: serious and graceful speech adapted to human thought and feeling.'

After rejecting Scaevola's claim that philosophy and rhetoric are mutually exclusive, Crassus makes the same argument with respect to the study of law. One can get far by specializing in philosophy or law, but that does not mean they are off-limits for the orator.

'Therefore, if anyone seeks both a general and particular definition of the term "orator", in my opinion the orator who really deserves such a dignified name will be the person who, whatever the topic being discussed, will speak in a wise, orderly, polished and accurate manner, while comporting himself with a certain dignity. And if my expression "on whatever topic" seems too broad, it can be clipped and pruned as each person pleases. Nevertheless, I will persist in claiming that even if an orator is ignorant of the contents of the other arts and sciences and only grasps what's relevant to political and legal debate, still if it does become necessary for him to speak about other matters, once he has learned the particulars from the specialists, he will speak about them much more effectively than those whose special competency they are.'

WHAT IS RHETORIC?

The philosopher Aristotle sought to provide a comprehensive account of almost all of the arts and sciences known to the Greeks. Delineating the proper function of each art was an important part of his task. Thus in the opening sections of his treatise On Rhetoric *he restricts rhetoric to 'the power of observing in each instance the possible means of persuasion'. From the broader vantage point of classical antiquity, this is a rather narrow definition of the subject, as the subsequent excerpt, from the Roman writer Quintilian, makes clear, and the opening of Cicero's* On the Orator *also argues. Yet his narrow focus, which he explains and justifies in this selection, allows Aristotle to explore in some detail the techniques involved in constructing explicit arguments (called enthymemes) that aim to persuade an audience of what is probably true. Quintilian, on the other hand, reviews more than twenty definitions that he finds in earlier treatises, settling on the expression 'rhetoric is the science of speaking well'. As simple as it may seem, the definition allows Quintilian to refute objections to rhetoric as a technique that can be put to bad as well as good ends. Deeply influenced by Stoic teaching, Quintilian suggests that speaking well is speaking in accordance with the moral order of the universe. The aesthetic and the moral aspects of eloquence are for him fully integrated.*

Aristotle
Rhetoric
I.I.I–I.2.I

Rhetoric is a counterpart of dialectic.[1] Both concern matters that are in some way available to everyone's discernment; neither is defined by any special knowledge. And so everyone in some sense has a share of both; for everyone, to some degree, attempts to criticize or sustain an argument and to speak in defence or to make an accusation. Of the many, some do these things hit or miss, others through familiarity arising from habit. Since either way is possible, it is clear that these goals could also be achieved systematically. For it is possible to observe the reason why some succeed through habit, others at random; and such, all would agree, is the task of an art.

Now, previous compilers of handbooks on speaking have supplied not even a small portion of the art (proofs being the only artistic element, the rest supplement). They don't even speak about enthymemes (explicit arguments), which are the body of proof, but they concern themselves by and large with extraneous business. For slander and pity and anger and other such passions are not pertinent to the issue, but directed towards the juror. So that if all trials were conducted as they are in some cities and especially those that are well governed, professional speakers of this sort would have nothing to say! And as it turns out, everybody thinks the laws should say as much, and some even adopt the practice and prohibit speaking off topic, as in the court of the Areopagus.[2] And they are right to think this way. One must not mislead the juror, turning him to anger or envy or pity. It would be like making a straight ruler crooked before putting it to use. In addition, it is clear that the only role of the litigant is to make clear whether something is or is not so, whether it happened or didn't happen. Deciding whether it is significant or insignificant, just or unjust, assuming the lawgiver has not specified, must be left to the juror without instructions from the litigants.

It's especially fitting, therefore, for well-composed laws, to the extent possible, to make all specifications, and to leave as little as possible to the judges, first because it is easier to find one or a few, as opposed to many, who think clearly and are capable of establishing laws and passing judgement. In addition, lawgiving takes place after a long process of consideration, while judgements occur on the spur of the moment, so that it is difficult for judges to determine appropriately what is just and what is advantageous. Most important of all, the judgement of the lawgiver is not given piecemeal, but pertains to the entirety of what will happen in the future, whereas the assembly-man and the juror pass judgement on specific issues in the present, on which they often already have a positive or negative outlook or some personal stake, so that they are unable to observe the truth sufficiently, since their personal pleasure or pain clouds their judgement.

About the rest, as we have said, it is necessary to make the judge the determiner of as little as possible; but as to whether something happened or didn't, or will be or won't be, or is or isn't, it is necessary to leave the matter to those assigned to make the decision. After all, it is impossible for the lawgiver to foresee these things. And if this is so, then clearly those who offer specific guidelines concerning the content of a proem or narrative or any other part are filling their manuals with material outside the subject. For they should not be concerning themselves with anything other than disposing the judge in a certain way. Yet they reveal nothing concerning the proofs based in art, even though this is the means through which one becomes skilled in the handling of enthymemes.

For this reason, although the method for deliberative and judicial speeches is the same, and deliberative topics are more noble and better suited to a public figure than contracts and exchanges, they say nothing about the former, but all strain to present a scientific discourse about judicial speaking, because it is of less use in deliberative oratory to speak outside the topic (because it concerns matters of common interest) and there is less opportunity for mischief. This is because in a deliberative context the person making a decision decides about his own affairs, so that there is no need to demonstrate anything other than that matters are as the speaker giving advice says they are. In court cases, on the other hand, this is not sufficient, but it is advantageous to win over the listener. Judgement is about affairs of others, so that the listeners, looking to their own interest and listening for pleasure, give in to the speakers but do not really judge. That's why, as I explained before, the law often forbids speaking off topic [in judicial cases], for in deliberative matters, the judges themselves keep sufficient watch.

Since it is clear that a scientific system is one that concerns proofs, and that a proof is a demonstration (for our confidence is strongest when we acknowledge that something has been demonstrated), there is a rhetorical type of demonstration, namely the enthymeme, and this is, to put it simply, the most authoritative of the proofs. The enthymeme, in turn, is a type of syllogism.[3] As it is the function of dialectic, as a whole or in one of its subdivisions, to consider every kind of syllogism in a consistent manner, it is clear that whoever is most capable of observing from what and by what means a syllogism comes to be would also be the most skilled at enthymemes, grasping in addition the subject matter of a given enthymeme and their differences from logical syllogisms. For the same faculty is employed in understanding what is true and what resembles the truth, and human beings are naturally and sufficiently inclined towards the truth and for the most part hit upon it. Therefore the person who is skilful in attaining the truth is similarly skilful in attaining what is likely to be true.

In short: other writers of treatises on rhetoric discuss matters outside the subject, and for this reason have inclined towards judicial oratory.

Still, rhetoric is useful, because truth and justice are naturally stronger than their opposites, so that if ever judgements are made improperly, they must have been bested by the latter, which is disgraceful. In addition, with some persons, even if we should possess the most secure sort of knowledge, it is not easy to persuade them merely by speaking thereof. Speech in accordance with [scientific] knowledge aims to provide instruction, but with such people this is impossible. Of necessity (as we also explain in *Topics*)[4] proofs and speeches must be constructed from common knowledge in the case of interaction with the multitude. In addition, it is necessary to be able to argue opposite positions, as with syllogisms, not in order to do so in practice (for one must not argue for what is wrong), but to understand the real state of the case and to be able to refute an opponent who is using such arguments contrary to justice. None of the other arts reasons to opposite conclusions; only dialectic and rhetoric do this, for they are similarly concerned with opposites.

But it's not the same with regard to the underlying subject matter. To put it simply, what is true and better is naturally easier to demonstrate and more plausible. In addition, it would be a bizarre state of affairs if it were shameful to be unable to defend yourself with your body, but not shameful to be unable to do so through language. After all, language is more particular to human beings than use of the body. But if it's objected that someone using such power of language unjustly could do great harm, the claim applies generally to all good things, except virtue, and especially to those that are most useful, for example strength, health, wealth or position of commander. The person who deploys these advantages in a just manner provides the greatest benefit; if unjustly, he does the greatest harm.

Clearly, rhetoric, like dialectic, is not limited to any one type of subject. It is useful; its task is not to persuade but in each instance to identify the actual means of persuasion. In this respect it resembles the other arts, for example medicine, the task of which is not to create health but to promote it as far as possible (for even those who are unable to recover health can still be treated properly). In addition it is the task of rhetoric to identify both the real and apparent means of persuasion, as it is of dialectic to identify the real and apparent syllogism. For sophistry is defined by moral intent, not ability.[5] In contrast, one can be a rhetorician on the basis of knowledge and moral intention, while a dialectician is defined by ability, not moral intent.

Let us now try to describe the system itself, explaining how and by what means we will be able to attain our objectives. Having established our definition, let us proceed, starting, as it were, from the beginning once again. Let rhetoric be the power of observing in each instance the possible means of persuasion. For this is the task of no other art. For each of the others can instruct and persuade regarding its own subject matter, for example medicine about health and sickness, geometry about the properties of magnitudes, arithmetic about numbers, and similarly the rest of the arts and sciences. But rhetoric seems to be able to find the means of persuasion regarding any given topic, so to speak, which is why we say that its technique is applicable to no particular or limited type of topic.

Quintilian
Oratorical Instruction
2.15.1–38

First of all, what is rhetoric? It has been defined in various ways, but there are two basic issues: disagreement about the nature of the thing itself, and disagreement about the terms in which it is defined. In the first and most important disagreement, some consider it possible even for wicked men to be orators, while others, myself included, prefer to restrict both the term and the art to those who are morally respectable.

Of those who separate competence at speaking from that greater and more desirable basis for renown, some say it is merely a power, some a science but not a virtue, some a practice, some an art divorced from knowledge and virtue, some a depraved art, or kakotekhnia. Such thinkers have generally identified the task of oratory as persuading or speaking in a manner suited to persuading. This can be accomplished as well by someone who is not a good man. Thus the common definition: 'rhetoric is the power of persuasion'. Where I say 'power' some say 'ability' or 'capacity'. To avoid ambiguity, by 'power' I mean the same as the Greek term 'dynamis'.

This opinion had its origin with Isocrates,[6] if the handbook attributed to him is in fact his. Although in intent he differs greatly from those who defame the function of the orator, his definition – that rhetoric is the craftsman of persuasion, or peithous demiourgos – is too bold. Nor would I allow myself to use the Ennian variant, 'the marrow of persuasion'.[7]

Gorgias, in the Platonic treatise named after him, says pretty much the same thing as Isocrates, but Plato wants it to be understood as Gorgias' definition, not his own. Cicero in many instances writes that the task of the orator is 'to speak in a manner suited to persuading'; in his *Rhetorica*, which he himself does not approve,[8] he made persuasion the aim of rhetoric. But the money and influence and prestige and status of the speaker are also persuasive. Even a voiceless image can persuade – as when memory of a person's good deeds, or a pitiable expression or physical beauty affects our thinking.

For example, when Antonius, during his defence of Manius Aquillius,[9] tore open his client's robes and exposed to sight the scars he had sustained on his chest while fighting for our country, he did not rely on eloquence, but instead assaulted the eyes of the Roman people. It is generally believed that the defendant's acquittal was due to the emotional impact of what was shown. One of Cato's speeches (not to mention other records) reports that Servius was saved by the pity he roused not just by bringing his own small sons into the assembly but even by carrying in his arms the son of Sulpicius Gallus.[10] So too, it's generally thought that Phryne was released no thanks to the speech of Hyperides,[11] admirable as it was, but due to the sight of her remarkable body, which she revealed by opening her tunic just a little.

If all these things persuade, then persuasion is not the distinctive goal we have been discussing. More precise are those who consider rhetoric the power of persuading by means of speech. This is the definition Gorgias was in essence coerced by Socrates into providing in the book mentioned above. Theodectes[12] is in agreement, whether the treatise *On Rhetoric* ascribed to him is in fact his or, as is believed, by Aristotle. There the goal of rhetoric is said to be 'to lead men by speaking to the conclusion intended by the speaker'.

But even this definition is inadequate. Others, besides orators, persuade by speaking or by speaking lead where they intend, such as prostitutes, flatterers or seducers. In contrast, the orator is not always engaged in persuasion, so that sometimes this is not his particular goal, and sometimes he shares this goal with those who are quite different from him. And yet Apollodorus[13] is not far from this definition when he says that the task of a judicial oration is first and foremost to persuade the judge and lead his opinion where one wishes. He too subjects the orator to fortune, so that if he doesn't persuade, he can't retain his own title!

Some pay no attention to the outcome, as when Aristotle says 'rhetoric is the faculty of finding all means of persuasion in speech'.[14] This definition has the fault we have already mentioned; what's more, it includes only the development of arguments, which, in the absence of style, hardly counts as eloquence. To Hermagoras,[15] who defines rhetoric as speaking persuasively, and others who express the same view, but in different words, saying it consists of 'speaking everything necessary for persuading', I have made sufficient response above, when I showed that persuasion does not characterize the orator alone.

Various additions have been made to one or the other of these definitions. Some say rhetoric is concerned with all affairs, others limit it to civil or political issues. Which of these is closer to the truth I will discuss in the appropriate place. Aristotle seems to assign everything to the orator when he says rhetoric is the power of seeing the means of persuasion in any matter; and Iatrocles,[16] although he does not use the words 'in any matter', shows that he means the same thing, because he excludes nothing. These definitions, like the one above, only take into account invention. To avoid this mistake Eudorus[17] thinks rhetoric to be the power of finding and speaking elegantly whatever is credible in every type of speech. Yet inasmuch as a person who is not an orator can discover what is credible as well as what is likely to persuade, his addition of 'in every type of speech' concedes – even more than the others – the beautiful term 'of eloquence' even to those who persuade others to commit crimes! Plato's Gorgias says he is the artificer of persuasion in trials and other such gatherings, and that he treats what is just as well as what is unjust. To him Socrates concedes the power of persuading, but not of teaching.

Those who would rather not assign all subject matter to the orator have introduced certain distinctions (more elaborate and verbose than necessary): for example, Ariston, the student of the Peripatetic Critolaus,[18] whose definition is 'the knowledge of finding and expressing through language what is likely to persuade a popular audience in public inquiries'. Being a Peripatetic, he considers rhetoric a science, not, as the Stoics[19] would have it, a virtue. And in referring to a popular audience, he expresses hostility to the art of pleading, which he considers unpersuasive to the educated. Let it be said of all who limit the orator to civil proceedings that they have excluded most of the duties of the orator, for example, the whole area of panegyric, which is the third branch of rhetoric.

To come now to those who think rhetoric is an art but not a virtue, there is the rather cautious definition of Theodorus of Gadara.[20] He says – I quote the words of those who have translated them from the Greek – 'rhetoric is the art that discovers, evaluates and proclaims, with a duly apportioned eloquence, the relevant means of persuasion on topics of civic interest'. Cornelius Celsus[21] also says that the goal of rhetoric is 'to speak persuasively on doubtful matters of civic interest'. Others give similar definitions, such as 'the power of understanding and addressing matters of public interest brought before it, and of doing so with a certain capacity to persuade, a certain bodily disposition and a certain delivery of what is being communicated'. There are thousands of other definitions, either the same or with the same elements, to which I will respond when I discuss the subject matter of rhetoric.

But some have regarded rhetoric as neither a capacity nor a science nor an art, with Critolaus referring to a 'practice, or knack, of speaking' (for this is the meaning of the Greek word *tribe*), Athenaeus[22] saying it is the 'art of deceiving'. The majority, however, are content to read a few incompetently excerpted passages from the *Gorgias* of Plato, and because they fail to unroll the whole dialogue or read his other works, have fallen into the greatest error. They believe that Plato is of the view that rhetoric is not an art but 'a knack for producing delight and pleasure' and elsewhere 'an image of a minute portion of civic life, the fourth part of flattery' because he assigns two parts of politics to the body, namely medicine and what they call gymnastics, two to the mind, namely the law and justice, while cooking is a flattery of medicine, and the practice of slave sellers a flattery of gymnastic training, because they falsify complexion with colouring and health with useless fat; quibbling is the flattery, or false version, of law, rhetoric of justice.

All such remarks found in the *Gorgias* are spoken by Socrates,[23] in whose character Plato seems to transmit his own opinion. But of his dialogues, some, called elenchic, or refutational, were composed to refute the opinions of Socrates' interlocutors, others, called dogmatic, were composed for the purpose of teaching doctrine. Socrates, or Plato, thinks only that rhetoric as practised in his day is of such a sort, for he even uses the words 'the manner in which you conduct public affairs'.[24] Genuine rhetoric he knows to be morally upright. Thus the dispute with Gorgias concludes as follows: 'therefore the rhetorician must be a just man, and the just man must intend to do what is just.'[25]

To this, Gorgias makes no answer, but Polus, reckless with his youthful passion, takes up the conversation, and it is against him that the claims about false image and flattery are made. Then Callicles, who is an even more turbulent character, is nonetheless led to the following conclusion: 'whoever truly intends to be a rhetorician must be just, and possess knowledge of what is just.'[26] Thus it would appear that Plato does not regard rhetoric as an evil, but believes that true rhetoric is available only to a person who is just and good. In the *Phaedrus* he makes it even more apparent that this art cannot be attained in full without knowledge of justice. And I concur. How else could Plato have written the *Apology of Socrates* or his praise of those who died for their country?[27] Surely these are the writings of an orator.

Plato believed that teachers of rhetoric were ill-suited to their subject, in that they would separate rhetoric from justice and prefer what was plausible to what was true. This is also in the *Phaedrus*. Cornelius Celsus seems to concur with the earlier rhetoricians when he says, 'the orator seeks only what is like the truth' and then later, 'the orator's reward is not a clear conscience but the success of the litigant'. If that were true, only the worst of men would give such dangerous instruments to terrible criminals and through their teachings offer assistance to villainy. But let those who consider such behaviour acceptable provide their own justification.

For our part, we have undertaken to form the perfect orator, whom we intend first and foremost to be a man of moral integrity. So let us return to those who offer better advice on the matter. Some consider rhetoric the same as politics. Cicero calls it a branch of political science[28] (with political science being the same as wisdom), some – including Isocrates[29] – say it is the same as philosophy. The definition best suited to the essence of rhetoric considers it 'the science of speaking well'. The definition given by Chrysippus,[30] who derived it from Cleanthes,[31] has the same meaning: 'the science of speaking correctly'. The same philosopher gives many other definitions, but they are more relevant to other issues. The same meaning is conveyed by the expression 'persuading what ought to be done', except that it limits the art to its outcome. Areus[32] said it well: 'to speak in accordance with the particular excellence of speech'.

Those who consider rhetoric to be the science or knowledge of civil responsibilities also exclude evil-doers, assuming they consider science a virtue, but they narrowly restrict rhetoric to political or civic issues. Albucius,[33] a well-known professor and author, agrees that rhetoric is the knowledge of speaking well, but errs in specifying 'about political questions and with credibility'. (To both of these restrictions I have already responded.) Those who said that the function of rhetoric is to think and speak correctly seem to have the right idea.

These are pretty much all of the well-known definitions, especially those that have been debated. It isn't relevant or possible for me to track down each and every one. It's a bad habit on the part of textbook writers these days never to define a term in the same words used by a predecessor. There will be no such pointless display on my part. I will use the definition I approve of, not necessarily the one I have invented, as follows: rhetoric is the science of speaking well. For when the best has been discovered, to seek an alternative is to seek something worse. Now that we understand these things, it's also obvious what constitutes the goal or the highest aim, or the ultimate outcome of rhetoric, that is, in Greek, its *telos*, which every art strives for. For if rhetoric is the science of speaking well, its end and highest aim is speaking well.

THE SYSTEM OF RHETORIC

Over the course of the years, rhetorical teaching came to be systematized into specific branches. Sometimes it was organized on the basis of the main modes of persuasion, namely character (ethos), emotion (pathos) and argument (logos). Other times an organization based on the tasks of the orator prevailed, specifically invention, arrangement, memory, style and delivery. Aristotle generally follows the first pattern of organization, in accordance with his greater interest in the sources of persuasion than in the practical activities of the speaker. Since the remainder of the present book will be organized around the second pattern, it seems appropriate to begin with Aristotle's more philosophical account. In the course of his treatment of ethos, pathos *and* logos, *he introduces a number of other distinctions that will be relevant throughout the history of rhetoric as well, specifically, the contrast between inartificial proofs (such as documents and testimony) and artificial proofs (of the sort developed by the speaker), and, within artificial proofs, the distinction between paradigms or examples, and enthymemes, or arguments. He also notes that rhetorical argumentation can take place in three very different contexts and with three very different aims: deliberative, that is discussion of a possible course of action; judicial or forensic, that is prosecution or defence of someone charged with a crime; and epideictic, that is praise or blame of a person, place or thing. As Aristotle tells it, his strong emphasis on deliberative oratory is an innovation in rhetorical theory. It fits his understanding of rhetoric as closely related to politics, since the type of deliberation that interests him is public debate about issues of policy, of the sort that would have been familiar to his Greek (and later Roman) readers.*

Despite his emphasis on rhetoric as a system of inquiry, Aristotle's presentation can be somewhat difficult to follow in its logic and organization. But it is worth following the twists and turns of his discussion, since it contains much within it of continuing interest, including a theory of human motivation, an analysis of differences between the young and the old, and a detailed list of topics of importance to decision-makers in ancient city-states.

Aristotle
Rhetoric
Selections from Books 1, 2 and 3[1]

The Bases of Persuasion

Now as for arguments, or means of persuasion, some are not the product of art, others are. By the former I refer to proofs that are not supplied by us, but pre-exist, such as witnesses, testimony obtained by torture, contracts and the like. By the latter, or artistic proofs, I refer to those that can be developed methodically by us. The former we use, the latter we devise.

Of the means of persuasion enacted through speaking, there are three types: some have to do with the character of the speaker, some entail disposing the listener in a certain way, others involve logical demonstration or apparent demonstration through speech itself.[2]

Character is the basis of persuasion whenever language is spoken so as to make the speaker believable. For we have confidence more readily and to a greater degree in people who are reasonable, confidence about matters in general and entirely so when the issue is uncertain and there is room for doubt. This confidence is to be achieved through speech and not through any prior conception of the speaker's character. For it is not, as some writers of manuals would have it, that the reasonableness of the speaker is not part of our art, as it contributes nothing to his plausibility. To the contrary, character might be called the most effective type of proof.

Persuasion occurs through the audience when they are led to an emotion by means of speech. For our decisions are not the same when we are grieving as opposed to rejoicing, or loving as opposed to hating. And this is the only topic that interests present-day writers of manuals. We will clarify our position in detail when we consider the emotions.

Speech itself is the basis of persuasion when we demonstrate the truth or apparent truth from plausible statements about each particular.

Now since the means of persuasion are of these sorts, it is clear that to possess them one must be able to reason syllogistically; to understand characters and virtues; and with respect to emotions, to know what each one is, its quality, and the means and manner of bringing it into existence. So it turns out that rhetoric is an offshoot of dialectic and of ethics, or, as it might rightly be called, politics. This is why rhetoric presents itself as politics, as do its adherents, whether through miseducation, boastfulness or some other human failing. In fact, rhetoric is a subdivision of dialectic, and resembles it, as we said at the outset. For neither one entails scientific knowledge of any one delimited domain, but both are means of furnishing arguments. About their power and relationship to one another, almost enough has been said.

For purposes of demonstration or apparent demonstration, dialectic has two techniques: induction and syllogism, or apparent syllogism. Rhetoric is similar.

For the paradigm, for example, is a form of induction, the enthymeme a form of syllogism, and the apparent enthymeme comparable to the apparent syllogism. I call enthymeme a rhetorical syllogism, a paradigm rhetorical induction. All speakers fashion proofs through demonstration or by speaking either paradigms or enthymemes, and nothing besides these. And if demonstration is only possible through syllogism or induction, as is clear from the *Analytics*,[3] then enthymeme and paradigm must be versions of the same.

The difference between paradigm and enthymeme is clear from the *Topics*[4] (where there is an earlier discussion of induction and syllogism). To show on the basis of many similar instances that something is so is there treated as induction, here as paradigm. But to show that, with certain things being the case, something else besides these turns out to result from these being the case, either universally or in general, in dialectic is a syllogism, in rhetoric is called enthymeme.

It is clear that each type of rhetoric has value. As stated in the *Methodics*,[5] there are some rhetorical expressions that take the form of paradigms, others enthymemes. In a similar vein, some orators prefer paradigms, others enthymemes. Speeches relying on paradigms are no less persuasive, but the type filled with enthymemes receives greater approval. The reason, and how each is to be used, we will explain later. But now let's differentiate them more clearly.

Since a persuasive statement is persuasive to someone, and either immediately in itself persuasive and plausible, or shown to be so through other persuasive statements, and since, in addition, no art looks to the particular (for example medicine just to what is healthy for Socrates or Kallias), but instead considers a person or persons of such and such a sort (for this is artistic, whereas concern for the particular is boundless and unknowable), then rhetoric considers what seems likely not to an individual, such as Socrates or Hippias, but to people of a certain sort. This is also the case with dialectic. It does not reason syllogistically from any random premise (for even madmen make truth claims) but from those respected by people who value rational argument. So too rhetoric is aimed at people who are already accustomed to deliberation.

Rhetoric concerns subjects we deliberate about but for which we lack other arts. It is practised in the presence of listeners who are unable to see many things simultaneously or to reason from a distant starting point. We deliberate about matters that seem to admit of two possibilities. For no one deliberates about matters that could not be different, whether past, present or future, at least according to his understanding. For there is then nothing to discuss.

Now it is possible to argue syllogistically and draw inferences either from prior syllogisms or from premises that are not syllogisms themselves but require syllogisms because they are not widely accepted. The first approach is hard to follow on account of its length (for the judge is understood to be an ordinary person), the other not persuasive because it relies on premises that are not generally agreed upon. Of necessity, then, the enthymeme and the paradigm concern things that could, generally speaking, be otherwise, with the paradigm being an induction, the enthymeme a syllogism, but one constructed of few, and often fewer premises than a syllogism per se. For if the premise is familiar, there is no need to articulate it. For example, to show that Dorieus has won a crown contest it is sufficient to say that he won an Olympic contest and not necessary to add that an Olympic contest is a crown contest, because that is something everyone knows.

Since few of the propositions of rhetorical syllogisms are necessarily true, in that most of the matters treated in trial and inquiries could be one way or another (for people deliberate about and examine activities that are specific but need not be the way they are), and so are demonstrated with claims that are only generally so, whereas necessary propositions can only be demonstrated on the basis of other necessary propositions (as discussed in the *Analytics*), it is clear that of the premises or stages of an enthymeme some will be necessarily so, but most only generally so. And since, as we know, enthymemes are argued from probabilities and signs, each of these must correspond to one or the other of the preceding [i.e. general or necessary statements].

[. . .]

Three Types of Oratory: Deliberative, Judicial and Epideictic

But first let us take up the types or genres of rhetorical speech, so that having defined them we can understand their elements and premises. There are three types of rhetoric, corresponding to the different audiences of speeches. Of the three components of a speech, namely speaker, subject and audience, the audience is the goal. Now the audience can be a spectator[6] or a judge, and a judge of the past or of the future. The assembly member passes judgement concerning future events, the juror concerning the past and the spectator concerning the ability of the speaker. As a result, there are three types of rhetorical speech: symbouleutic (deliberative), judicial and epideictic.

Deliberation entails a turning towards or a turning away

(called protreptic and apotreptic). Those who deliberate in private or in public always have one or the other of these aims. A legal speech entails either accusation or defence. For the litigants must either accuse or defend. Epideictic entails either praise or blame.

The time frame of each type is as follows: the future for deliberative oratory (for one advises either pro or con about future actions); the past for forensic (for one accuses or defends always about past actions); for the epideictic chiefly the present (for all who praise or blame address the current situation), although epideictic speakers often recall the past and anticipate the future.

Each type of oratory has a distinctive aim. Since there are three types of oratory, there are three aims or ends. In a deliberative speech, the aim is the advantageous and disadvantageous, for the speaker recommends a course of action as better, opposes it as worse, aligning other considerations with these, such as whether the proposed action is just or unjust, noble or disgraceful. In a judicial speech, the end is justice and injustice, and speakers align other considerations with these. In speeches of praise and blame the aim is the noble and the disgraceful, and speakers relate other aspects to these.

The following is a good indicator of the validity of our identification of ends. Sometimes speakers do not even argue about other matters, for example a judicial speaker may ignore the question whether an act happened or not or caused harm or not. But he and his opponent will never agree as to the justice or injustice of the disputed act. If that were the case, there would be no reason to hold a trial. So too with deliberative orators: they may pass over everything else, but they would never agree that what they are recommending is disadvantageous or try to dissuade the audience from an advantageous course of action. Often such speakers fail to consider the justice or injustice of enslaving neighbouring communities, even those that have done no wrong. So too, those who praise or blame do not ask whether someone has done what is advantageous or harmful but in the course of praise often establish that he has made light of his own advantage in doing what is noble, for example, if they praise Achilles for coming to the assistance of his comrade Patroclus,[7] even while knowing that he would have to die, although he might otherwise have lived. To Achilles such a death was more honourable, although continuing to live was of course advantageous.

It is clear from what has been said that it is necessary in the first place to have propositions pertaining to the various aims. Rhetorical propositions consist of self-evident claims (called tekmeria), probabilities, and signs or indicators. For the syllogism consists entirely of propositions, and the enthymeme is a syllogism based on the propositions just listed.

But since what is impossible cannot be done or have been done (only the possible can) and what has not happened or will not happen cannot either have happened or be about to happen, the deliberative, judicial and epideictic orators must have propositions about the possible and impossible, and whether something has or has not happened, or will or will not happen. Yet since all speakers – those who praise or blame, those who recommend or oppose a course of action, those who accuse or defend – attempt not only to prove what they are saying but also to show that it is great or small, good or bad, noble or disgraceful, just or unjust, either in itself or in comparison with something else, it is clear that they must have at the ready propositions about the great and the small, the greater and the lesser, the universal and the particular, for example what is the greater or lesser good, just or unjust course of action, and likewise about the rest.

So much for the issues about which the orator must acquire propositions.

Next we must consider individually the issues at stake in each category of speech, namely, deliberative, epideictic and judicial.

Topics of Deliberation

With respect to deliberative oratory, we must first understand the types of good and bad things the adviser advises about. He can't advise about everything, only about things that can possibly happen or not. About things that necessarily are or will be, or impossibilities, or things that just are or have already happened, there is no advice to be given. The deliberative speaker doesn't even advise about every single possibility, for some good possible outcomes happen naturally or by chance, and there is no point in advising about them. The real subjects of deliberation are clear: they are actions that affect us and have their origin in us. And we consider whether they can or cannot be carried out.

[. . .]

Generally speaking, there are five main topics of deliberation and public counsel, namely resources, war and peace, defence of territory, imports and exports, and legislation.

The speaker who intends to advise about resources needs to know the revenues of the city, their nature and amount, so that if any has been omitted it can be added and if any is too small it can be augmented, and also all the expenses of the city, so that if any is superfluous it can be eliminated, and if too great reduced. For cities become richer not only by increasing resources but also by eliminating expenses. It is possible to become knowledgeable about deliberative topics from personal experience, but it's also essential to be informed about the findings of others in order to offer advice in these areas.

With regard to war and peace, the speaker must know the power of the city, the size of its available resources and how much it can acquire in addition, the nature of both current and potential resources, the wars it has already waged and how it has fought. He must know these things not just about his own state but also those nearby and those with whom conflict is likely, so as to recommend peaceful conduct towards the stronger. And as for the weaker, against whom the city can decide for itself whether to fight or not, he must know their resources as well, and whether they are like or unlike those of his city, for advantage or disadvantage is identified in this way. And he must study all of these issues as they pertain to the wars fought by his own state, but also wars involving others, in particular their outcomes. For from similar circumstances similar results naturally follow.

As for defence of one's territory, the speaker must not overlook the mode of defence, the size and nature of the guard, the locations of the guard posts (which is impossible for one unfamiliar with the territory), so that an inadequate guard can be strengthened, an excessive one pruned, and the appropriate places better guarded.

On the topic of food, he must know how much and of what sort the city requires, what it produces on its own and what it imports, what exports and imports are necessary and from whom so that contracts and agreements can be secured. For there are two groups towards whom citizens must behave unimpeachably: those who are stronger and those who handle imports and exports.

To advance the security of the state, all such matters must be studied, and lawmaking no less. The salvation of the city is in its laws, so that it is necessary to know the various types of constitutions, what is advantageous for each, and through what means each is susceptible to destruction, either from within or as a result of opposition. When I speak of destruction by forces within or intrinsic to a constitution, I mean that with the exception of the best constitution, all others are destroyed by relaxation or straining. For example democracy, by relaxing or straining too much, becomes weaker and ends up as oligarchy. In like manner, a hooked or snub nose, if the defect is relaxed, approaches the mean. If the defect is exaggerated, it no longer seems like a nose.

When establishing laws, it is useful to know not only what kind of constitution is advantageous, based on observation of the past, but also to know how the constitutions of other states are suited to other populations. Clearly, then, travel narratives are useful for establishing laws, since they make it possible to learn the customs of other states; and history is useful in political deliberation: although both are more the purview of politics than of rhetoric. Such are the topics about which the would-be deliberator must be well informed.

[. . .]

Praise and Blame

Next let us consider virtue and vice and the noble and the disgraceful, for they are the points of reference for the speaker who praises or blames. In discussing such topics we will also clarify the sources of character-presentation, which was our second major mode of persuasion. Having such knowledge, we will be able to make ourselves and others credible with regard to virtue. But since it happens that we sometimes praise, seriously or in jest, not just persons or deities, but even inanimate objects or random creatures, we must have propositions concerning these topics.

[. . .]

A speech of praise celebrates great virtue or excellence. It is therefore necessary to explain that the actions of the person being praised are of a particular sort. Encomium concerns accomplishments and thus those who accomplished them: other topics, such as birth or education, contribute to plausibility, in that good people are ordinarily of good birth, and people in general are as they were brought up to be. Achievements are at best indicators of disposition; after all, we would praise a person we believe to be of a certain disposition or character even if he had achieved nothing. Blessing and congratulating are the same thing, but not the same as praise or encomium. Rather, just as well-being includes virtue, so congratulating implies praise or encomium.

Praise and deliberative oratory can resemble one another, for a recommendation made in a deliberative speech can, with alteration of language, become an encomium. Thus when we know what needs to be done and what kind of people we should be, the one recommending such things simply needs to change the language, for example, instead of recommending that we ought to have higher regard for what we have acquired on our own rather than by chance, say, as an expression of praise, 'this fellow has a higher regard for his own accomplishments than for chance acquisitions'. So when you wish to praise, see what the underlying recommendation or proposition would be. And when you recommend, determine what you would praise – and vice versa, when you are arguing the opposite.

[. . .]

Speaking in general about approaches common to all speeches, augmentation or amplification is best suited to epideictic oratory, in that it considers actions that are not in dispute, so that what remains for the speaker is to express magnificence and beauty. Paradigms are best suited to deliberative speeches, because we make our decision by divining the future on the basis of the past. And enthymemes are best suited to legal speeches, for dispute over a past event invites causal explanation and clarification.

Such, then, are the bases for virtually all praise and blame, the necessary considerations for a speaker of praise and blame, and the sources of encomium and invective. For when we understand praise or encomium, we understand its opposite, inasmuch as the bases for invective are the opposite of those for encomium.

Judicial Oratory (Accusation and Defence)

We should next consider speeches of accusation and defence, specifically the nature and number of the propositions that provide the material for syllogisms in them. There are in essence three sources of syllogisms in such speeches: the nature and number of the motives for unjust conduct; the disposition of those who commit injustice; and the character and disposition or situation of their victims. Let's first define injustice, then consider these sources in order.

Injustice is defined as willingly causing harm in violation of the law. Law can be either specific to a community or general. By specific to a community I mean the written laws by which people conduct affairs, by common I mean the unwritten rules that seem to be shared by everyone. To act willingly means to do so knowingly and without being forced. Those who act knowingly do not always act with premeditation, but to act with premeditation is always to act knowingly. For no one can premeditate unawares. People deliberately cause harm and do wrong against the law because of wickedness and lack of control. Whenever people have one or more vices, they are unjust in line with their vice.

For example, a stingy person will be unjust with regard to money, an indulgent person with regard to the pleasures of the body, a passive person with regard to ease, a cowardly person with regard to dangers (for fear makes him abandon his comrades), the ambitious with regard to honours, the ill-tempered with regard to anger, the competitive with regard to victory, the bitter with regard to vengeance, the witless through confusion about right and wrong, the shameless through lack of concern for reputation, and so on, with each doing wrong in line with his particular vice.

All of this is clear from what we have said about virtues and will say about emotions. It remains to explain the motives, character and victims of those who commit injustice.

First let us determine what those who intend to do wrong are seeking or avoiding. For it is clear that the accuser must examine the number and nature of the motives that lead people to harm their neighbours, especially as pertain to his opponent; while the defence must examine the number and nature that do not apply. Everything people do they do either on their own initiative or not. Of those actions taken not on their own initiative some occur through chance, others through necessity, whether by force or nature, in other words, through chance, nature or force. Those taken on their own initiative, and for which they are responsible, come about through habit or desire, with some instances of desire being rational, others irrational. Active preference is a desire for the good, for no one prefers something unless he considers it to be good, but anger and longing are irrational desires.

Thus there are seven possible motivations for any given action: chance, nature, compulsion, character, reasoning, anger and desire. There is no point in making further distinctions concerning age or disposition or anything else. For if young people happen to be angry or full of desire, their actions stem from anger or desire, not from youth. So too with wealth and poverty: because they are poor, poor people have a desire for money, because they are rich, rich people have a desire for unnecessary pleasures. Their actions are motivated not by wealth or poverty but by desire. So too the just and unjust and

others who are said to act according to moral disposition in
fact act through reason or emotion, some through good character and emotion, some through the opposite. Granted, it
does happen that certain actions follow from certain moral
dispositions; for example from a temperate person due to
his being temperate proper opinions and desires concerning
pleasant things follow, and from the intemperate person the
opposite. So let us set aside such distinctions and consider
what kinds of actions follow from what kinds of conditions.
For if a man is light or dark, tall or short, nothing of the sort
follows from that, but if he is young or old, fair or unfair, it
does make a difference. And in general circumstances that
shape character, for example, considering oneself rich or poor,
fortunate or unfortunate, will make a difference.
  [. . .]
Such are the bases on which we persuade and dissuade, praise
and blame, prosecute and defend, and the opinions and propositions useful for generating acceptance in speeches. For
enthymemes concern these matters and are derived from them,
in accordance with each particular type of speech.

Character and Emotion as Bases for Persuasion

Because rhetoric exists for the sake of judgement (for audiences
make a decision in response to deliberative oratory, and a trial
is itself an occasion for judgement), the speaker must have in
mind not just the explanatory force and believability of his
language, but also how to situate himself with respect to the
audience and vice versa. For it has a great effect on credibility,
especially in deliberative speeches but even in trials, that the
speaker appear to be a certain sort of person and that the audience understand him to be disposed towards themselves in a
certain way and in addition that they be disposed towards him
in a certain way.

  For the speaker to seem to be of a certain sort is more useful
in deliberative oratory, how the listener is disposed matters
more in trials. For things appear quite different to those who
love and those who hate, to those who are angry and those

who are calm and gentle. A person who is kindly disposed towards the defendant either assumes he does no wrong or that any wrong he does is insignificant; but a judge who is hostile makes the opposite assumption. A listener who is in an upbeat and optimistic mood, if the proposal being deliberated is appealing, will anticipate a favourable outcome; but if the audience is apathetic or worse, it will have the opposite expectation.

There are three ways (apart from demonstrations) in which a speaker establishes his credibility: good sense, virtue or excellence, and good intentions. Speakers are unreliable in what they say or advise, based on their lack of one or all of these characteristics. Either through foolishness they hold incorrect opinions, or although holding correct opinions, through malice they refrain from expressing them, or they are sensible and fair-minded but lack good intent – which is why it is possible for people who know what is best not to advise it. But besides these there is nothing.

The one who has all three positive qualities cannot help being credible to the audience. The means for conveying good sense and moral integrity can be inferred from our discussion of the virtues. He should present himself in this regard just as he would present someone else. As for good intent and friendship, they are to be considered under the heading of emotions.

Emotions are the means through which opinions are changed with respect to judgements, and are accompanied by pain and pleasure. The emotions include anger, pity, fear and others like these as well as their opposites. Each is to be discussed in three aspects, for example regarding anger, how are angry men disposed, with whom are they likely to be angry and about what sorts of things. For if we understood one or two of these, but not all, it would be impossible to arouse anger. And likewise for the rest. Just as we have listed propositions about earlier subjects, let us do the same concerning emotions and analyse them in the manner described.

[. . .]

Let us next describe characters in terms of their emotions, habits, ages and circumstances. By emotions I mean anger, desire

and the others we have discussed; by habits, I mean virtues
and vices, also discussed earlier, as well as preferred activities.
Ages are youth, maturity and old age. By circumstances I mean
good birth, wealth and talents, and the opposite to these, and,
more generally, good and bad fortune.

Psychology of the Young and the Old

Now young men have a character that is desirous, and such as to
act on the basis of desire. Their desire for sex is of all the physical
desires the strongest, and they have difficulty controlling it. They
are quick to change and easily sated in their desires, quick to feel
a longing and to stop feeling it as well, for their will is keen but
not strong, like the hunger and thirst of the sick. They are passionate, impulsive and inclined to act on their emotions.

Because they are obsessed with honour, they cannot stand
to be slighted, and become outraged when they think they are
being wronged. They are eager for honour, but especially eager
for victory (for youth desires supremacy, and victory is supremacy), and they desire both honour and victory more than they
desire money. (Their desire for money is limited because they
have not experienced real need, as Pittacus said in regard to
Amphiaraus.)[8]

Their temperament is not wicked but simple because they
have not yet experienced many instances of bad behaviour.
They are credulous because they have not often been deceived.
They have high hopes: like drinkers of wine the young are hot-
tempered by nature, and besides, they have not experienced
much in the way of misfortune. Indeed, they live for the most
part in a state of hope, for hope concerns the future while
memory is of the past, and for the young the future is long, the
past is short. At the dawn of life, there is nothing to remember
and everything to hope for.

They are easily deceived for the reason stated (for they hope
so freely), and they are especially courageous, being impetuous
and full of hope, the one quality making them fearless, the
other making them bold – for no one who is angry feels fear,
and expectation of a good outcome boosts confidence. They

quickly feel ashamed, for they have not yet understood other fine things but have been fashioned only by convention. And they have greatness of soul, for they have not been beaten down by life or experienced need, and greatness of soul means considering oneself worthy of great things. It is a characteristic of the person with high hopes.

They prefer noble actions to those that are merely advantageous. For they live in accordance with their character rather than calculation, and calculation concerns advantage while excellence concerns what is fine and noble. And they enjoy friends and comrades more than other age-groups do because they enjoy associating with others and do not yet judge anything on the basis of advantage, including friendships.

All of their mistakes are due to excess and overzealousness, in contrast to the precept of Chilon.[9] In fact, they love in excess and hate in excess and do everything else in excess, and they think they know everything and confidently affirm as much. And when they do wrong they do so out of insolence rather than mean-spiritedness. And they are inclined to pity because they suppose everyone is good, or even better. They judge their neighbours according to their own lack of viciousness so that they assume that others must be suffering undeservedly. And they enjoy laughter, and thus a good joke. For wit is a kind of educated insolence.

Such is the character of the young. Older people and those past their prime have a character that is generally speaking the opposite. Because they have lived many years and more often been deceived and more often made mistakes, and most of their dealings turn out badly, they maintain nothing with certainty and show less regard for everything than is right. They 'think' such-and-such, but 'know' nothing. They constantly express doubt, prefacing every statement with 'perhaps' and 'maybe', always speaking this way and never asserting anything without reservation.

They have a nasty disposition. For nastiness consists of thinking the worst about everything. Also they are suspicious because of their lack of trust, and untrusting because of experience. As a result, they neither love nor hate with any intensity, but following the saying of Bias, they love as if they will one day hate and hate as if they will love. They are cramped in spirit, having been laid low by life. They desire nothing great or special but just the necessities of life.

They are stingy. For property is one of the necessities of life, and at the same time through experience they know how difficult it is to acquire property and how easy to lose it. They are cowardly and fearful about everything. Their disposition is opposite to that of the young. They are cold while the young are hot, and thus their age leads to cowardice, since fear is a kind of chilling. They love life especially as they approach the end, out of longing for what is gone. What they lack they desire most of all.

They love themselves more than they should – another instance of their small-mindedness. And they focus on what is advantageous rather than on what is noble or fine to a greater extent than is necessary, on account of their self-regard. For advantage is good for some person, whereas the noble is noble all by itself. And they are shameless rather than properly ashamed. Because they do not concern themselves equally with advantage and fineness, they make light of reputation. And they are disinclined to be hopeful, based on experience, since most enterprises amount to little and many make matters worse, and also out of cowardice.

They live in a state of recollection rather than hope. For the remainder of their life is small, what has passed is great, and hope is for the future while memory is of the past. This is also the reason for their idle chatter: they ramble on about the past, for they enjoy the process of remembering.

Their angry outbursts are keen but of no consequence; their desires have either gone away or are ineffectual, which means they aren't energetic in pursuing their desires, except for profit. Thus men of this age appear self-controlled, for desires have lessened and they are slaves to gain. And they live more according to calculation than according to character, for calculation aims at profit while character aims at excellence.

When they commit an injustice, they do so out of mean-spiritedness rather than insolence. They too are inclined to pity, but not for the same reasons as the young. The young take pity out of a fondness for humanity, the old out of a sense of weakness. For they think that they themselves are on the verge of suffering everything, and this turns out to be a source of pity. They are full of complaints, not at all witty, not at all given to laughter. For love of complaint is the opposite of love of laughter.

So much for the character of the old and the young. Therefore since all people welcome speeches spoken in their own character by speakers similar to themselves, it's clear that language is to be used to make the speech and the speaker seem to be of a certain kind.

The character of those in their prime will be midway between that of the others, lacking the excess of each. They aren't overly bold (for that shows rashness) or excessively fearful, but properly inclined towards both. They don't trust everybody, or distrust everybody, but decide in accordance with the truth. They don't orient their lives solely towards what is fine or solely towards what is advantageous, but towards both. They are neither stingy nor spendthrift but seek a mean. Similarly with respect to anger and desire. Their restraint is accompanied by courage, their courage accompanied by restraint. For among the young and the old these qualities are found separately, with the young being brave and reckless, the old restrained and fearful. To speak in general terms, as many advantages as youth and old age possess separately, those in their prime hold simultaneously, and what the young and old have in excess or insufficiency, of these they have a mean and measure. The body is in its prime from about thirty to thirty-five, the mind around the age of forty-nine.

So much for the respective character types of the young, the old and those in their prime.

[. . .]

Examples and Enthymemes

It remains to speak about all of the common proofs, since we have spoken about those specific [to the different branches of rhetoric]. Common proofs are two in kind, example and enthymeme. (For the maxim is a part of an enthymeme.) First let us speak about the example. For examples are similar to induction, and induction is a starting point.

There are two types of examples: historical and fictional. The latter include comparison and fable, like those of Aesop and the Libyan tales.[10] It's an instance of describing past events if someone argues that it is necessary to make preparations against the king and not allow him to overpower Egypt by pointing out that in the past Darius did not cross over to Greece until he had seized Egypt, whereupon he crossed over, and Xerxes[11] also did not invade Greece until he had seized Egypt, at which point he crossed over, and concluding that if the present king seizes Egypt, he too will cross over, which must not be permitted.

Comparison includes Socratic sayings, for example, if someone should say that a ruler ought not be chosen by lot. For this would be like saying that athletes should be chosen by lot and only those so chosen allowed to compete, or that among sailors the pilot should be chosen by lot, the position going to the winner of a lottery and not to an expert.

An example of a fable is the story told by Stesichorus concerning Phalaris[12] or Aesop's defence of a demagogue. For Stesichorus, when the Himerans had chosen Phalaris as sole ruler and were about to give him a bodyguard, made various arguments then told them a story about a horse that had sole possession of a meadow. When a stag happened along and damaged the pasture, the horse was eager to take vengeance on the stag and asked a man if he would help him. The man agreed on condition that the horse accept a bit and let the man mount him, spear in hand. The horse agreed and the man mounted him, but instead of getting vengeance on the stag, the horse became the man's slave. 'Just so,' he said, 'see to it that in your eagerness to take vengeance on your enemies you don't suffer the same outcome as the horse. You already have a bit, having selected Phalaris as sole ruler; if you give him a bodyguard and let him mount you, you will become his slaves.'

As for Aesop, he was speaking at Samos on behalf of a

popular leader charged with a capital offence. He told the following story: 'A fox while trying to cross a river was swept into a gully. Unable to climb out, she suffered for a long time and became infested with ticks. A hedgehog happened to be wandering by, and when he saw the fox, felt sorry for her and asked if he could remove the ticks. But the fox declined the offer.

'When the hedgehog asked why, the fox said, "These ticks are already full and no longer draw much blood, but if you remove them, other, thirstier ones will come, and they will drink the rest of my blood." The same is true of you, men of Samos. This man is already rich and will cause you no more harm. But if you execute him, needier men will come, and drain away the rest of your resources.'

Fables are suited for speeches in front of the assembled people and they have the advantage of being easy to invent, whereas historical precedents can be hard to find. They should be constructed on the model of comparisons, as long as you can locate the similarity, which is easy through philosophical study. Fables are easier to supply, but historical precedents are more useful for deliberation. For in general the future resembles the past.

If we don't have enthymemes, it is necessary to use examples as demonstrations (for persuasion comes through these). If we do have enthymemes, then we use examples as evidence, letting them serve as epilogue to the enthymemes. Placed first, they will seem like induction, which is not suitable for rhetorical speeches except on occasion; placed last, they will resemble evidence, and evidence is always compelling. If placed first, there must be many such examples; if placed last, one is sufficient. For even one reliable witness is useful.

[. . .]

Let us now consider how to find enthymemes more generally, and then consider their topics. For these are two different inquiries.

It was explained earlier that the enthymeme is a syllogism, how it is a syllogism and how it differs from the syllogisms of dialectic. For it must not draw its conclusion by reaching too far back or including everything. Length leads to lack of clarity, and saying things that are obvious is just useless verbiage. This is the reason why the uneducated can be more persuasive than the educated when speaking to large groups. As the poet says, 'the ignorant are better at enchanting the crowd.'[13] The educated speak in general and abstract terms, while the uneducated talk about what they know, especially matters close at hand. Thus we must base our arguments not on any possible opinion, but on a defined set, such as those accepted by the audience or by those of whom the audience approves (and even the latter must be acceptable to most or all). And our conclusions are to be based only on premises that are generally true, not on those that are necessary. Thus it is of prime importance to understand the subject about which we are speaking or reasoning. Whether it is a political subject or something else, we must have the facts, either all or at least some. For having nothing, you would only be able to draw conclusions from nothing.

For example, how would we be able to advise the Athenians about waging war or not if we don't know what sort of power they have, whether they have navy or infantry or both, how large each is, their revenues, who are their friends and enemies, finally what wars they have waged and with what results and other such matters?

Or how could we praise them, if we knew nothing of the naval battle at Salamis, or the battle of Marathon, or the achievements of the Heracleidae and so forth?[14] For all who praise do so on the basis of beautiful deeds, or deeds that seem to be beautiful. Similarly, those who blame do so on the basis of the opposite sorts of actions, seeking some such that applies to their target, or seems to, for example, that they subjugated the Hellenes and sold into slavery the Aeginetans and Potidaeans[15] who fought as their allies against the barbarian, and any other such matters as may apply to them. In the same way prosecutors and defenders prosecute and defend on the basis of the discoverable facts.

It makes no difference whether the discussion is about Athenians or Spartans, human or divine: the same approach must be taken. For example in advising Achilles, in praising or blaming, in accusing or defending him, we must lay hold of what pertains or seems to pertain, so as to speak on this basis, praising or blaming if there is something fine or disgraceful, accusing or defending if something just or unjust, advising if there is something advantageous or harmful. Likewise about any matter whatsoever, for example about justice, whether it is a good thing or not, [we must derive our arguments] from the things that inhere in justice and goodness.

Since speakers seem to demonstrate in this way, whether they argue strictly or loosely, (for they don't argue on the basis of any and every thing, but on the basis of facts pertaining to the topic at hand), and it is clearly impossible to do otherwise in language, it is evidently necessary, as explained in *Topics*, first, on any given issue, to have on hand a selection of premises about what is possible and most fitting, and about issues that arise on the spot to seek out premises in the same manner, looking not to general principles but to the actual circumstances addressed in the case, applying as many as possible, especially the most relevant.

Now, the more particulars one has, the easier the demonstration, and the more closely connected to the case, the more suitable and less general. By general I mean, for example, praising Achilles as a man and one of the demigods and a warrior at Troy. For these observations apply to many others, and the one who cites them praises Achilles no more than Diomedes. Particulars are those that characterize no one but Achilles, for example that he killed Hector, the best of the Trojans, and also Cycnus,[16] who prevented all the invaders from disembarking, being invulnerable, also that Achilles was the youngest of the warriors and not obligated by oath to fight, and other such details.

[. . .]

Style and Delivery as Elements of Persuasion

Three things must be considered in speech-making: first, the sources of arguments; second, style; and third, the arrangement of the parts of a speech.[17] We have already spoken about arguments, that their sources are also three in number, what they are, and why they are only three – for all persuasion occurs either because the judges themselves have an emotional reaction, or they understand that the speakers have a certain character, or something has been demonstrated to them. We have also spoken of enthymemes and their sources (for there are different types of enthymemes as well as common topics).

It remains to discuss style. For it is not sufficient to know what to say, it is also necessary to know how to say it – which contributes greatly to making the speech appear to be of a certain sort. Following the natural order, there has been, first, an examination of that which naturally comes first, the means of attaining persuasion, second, the arrangement of these things through style, third – and most important yet not yet attempted, delivery. This is because delivery only became an issue late with respect to tragedy and rhapsody.[18] For originally the poets themselves performed the tragedies. So it is clear that there is something of the sort in the study of rhetoric as in poetics, such as others have treated, including Glaucon of Teos.[19]

Delivery[20] involves the voice, how to employ it for each emotion, for example when it should be loud or quiet or in between, and how to use the tones, for example sharp and heavy and middle, and what rhythms to use in each situation. For there are three considerations: volume, harmony and rhythm. Prizewinners at the competitions understand these things. And just as actors at the competitions are more important than poets, so it is in political contests, due to the debased nature of the citizens.

No systematic treatise has yet been composed about these topics, since even discussion of style is of recent origin. And, correctly understood, it does seem rather meretricious, but since the entire study of rhetoric concerns the way a topic is presented, we must attend to this issue not because it is proper to do so, but because it is necessary. In fact, the only legitimate issue [concerning delivery of a speech] is to inquire how not to cause pain or incite pleasure. For it is legitimate to wrangle over facts, but anything other than demonstration is superfluous.

Still, as just pointed out, delivery makes a big difference due to the debased nature of the audience.

However in all instruction there is some slight necessity to consider style. For it makes a difference as to clarity to speak one way or another, although really not very much, but all is for appearance's sake and aimed at the listener. Nobody teaches geometry this way! But whenever style becomes a consideration it will have the same effect as delivery. Some have made a modest attempt to speak about this topic, such as Thrasymachus in his *Eleoi*.[21]

Delivery is also a natural talent and not subject to artistic rules, whereas it is possible to discuss style in a systematic way. So the prizes come in turn to those who are capable in this regard, just as they come to speakers on the basis of their delivery. For orations that are written in advance achieve their effects more through style than through thought. The poets, as is only natural, were the first to set in motion the study of style. For words are imitations, and voice turns out to be the most imitative aspect thereof. This is how the arts of rhapsody and acting and other such were developed. Since the poets, speaking nothing serious, seemed to make a good impression through style, the first oratorical style was poetic, such as that of Gorgias,[22] and even now many uneducated speakers think that this is the most attractive kind of style.

But this is not the case, and rhetorical and poetic style are different from one another. This is clear from what happened, for not even the writers of tragedy use the same approach as they once did. Instead they have changed from tetrameters to iambs, because the iambs are of all metres the most like speech, and they have abandoned words that are not in common usage, with which formerly they adorned their compositions. And now even writers of hexameters have abandoned such words. And so it is absurd to keep imitating the very people who no longer use that approach. It is clear, then, that it is not necessary to discuss in detail everything about style, but only to consider the style of which we are speaking. The rest has been treated in the *Poetics*.[23]

[. . .]

Style must be either strung out and linked with connectives, as in the prologues of dithyrambs, or turned around and similar to the antistrophes[24] of the ancient poets. The strung-out style is the ancient one, for example:

Of the inquiry of Herodotus of Thurii herewith the exposition.[25]

In the past everybody used this style, now hardly any do. I call the style strung-out because it has no foreseeable endpoint in and of itself, until the topic under discussion comes to an end. It is unpleasant because unlimited. For everyone longs to have an end in view. This is why in approaching the turning-point runners catch their breath and stop exerting themselves, although they do not grow tired in advance when they are looking towards the finish.

Such is the strung-out style. The turned-around style is composed of periods, or circuits. By period I mean an expression that has a beginning and an end in itself and a magnitude that can be taken in at a glance. This style is pleasant and easily intelligible. It is pleasant because it is the opposite of unlimited, and at any given moment the hearer thinks he has acquired something and a conclusion has been reached, whereas not foreseeing or completing anything is unpleasant. It is intelligible because it is easy to remember, in that periodic style has a certain regularity, which is easiest of all to remember. This is why people remember things in metre better than those that are just poured out. Metrical language has regularity. And a period must bring a thought to a conclusion and not be cut off, as happens in the iambic verses of Sophocles, for example:

This place is Kalydon, the land of Pelops

When the phrase is broken off in this way, it is possible to understand something different from what is intended, as if, in this case, Kalydon really were located in the Peloponnese.[26]

Now a period may be composed of cola, or simple. If composed of cola the period has a certain completeness and division and is easy to utter in a breath, not in part but in its entirety (for a colon is one of the parts of a period). By single I mean a period of one colon.

Cola and periods should not be either tapering or long. A shorter unit can trip up the listener, for when he has a measure in mind and is hurrying towards it, he must stumble at a pause, as if tripping over an obstacle. But cola and periods that are too long leave the listener behind. They are like runners who wearily continue past the finish line, leaving their fellow runners behind. So too, long periods become a kind of speech, and resemble a prelude, which is the origin of Democritus the Chian's joke at the expense of Melanippides, who, he said, wrote preludes instead of antistrophes.

> A man does harm to himself in doing harm to another. A
> lengthy prelude hurts the composer most of all.[27]

This observation also applies to those who speak in overly long cola. And if the cola are too short, then there is no period; instead they rush the listener headlong.

In periodic style the cola may be either divided or antithetical. As an example of divided cola:

> Often have I marvelled at those who summoned the general
> festivals and established the gymnastic competitions.[28]

In antithesis, either each colon is placed alongside the one to which it is opposed or contrasted, or a single expression unites the opposites, for example:

> They benefited both kinds, those who remained and those who
> followed: for the latter they gained more than they had at home;
> for the former they left what was sufficient at home.

The opposite terms here are 'remained', 'followed', 'sufficient', 'more'. In the expression

> For those who need money and those who wish to enjoy it

enjoyment is set in opposition to acquisition. Other examples follow:

> For it often happens in such situations that the prudent fail while the foolish succeed.

> Immediately they were thought worthy of the prizes for courage; not much later they seized control of the sea.

> Sailing through the mainland, marching through the sea, linking up the Hellespont, digging straight through Athos.

> By nature being citizens, by law deprived of their state.

> Some perished wretchedly, others survived disgracefully.

> In private they use barbarians as slaves, in public they ignore many allies who have been enslaved.

> To possess it while living, to abandon it while dead.

And as someone said against Pitholaos and Lycophron in the law-court:

> At home they sold you, here they bought you.[29]

All of these are instances of antithesis. This kind of style is attractive, for opposites are easily understood, more so when placed side by side; and it resembles syllogism, for refutation is a bringing-together of contraries or opposites. So much for antithesis.

Parisosis is when cola are equal in length, paromoiosis when each colon has words of matching shape. The matched pair can be placed either at the beginning or at the ending. In the beginning, entire words are parallel, at the end, final syllables or inflections of the word, or the word itself. For example, at the beginning:

> farmland he took, fallow from him

or

> awaiting their gifts, berating their guests[30]

or at the end:

> you didn't know he was so rotten, you just assumed he had forgotten

or

> with an abundance of aspiration, a minimum of expectation.

And from word ending as follows:

> deserving prizes, but not at those prices

or using the same word:

> when he lived you spewed abuse, and now you scribble abuse

or syllable:

> you suffered something dreadful if you saw a man act slothful.

It's possible to use all at once, and for an antithesis to display both parison and homoioteleuton. Almost all the beginnings of periods have been enumerated in the treatises of Theodectes.[31] There are even false antitheses, for example when Epicharmus[32] says:

> at times I was with them, at times among them.

INVENTION OR DISCOVERY
OF ARGUMENTS

In the majority of handbooks, the first branch of rhetoric dis-cussed is invention, that is the finding of arguments and approaches appropriate to the matter at hand. We have already encountered one approach to invention in Aristotle's discussion of enthymemes and paradigms. Other writers, without rejecting Aristotelian teaching, developed an approach based on the identification of the critical or decisive issue in a case and the development of a certain stance towards it. The passage presented here, from the anonymous Rhetoric to Her-ennius, *is fairly typical in its analysis of issues and stances. Once the speaker, following the guidelines presented, identi-fies the key point of contention and adopts a stance towards it, he can develop appropriate arguments of a positive or negative sort. The lists of issues, sub-issues and stances pro-vide a kind of scaffolding for the construction of a case.*

This passage, as well as others from the Rhetoric to Heren-nius, *is also of interest for the examples presented by the author. Some are of the fictional sort that would have been used in preliminary school exercises, but others closely track real-life cases in the Roman courts of the late republic.*

Rhetoric to Herennius

1.18–27

Now let's proceed to proof and refutation. All hope of success and the entire justification for one's position are based on proof and refutation. For when we have explained the points in our favour and refuted those in opposition, we have accomplished in its entirety the task of the orator. We will be able to succeed at both proof and refutation, provided we identify the issue in the case. Others have specified four central issues.[1] My teacher claimed there were three, not to detract from others' discovery, but to show that a type they had made double and bipartite should in fact be taught as one.

An issue consists of the primary plea of the defence understood in conjunction with the charge of the accuser. As I have said, there are three such issues: factual,[2] legal and juridical.

An issue is factual when there is dispute as to what happened. For example:[3]

> Ajax is in the woods, and after realizing what he had done while out of his mind, falls on his sword. Ulysses comes upon him, sees that he is dead and removes the bloody weapon from his corpse. Teucer arrives and, seeing his brother dead and the enemy of his brother with a bloody sword, accuses Ulysses of murder.

Here the truth is sought by inference; the dispute will be over the facts. And so the issue of the case is said to be factual.

An issue is legal when a dispute arises over a text or the implication of a text. There are six potential problem areas: text and meaning, contrary laws, ambiguity, definition, transference and analogy.

A dispute about text and meaning arises when the intent of the writer seems to conflict with the text itself. For example:

> Suppose the law orders that those who abandon a ship on account of bad weather lose everything, and that their goods, including the ship if it has been saved, become the property of those who remained on board. During a huge storm, everyone flees a ship in terror and gets into a lifeboat except one invalid. Due to his illness he cannot leave or escape. By chance and luck the ship is carried undamaged into port. The invalid is now in possession of the ship. The previous owner sues to get it back.

This is an issue based on text and meaning, or, we might say, letter and intent.

A dispute over conflicting laws arises when one law requires or permits what another forbids, for example:

> The law forbids anyone convicted of extortion from speaking in the public assembly. Another law orders an augur to identify by name in the assembly the candidate to replace a deceased augur.[4] A certain augur convicted of extortion has designated the candidate for replacement of the deceased. There is a petition to punish him with a fine.

This is a legal issue arising from conflicting laws.

A dispute arises from ambiguity when what is written has two or more meanings, for example:

> The head of a family named his son as heir, but in his will he bequeathed silver vessels to his wife as follows: 'Let my heir convey silver vessels weighing thirty pounds, such as will be selected.' After his death his widow demands certain precious vessels with beautiful relief work. The son says that he is only obliged to give her thirty pounds' weight of vessels, such as will be selected – by himself.

This is a legal controversy arising from ambiguity.

The case hinges on definition when the term to be assigned to an act is in dispute. For example:

> When Lucius Saturninus was about to propose a law setting the price of grain at five-sixths as, Quintus Caepio, who was at the time urban quaestor, told the senate that the treasury could not afford such an outlay.[5] The senate decreed that if Saturninus should refer the matter to the people, he would be considered an enemy of the republic. Saturninus initiated the referral. Caepio, seeing him act against the republic despite the veto of his colleagues, makes an attack with the help of fellow conservatives: he destroys the bridges,[6] overturns the ballot-boxes and prevents further consideration of the motion. Caepio is charged with treason.

This is a legal issue based on definition. For it is a question of defining the term 'treason'.

A dispute arises from transference when the defendant seeks a postponement, a change of prosecutor or a change of judges. The Greeks used this type of issue in actual trials, we Romans in preliminary proceedings. Still, we do sometimes raise this issue even in trials. For example, suppose someone is accused of embezzlement, having removed silver vessels belonging to the public from a private venue. He might argue, once he has defined theft and embezzlement, that he should be tried on the former charge but not the latter.[7]

This subset of legal issue rarely arises in such cases because while in a private action the praetor[8] hears counterpleas and the plaintiff loses the case unless he has a cause for action, in hearings on public matters, the laws provide for a prior ruling, if it suits the defendant, as to whether his opponent is or is not entitled to make an accusation.

Analogy is the issue when a matter comes to trial that is not mentioned in any specific law, but is pursued nonetheless on the basis of similarity to other laws. Here is an example:

> The law states: if a man is insane, let control of his money be in the hands of his paternal relatives and members of his extended

family. Another law: Anyone convicted of killing a parent is to be wrapped and bound in leather and thrown into rushing water. Another law: whatever a head of family has directed regarding his money and his household, let the law sustain. Another law: if a head of family dies without a will, his household and money fall to his paternal relatives and members of his extended family.

Malleolus[9] is convicted of killing his mother. As soon as he is convicted, his face is wrapped in the skin of a wolf and wooden shoes are placed on his feet. He is then taken to prison. His defenders bring tablets to prison and transcribe his will in his presence, with the required witnesses. He is then executed. Those named heirs in his will enter into the inheritance. The younger brother of Malleolus, who opposed him at his trial, invokes his right of inheritance on the basis of the law concerning paternal, or agnate, relations.

Here no specific law is applicable, yet many are treated as applicable, and from them inference is developed, as to whether the will can or cannot be legal. This is a legal issue of analogy.

We have discussed the subheadings of legal issue, now let's consider juridical issue. The issue is juridical when there is an agreement as to what happened, but there is a question as to the justice or injustice of the act. There are two versions of this issue, one absolute or instrinsic, the other assumptive or extrinsic.

The juridical issue is absolute when we assert that the disputed action was correct, independent of any external consideration. For example:

A certain mime verbally attacked the poet Accius[10] by name from the stage. Accius claims injuries in court. The mime makes no defence except that it is legal to call out by name someone in whose name plays are offered for production.

The juridical issue is of the extrinsic sort when the defence is weak on its own, but compelling if extraneous considerations are brought to bear. Such extraneous considerations are of four sorts: acknowledgement, rejection of responsibility, transfer of responsibility, comparison.

It's acknowledgement when the defendant asks to be pardoned. This is divided into exoneration and an appeal for clemency. Exoneration is when the defendant claims that his action was not intentional. It can be based on ignorance, misfortune or necessity: misfortune as in the case of Caepio before the tribune of the plebs concerning the loss of his army;[11] ignorance, as in the case of the man who had a slave killed for killing his master, the man's brother, before he opened the will in which the slave had been set free;[12] necessity, as in the case of the man who failed to return on time from a leave because a flood had blocked his way.

A plea for mercy occurs when the defendant admits that he committed a crime and did so intentionally but asks for pity. This doesn't usually happen in court unless we are arguing on behalf of someone known for his good deeds. For example, we might amplify our argument by supplying a commonplace, such as: 'If he had committed this act, it would still be right to pardon him for his prior good deeds, and yet he does not ask to be pardoned.' This approach isn't used in court, but can be used in the senate, before a general or in the meeting of an advisory group.

The argument arises from transfer of blame when we do not deny the act, but say we were forced to do it by the criminal behaviour of others. For example, Orestes, when defending himself, transferred responsibility to his mother.[13]

The argument consists of removal of the charge when we shift blame to some other person or thing. Here is an example of transfer to a person:

If the one who is accused of killing Publius Sulpicius[14] admits it, but also explains the reason why the act was permissible.

Of transfer to a thing:

If someone is forbidden by plebiscite to do what is required of him as heir.

The argument is from comparison when we say it was necessary to do one thing or another, and that the action we took
was preferable. Here is an example:

> Gaius Popilius, when he was surrounded by the Gauls[15] and
> unable to escape by any means, entered a colloquy with the
> enemy generals. The upshot was that he could lead his army off
> as long as he abandoned their baggage. He reasoned that it was
> better to abandon the baggage than the army. And so he led the
> army off, but left the baggage behind. He is being charged with
> treason.

I believe I have explained the key issues and their subdivisions.
Next to be considered are the strategies for treating issues,
once both sides have reached agreement as to the focus of the
case.

As soon as the key issue has been determined, we must seek
the motive or rationale. The motive is the cause of the alleged
criminal action and structures the defence. For example, to
stay with the case of Orestes for instructional purposes:

> Orestes admits that he killed his mother. If he doesn't advance
> a rationale for the deed, he undermines his defence. And so he
> describes the action without which the alleged crime would not
> have taken place: 'She killed my father.'

Therefore, as I pointed out, the motive or rationale structures
the defence. Without it there is not the slightest doubt that
would delay conviction.

Once the rationale has been discovered, we must determine
the basis of the accusation. This structures the prosecution case
and is presented in opposition to the defence. It is established in
the following manner. When Orestes presents his rationale,
saying, 'I was within my rights to kill her, for she killed my
father', the accuser will use a basis like this: 'But it was not right
for her to be killed by you, or to pay the penalty without being
convicted.'

The decision at trial necessarily hinges on the rationale

presented by the defence and basis presented by the prosecution. We call this the point of contention, for which the Greek term is *krinomenon*. It is established by bringing together the basis and the rationale, as follows:

> Because Orestes says that he killed his mother to avenge his father, the point of contention is whether it was right for Clytemnestra to be killed by her son without a trial.

Thus we absolutely must find the point at issue and organize our entire presentation around it. This is how we find the key point of contention, regardless of the issues and subdivisions under consideration. This is especially true with disputes as to fact, which lack either a defence rationale, since the act is denied, or a prosecutorial basis, since there is no rationale to refute. The point of contention, instead, is assertion and denial of the act. For example:

> Assertion: You killed Ajax.
> Denial: No I didn't.
> Point of contention: Did he or didn't he?

As explained earlier, the entirety of each speech must bear on this point of contention. If there are many issues or sub-issues in a single case, then there will be many points of contention, but all will be identified in a similar manner.

We have tried very hard to discuss clearly and concisely the topics addressed thus far. Now, because the size of this volume has grown quite enough, it is better to take up the remaining topics in another volume, so that the number of letters does not tire you out. But if you think your studies are going too slowly, you can blame the magnitude of the subject as well as my other occupations. Nevertheless, I will try to speed the process and compensate for the time lost to other business. It's only right for me to treat you with generosity, given your service to me and my warm regard for you.

ARRANGEMENT

Once the speaker has settled on the arguments to be deployed in a case, it becomes necessary to arrange them in such a way as to maximize their effect on the audience. This means helping the audience get a clear grasp of the relevant facts of the case, advancing one's own arguments while refuting those of the other side and summoning the appropriate emotions. The account of arrangement presented in Cicero's early treatise called, somewhat confusingly, On Invention, *outlines the standard structure of a judicial speech as found in surviving Roman oratory. Because many of the members of the jury at a trial would have undergone the same rhetorical training as the speakers, a certain conventional pattern of presentation came to be expected. Rather than constraining the speaker, the conventional order of a speech allowed him to display his rhetorical virtuosity without losing the attention of the audience. At the same time, the guidelines presented here helped the speaker to consider the range of possibilities available to him for each part of his speech, thus moving him closer to the composition of a finished product. The speaker who wished, for example, to summon a sense of indignation on the part of his audience wasn't expect to use all fifteen bases or sources of indignation listed here, but, by reviewing the list, he could be reasonably certain he wasn't leaving anything out.*

Cicero
On Invention
Selections from Book 1[1]

Therefore when the focus of dispute and the arguments pertaining to it have been carefully discovered in accordance with our method, then and only then are the remaining parts of the speech to be set in order.

In our view there are altogether six parts: preface or exordium, narration, division, confirmation, refutation and conclusion. Since the exordium comes first, we'll first give guidance on it. The exordium prepares the listener for the rest of the speech; it will succeed if it makes him positively inclined, attentive and open to instruction. Constructing a good exordium requires first determining the nature of the case. Cases are of five types: ethical, surprising, trivial, ambiguous and obscure. With an ethical case the listener is favourably inclined even before we begin to speak. A surprising case is strange or unfamiliar to the listener. A trivial case is one that the listener considers insignificant and not worth paying attention to. In an ambiguous case the point at issue is uncertain and the case is partly shameful, partly honourable, so as to prompt both goodwill and opposition; an obscure case is one in which either the listeners are not very intelligent or a verdict requires understanding of challenging material. Because the types of cases are so different, a different approach is necessary for each type.

[. . .]

In sum, an exordium should be thoughtful and serious and employ all devices that contribute to a sense of dignity, since the best outcome is for the speaker to win the favour of the audience. Brilliance, wit and stylistic polish should be kept to a minimum because they can arouse suspicion of over-preparation and feigned concern, which diminish confidence in the speech and the speaker.

[. . .]

The narration is a presentation of the events that have occurred or are alleged to have occurred. There are three kinds of narration. The first is limited to the case and points of controversy. The second includes some digression beyond the case and charge, either to attack someone or to draw a comparison or to provide some amusement, but in a manner not inappropriate to the matter at hand, or just for the sake of making the affair seem more important. A third kind of narrative has nothing to do with civil affairs but is written and spoken for the sake of entertainment, although it also provides useful practice. [. . .]

With regard to narration in a civil case, there are three requirements: it must be brief, clear and plausible. It will be brief if it starts where necessary and doesn't go back to some remote point; if it will not discuss in detail anything that can be summarized, for example it's often sufficient just to say what happened, not how it happened; if it doesn't extend beyond what is essential; and if it doesn't cross over to some other legal matter. Also brevity is achieved if sometimes a point is left unstated but can be inferred from what has been expressed; if we omit both what hinders the truth and things that neither hinder nor help; if each point is stated only once; and if the narrative does not return to matters that have already been discussed. [. . .]

A narration will be clear if what happened first is presented first and if the temporal sequence of events is preserved, so that the story is told as it happened or could have happened. We should take special care not to mention anything out of order or with twists and turns or to wander to another topic, or start too far back or extend the story too far forwards, or omit anything that is pertinent. The rules about brevity apply to clarity as well. Often the case is hard to follow due to the length of the narrative rather than any obscurity. And we must use words that are clear and precise – a topic to be treated when we cover style.

A narration will be plausible if the things that happen in it are the sorts of things that happen in reality; if the behaviour described conforms with the status of the individuals involved; if motives for actions are clear; if there seem to have been means for the actions; if the time can be shown to be appropriate, the space sufficient, the location convenient for carrying out the act to be narrated; if behaviour matches the nature of the agents, the practice of ordinary people and the expectations of the audience. A narrative that seems likely to be true is constructed on the same bases. [. . .]

Let us now consider the division or partition. A properly handled partition makes the entire speech clear and illuminating. There are two versions, both of which are a great resource for clarifying the case and establishing the key point of disagreement. One approach is to show how we agree with the opposition and how we differ. In this way the mind of the auditor is focused as it should be. The other approach is to briefly lay out, point by point, the topics we will be discussing. The auditor then holds in mind specific topics and will know that the speech is over once they have been covered. [. . .]

Confirmation is the part of the speech in which, through argumentation, we establish the believability and authority of our case. [*The author then proceeds to discuss the strategies for developing arguments, along the lines presented in the section called 'Invention or Discovery of Arguments' above.*]

Refutation is the part of the speech in which, through argumentation, we refute or weaken or make light of the opponent's own confirmation. It uses the same resources for invention as confirmation does, for whatever techniques are used to support an argument can be used to refute it. [. . .]

Generally speaking, an argument is refuted either by refusing to accept its underlying assumptions, or if one or several of the assumptions are accepted, but we deny that a particular conclusion follows from them, or if the form of argumentation is shown to be faulty, or if against a strong argument we set another that is just as strong or even stronger. [. . .]

The conclusion or peroration is the finale and end point of the entire speech. It has three aspects: enumeration, summoning of indignation, appeal to pity. Enumeration or summing-up entails gathering in one place everything discussed throughout the speech for the purpose of reviewing it all at a glance. If everything is treated in the same manner it will be evident to all that you have employed a certain artifice. If matters are handled with variation, it will be possible to avoid such an inference as well as boredom. Therefore sometimes it will be necessary to do what the majority do for simplicity's sake, namely touch on every point individually and briefly run through all arguments. Sometimes, however, it will be necessary to take the more difficult approach and review the issues you promised to discuss in your partition and recall how you addressed each one, for example: 'We have proven this, we have made this plain.' Sometimes it will be useful to ask what the audience ought to expect to be proven. In this way the listener will refresh his own memory and think that there is nothing more that he should be looking for.

In all of these approaches you will sometimes treat your own arguments individually, sometimes – which is more artful – match them with those of your opponent, and sometimes, having reviewed your own argument, proceed to show how you have also refuted what is said against it. Thus through brief comparison the audience will be reminded of what has been proven and what has been disproven. It will also be important to vary your delivery: sometimes you can conduct the summation in your own persona, reminding the audience of what you have said and in what order. Other times you will introduce a different person or entity, assigning to it the entire enumeration. As an example of a different person:

If the author of the law should appear before us and ask you why you are in doubt, what could you say, when such and such has been proven to you? [. . .]

An entity is used when summation is attributed to something like a law, a locale, a city, or a monument, for example:

> What if the laws could speak? Would they not beseech you in these words: 'What more can you ask for, judges, when such and such has been made clear to you?'

With either of these, the various methods of summation are all legitimate. An important lesson for any summation is that for each argument, because the entirety cannot be simply restated, you must choose what is most compelling, and run over such points as briefly as possible. The goal is to reinforce memory, not repeat the speech.

As for summoning indignation, this entails provoking hatred against a person or a sense of grave offence against a deed. [. . .] Any attribute of a person or event can be expanded upon and serve as a basis for indignation. Still, let's consider one by one instructions concerning indignation.

The first basis for an appeal to indignation is to commemorate the attention given to the affair by those who ought to have the greatest authority: immortal gods, as evidenced by lots, oracles, soothsayers, omens, prodigies, responses and so forth; also, our ancestors, kings, states, peoples, wise men, the senate, the people, the writers of laws. The second is to show, with passionate emphasis, who will be affected by this affair, whether everyone or almost everyone (in which case misconduct is atrocious) or superiors, such as those whose rank prompts indignation (in which case it's disgraceful), or those who are equals in mind, fortune, body (in which case it's unjust) or those who are of lower station (in which case it's the height of arrogance). The third technique involves asking what would happen if everybody else behaved in the same way, simultaneously showing that if the defendant gets off, there will be many ready to imitate his boldness. This allows us to describe the evil that will follow. The fourth technique is one in which we explain that many are eagerly awaiting the decision, knowing that what is permissible for one will be permissible for the rest in a similar situation.

A fifth involves showing that in other instances a bad decision can be revised once the truth is known, but that this case,
once decided, cannot be altered by any judgement or corrected
by any authority. A sixth consists of demonstrating that this
deed was performed intentionally and deliberately, then adding that no forgiveness is to be shown to voluntary bad conduct,
even if it is sometimes appropriate in a case of inadvertence.
The seventh involves showing our own indignation, calling the
deed foul, cruel, unspeakable, tyrannical, carried out by force,
direct violence, or wealth in complete contradiction of the law
and a sense of fairness. The eighth technique involves showing
that the crime is not a commonplace one, that it is not committed even by the most violent sorts of men, being unfamiliar to
savage folk, barbarian nations and monstrous beasts. These
will be crimes said to have been committed cruelly against
parents, children, spouses, blood relations, suppliants or against
elders, guests or hosts, neighbours, friends, companions of life
or education, mentors, the dead, those who are wretched and
deserving of pity, distinguished, noble and honoured men,
against those who could not hurt another or defend themselves
against such hurt, for example children, the elderly, women. In
such cases, the fierce arousal of indignation will summon the
greatest hatred against the perpetrators.
The ninth technique is to compare the alleged crime with
other deeds that all agree are crimes, thus showing how much
more atrocious and disgraceful is the charge in this trial. A tenth
involves gathering together everything that was done in the
course of the crime and subsequent to it, deploring and turning
into an accusation each and every point and with our language
as far as possible placing before the eyes the entire affair so that
the disgraceful act will be visible as if each member of the audience had been there in person. The eleventh involves showing
that the crime was committed by the person for whom it was
least right to behave thus and who would be expected to prevent
it at the hands of another. The twelfth involves expressing our
indignation that this has happened to us first, and that it has never
happened to anyone else. Thirteen is to show that insult was
added to injury, thereby stirring up hatred against insolence and

disdain. In the fourteenth we ask the audience to relate our injuries to their own situation, for example if children are involved have them think about their own offspring, if women, have them think about their wives, if old men, about their fathers or parents. In the fifteenth we assert that even opponents and enemies are undeserving of the treatment we have received. Generally speaking these are the ways in which indignation can be communicated most effectively.

Lamentation is an appeal to the pity of the listeners. The first task is to make the mind of the listener compliant and merciful so that he can be affected by the specific appeal. This will be achieved through the use of commonplaces[2] that reveal the power of fortune over everyone and the weakness of humanity. When such things are discussed gravely and thoughtfully the listener's spirit will droop and be ready to show pity since he will reflect on his own weakness while considering someone else's misfortune.

After that, the first theme or topic for inducing pity is demonstrating how those who were once happy and prosperous are now in a bad condition. A second involves temporal distinction, showing the evils they have experienced, are experiencing and will experience. A third consists of lamenting in detail each misfortune, for example when speaking of the death of a son, describe the charm of boyhood, the father's affection, hope, comfort, attention to his upbringing and anything that can be said by way of grieving over whatever misfortune. A fourth means is to describe the shameful humiliations they have endured and will endure, actions unsuited to their age, family, earlier fortune, status and generosity.

The fifth is to place everything, one by one, before the eyes so that the listener actually seems to see them and will be led to pity by the events themselves and not just by words. The sixth is to show how the subject is in distress contrary to what was expected, and that he has not only not achieved what he was hoping for but fallen into the greatest misery. The seventh involves turning to the audience and asking them when they see us to recall their children or parents or someone dear to them. The eighth is to say that something happened that should not have happened, or something hasn't happened that should have, for example: 'I was not present, I did not see, I did not hear his final words, I did not catch his dying breath.' Or: 'In the hands of enemies he died, in a hostile land he has been lying unburied, mutilated by wild beasts, lacking common dignity in death.'

A ninth consists of presenting someone as speaking to a mute or inanimate object, for example a horse, a house, a garment. The mind of listeners who have cherished something of the sort is greatly affected. The tenth puts on display poverty, weakness, isolation. An eleventh in which the speaker hands over to the audience his children, parents or the task of burying his body. A twelfth entails deploring forceful separation from someone you lived with most willingly, such as a parent, a son, a brother or a close friend. A thirteenth in which we angrily complain that we are being mistreated by those from whom we least deserve mistreatment, for example, relatives or friends we have treated kindly and we thought would help us, or by those from whom such ill treatment is unworthy, such as slaves, freedmen, clients or suppliants. A fourteenth consists of begging or beseeching, in which we pray that those who hear will show mercy. A fifteenth in which we present ourselves as mourning the misfortunes not of ourselves but of those who ought to be dear to us. Sixteenth, we show that we feel compassion for others yet remain and will remain generous, noble and tolerant of whatever evils may befall us. For often courage and grandeur, which carry a certain gravity and authority, are more effective at summoning pity than humility and grovelling.

Once the spirits of the audience have been aroused, it will not be necessary to dwell on lamentation for any great length of time. As the rhetorician Apollonius[3] said, 'Nothing dries faster than tears.'

STYLE

Style was of the utmost importance in differentiating rhetorical speech from other modes of communication, such as philosophical discourse, everyday conversation and poetry. Speakers sought to give their language a certain formality and distinction without turning it into an esoteric discourse comprehensible only to a few. The availability of finely calibrated stylistic registers also allowed speakers to signal subtle shifts in significance within a speech, such as the transition from a simple narrative to more vigorous argumentation. A speaker could also cultivate a personal style that differentiated his manner of writing and speaking from that of his peers and rivals. Indeed, most surviving classical authors display a readily identifiable individual style, even as they draw on the stylistic resources more generally available.

As the anonymous author of the Rhetoric to Herennius *makes clear in this passage, all style should be correct, in the sense of using proper Latin (or Greek), and clear, and should avoid unpleasant collocations or repetitions of sounds. Beyond that, style should be distinctive or polished, a goal achieved through the use of what he calls figures of language and figures of thought. Although it is not always clear why a given figure falls into one category as opposed to the other, generally speaking figures of language entail the manipulation of sound effects, word order or the meaning of specific words, whereas figures of thought have to do with the overall presentation of a key idea. Practice in generating and identifying figures of language and of thought expanded the student's sense of the communicative possibilities inherent in language.*

It will be useful to read the fairly mechanical discussion of stylistic devices presented here in conjunction with Cicero's more expansive treatment of rhetorical ornament (pp. 180–216 of this book). Polished speech, that is speech clearly differentiated from everyday conversation, is the goal of both treatises, but only Cicero considers why such speech matters and the principles underlying the rules for attaining it.

Rhetoric to Herennius
4.17–69

Now that we have discussed the genres of style,[1] let us consider
features that characterize a style that is effective and resolved.
Of particular importance to the orator are elegance (or selectivity), arrangement and distinction.

Elegance allows for each and every passage to be expressed
simply and clearly. It can be subdivided into Latinity and clarity. Latinity entails maintaining correct language free of fault.
Two faults diminish Latinity, namely solecism and barbarism.
Solecism occurs when a word does not agree with those preceding it in a group. (We will explain in our treatise on grammar[2]
how to avoid these errors.)

Clarity makes a speech lucid and easy to understand. It
entails using language that is customary and appropriate. Customary words are those employed in everyday conversation.
Appropriate words are those that correspond to the subject.

Arrangement (juxtaposition) entails the ordering of words in
such a way that all parts of an expression are equally polished.
We shall achieve proper arrangement if we avoid frequent
juxtapositions of vowels,[3] which make an expression gaping
and unarticulated, for example:

Many a alderberry oddly arranged

and if we avoid excessive repetition of the same letter, for
which the following verse serves as an example (there's no
reason not to take examples from the writings of others):

O Titus Tatius tyrant truly triply tormented[4]

and this from the same poet:

> who hadn't heard how he'd hidden his horse*5

and if we avoid too much repetition of the same word:

> When the reason of his reasoning is not really real,
> there's really no reason to rely on what he reasons[6]

and if we avoid words that have similar endings, as in:

> weepingly, whiningly, woefully, pray for me[7]

and if we avoid placing words in odd locations, unless suited to our subject. Coelius often makes this mistake, for example:

> In a previous book these things for you written we sent, Lucius Aelius.[8]

It is also necessary to avoid a long periodic expression, which strains the auditor's ears and the speaker's breath.

Setting aside these mistakes in arrangement, let us now consider the attainment of distinction.[9] Distinction makes a speech polished and richly varied. It can be divided into figures of language and figures of thought.

Figures of Language

In a figure of language, the adornment consists in the particular polish given to the words themselves. In a figure of thought, the adornment consists of a special quality in the expressed idea or thought.

[Let us first consider figures of language.][10]

In repetition, successive phrases begin with one and the same word, which may be used with the same or different meanings, for example:

To you must this deed be attributed, to you must we extend our
thanks, to yourselves will this deed of yours be a source of honour.[11]

or

Scipio razed Numantia, Scipio destroyed Carthage, Scipio sealed
the peace pact, Scipio saved the state.

or

You enter the forum? You see the light? You come into our presence? How dare you speak! How dare you seek! How dare you
beg forgiveness! What on earth can you say in your defence? What
on earth do you dare to demand? What on earth do you think we
should concede to you? Did you not ignore your oath? Did you not
betray your allies? Did you not raise your hand against your own
blood? Did you not wallow in every kind of filth?

This figure can be quite charming, while also conveying intensity and vigour.

In conversion, we repeat, not the first word, as in the preceding, but the last, in subsequent phrases, like this:

Against the Carthaginians the Roman people justly prevailed,
decisively prevailed, generously prevailed.

or

When civic harmony was destroyed, liberty was destroyed, trust
was destroyed, friendship was destroyed, the very republic was
destroyed.

or

Gaius Laelius was a self-made man, a talented man, a learned
man, to all responsible people and plans a supportive man – and
so within the state a leading man.

Intertwining employs both previous figures, repeating one word at the beginning and one at the end of successive phrases, for example:

> Who broke treaties time and again? The Carthaginians! Who waged war in the cruellest manner possible? The Carthaginians! Who destroyed our beautiful Italy? The Carthaginians! Who dares to demand forgiveness? The Carthaginians! Yet you have to ask if it's right to grant their request?

Another example:

> Whom the senate has condemned, whom the people have condemned, whom the judgement of everyone has condemned – will you really vote to set him free?

Transduction is repetition of a word in a manner that, rather than causing annoyance, in fact improves the harmony of the speech, as follows:[12]

> Anyone who thinks there is nothing in life more pleasant than life cannot possibly lead a virtuous life.

or

> You call him a decent man, but if he had been a decent man he never would have sought the cruel execution of another decent man. You say he was his enemy. Is that why he fought so hard to take vengeance on an enemy that he became an enemy to himself?

or

> Leave riches to the rich. You, on the other hand, should prefer virtue to riches. For if you are willing to compare riches with virtue, riches will hardly deserve to be among the entourage of virtue.

The same type of figure occurs when the same word is used in different functions, for example:

> Why do you concern yourself with something that causes you such great concern? [. . .]

or

> I will stay with you, if the senate will stay my execution.

In the four figures I have just described, it's not through the speaker's inadequacy that the same word is repeated, rather the repetition conveys a certain liveliness, more easily recognized by the ears than can be demonstrated in writing.

Contrast or antithesis occurs when a passage is constructed around oppositions. For example:

> Flattery starts out sweet, but ends up bitter.

or

> To enemies you are conciliatory, to friends unforgiving.

or

> When all is calm you are disturbed; when all is disturbed, you are calm. You are thrilled about the most boring matters; bored with the most thrilling. When silence is called for, you raise a shout; when it is time to speak up, you stay silent. You show up, you want to leave; you leave, you want to return. In peace you seek war, in war you long for peace. At public meetings you talk of courage, in battle you cannot endure the sound of the trumpet because you are a coward.

This figure gives our style distinction, making it impressive and ornate.

Outcry communicates pain or indignation through the direct address of some person, city, place or thing, in this manner:

You, Africanus, I now address – you whose name, even when dead, grants glory and lustre to the state. Your illustrious descendants have with their very blood fed the cruelty of their enemies.

or

Faithless Fregellae! How quickly your crime caused your collapse! Your brilliance once brightened Italy, now nothing remains of you but your ruins.

or

Enemies of the good! Bandits! Seekers of every innocent life! Do you now assume a right to slander, thanks to the perversity of our courts?

Provided that we use this type of outcry only rarely and when the significance of the subject seems to demand it, we will lead the listener to the state of indignation we intend.

Rhetorical question isn't always impressive or attractive, but it can strengthen a speech by recapitulating all the problems in the opponent's case, for example:

So when you were doing, and saying, and managing all of this, were you alienating the allies from the republic, or were you not? And should someone have been charged with putting a stop to you, or not?

It's called explanation by means of question and answer when we ask ourselves the basis for every statement we make and provide a reason for each and every claim. Here is an example:

Our ancestors, if they convicted a woman of one crime, regarded her, on the basis of a single judgement, as guilty of many. How so? If they convicted her of unchastity, she was also considered guilty of poisoning. Why was that? Because a woman who had committed her body to base desire would be afraid of many people. Whom do you mean? Her husband, parents and everyone else she would see as affected by her disgrace. What then? Obviously she would want to kill those she feared. Why 'obviously'? Because sound reason cannot constrain someone who is frightened at the magnitude of her crime, emboldened by immodesty and reckless due to her very nature as a woman. What then? What did they think of a woman who was guilty of poisoning? That she was necessarily guilty of unchastity. Why? Because nothing leads more easily to this crime than shameful love and violent lust. Besides, they thought that if a woman's mind was corrupt, her body could hardly be chaste. So what? Isn't the same true of men? Not at all. And why do you say that? Because different desires lead men to distinctly different crimes, whereas with women a single desire leads to all crimes.

Another example:

Our ancestors were right when they decided never to execute a king they had captured in battle. Why is that? Because in their view it wasn't right to waste the advantages granted by fortune on punishing people whom the same fortune had recently elevated. But didn't he lead an opposing army? I no longer recall. What on earth do you mean? A brave man, when victory is in doubt, considers his opponents enemies. But when they have been defeated, he thinks of them as fellow humans. His bravery lessens the war, his humanity augments the peace. And the enemy king – would he have done the same if he had been victorious? No, he would surely not have been so wise. Then why spare him? Because it is my practice to despise stupidity, not to imitate it.

This figure especially suits a conversational style and holds the attention of the listener with the charm of the exchange and anticipation of the explanations.

A saying or maxim is an expression drawn from life, which briefly expresses how things are or ought to be. For example:

Every beginning is difficult.

The man who always relies on luck is unaccustomed to honouring virtue.

A man is to be considered free when he is no longer slave to vice.

If nothing is enough for you, you're just as poor as someone who really doesn't have enough.

Choose the way of living that's best. Practice will make you like it.

Simple statements of this sort are not to be avoided. Their brevity, when no explanation is needed, gives much delight.

But also worth using is the type of maxim that provides confirmation along with an explanation. For example:

The entire basis for a good life is to be found in virtue. That's because only virtue is under its own control; everything else is subject to the rule of fortune.

or

Those who choose a friend on the basis of his good luck avoid him as soon as his luck changes. The reason they kept him company is gone, so there's no reason to keep his friendship.

Some maxims are in the form of double statements. Here is an example in which no explanation is given:

Successful people are wrong to think they've escaped the blows of fortune. Wise people fear adversity even when they're successful.

With an explanation, as follows:

Those who think it necessary to excuse the faults of adolescents are mistaken, for age is no impediment to good behaviour. Those who are harsh with adolescents are acting wisely: they want them to acquire at just the right time virtues they can practise all their life.

It's best to insert maxims sparingly. We want people to think of us as pleaders, not preachers. That way, too, when maxims are introduced, they have a big effect. The listener will silently approve a statement drawn from everyday experience that is applied to the specifics of the case.

Reasoning from the contrary occurs when one of two opposing statements is used briefly and conveniently to prove the other. For example:

> Do you imagine that a treacherous ally can be a trustworthy enemy? Would you expect a man who behaves with insufferable arrogance in private affairs to accept limits when he holds a position of power? Or that a man who never tells the truth among his friends will keep from lying at public meetings?

or

> We dislodged them from the hills. Are we now afraid to fight them on the plains? When they were numerous, they were no match for us. Now that their numbers are reduced are we afraid that they are stronger?

This figure ought to be brief and uninterrupted. Its brevity and completeness are satisfying to listen to, and it effectively establishes the speaker's point by establishing a contrast, arguing for what is doubtful on the basis of what is not at all doubtful. It either cannot be refuted or can only be refuted with great difficulty.

A colon, or limb, is a brief, self-contained unit that nonetheless does not convey the entirety of the idea but is instead continued by a successive colon. For example:

> You were both helping the enemy

This is a single colon, it needs to be supplemented by another:

> And hurting your friend.

Now this figure can consist of two cola, but the most effective and resolved contains three, for example:

> You helped your enemy, you hurt your friend and you did not consider your own advantage.

or

> You paid no attention to the republic, you gave no help to your friends, you offered no resistance to the enemy.

A comma, or digit, refers to the use of a differentiated sequence of individual words presented in a clipped style, as follows:

> With voice, looks, ferocity you terrified your adversaries.

or

> You destroyed your enemies with malice, abuse, manipulation, treachery.

This figure has a different sort of energy from the prior one. The prior attacks slowly and sparingly, the latter strikes quickly and repeatedly. Thus the former pulls back the arm and by a twist of the hand strikes the body with a sword, while with the second jabs the body quickly and repeatedly.

A period is a substantial and self-contained group of words in which all the thoughts are brought to completion. It's especially useful in three instances: for a maxim, for reasoning from the contrary and for drawing a conclusion. As a maxim, here is an example:

> Fortune cannot cause much trouble for a man who relies more heavily on virtue than on luck.

In argument from the contrary:

For if we don't place much confidence in luck, then how can luck get in our way?

To draw a conclusion:

But if fortune has the greatest power over those who have entrusted their plans to luck, then we must not so entrust our plans, lest fortune come to dominate us.

With these three types a compressed style must be used to match the force of the period. Indeed, the orator will seem incompetent if he doesn't express the maxim or argument from the contrary or the conclusion with close-packed words. To express other matters through periods of this sort isn't wrong, but it isn't necessary either.

The term conpar, or parallelism, refers to the use of several cola (of which we spoke previously) of roughly the same number of syllables. We don't achieve this by strict counting – that would be childish – but experience and practice will create such a facility that more or less instinctively we can match a colon to the one preceding, for example:

In battle the father was seeking death.
At home the son was arranging a marriage.
Here the omens were predicting disaster.

or

To another man fortune granted success.
For this man effort yielded virtue.

Often with this figure the number of syllables is not exactly equal, but still seems so, if one colon is shorter by one or two syllables, or if one colon contains more syllables, but a syllable or syllables in the other are longer or fuller, so that the length or fullness of the syllables in one colon balances the greater number of syllables in the other.

The figure is called matched inflection (homoioptoton) when in the same passage two or more words of the same case ending are used, for example:

He loves women, hates children, fears vixen.*13

or

In cash he puts all expectation, he has no time for contemplation. His diligence secures his wealth, his negligence corrupts his mind. And yet although he lives this way, he thinks that nobody – besides himself – counts as anybody.

It's called matched ending (homoioteleuton) when two words that don't decline nonetheless end with the same sound, for example:

You dare to act shamelessly and strive to speak aimlessly.

You live resentfully, you break the rules intentionally, you talk unrepentantly.

With boldness you rage, with meekness you fawn.

These two figures, one consisting of similar word endings, the other of similar case endings, are themselves quite compatible with one another. This is why those who use them often place them together in the same part of a speech. Here is an example of how it should be done:

To consort with lovers, cavort with brothers.
Prefer beauties, defer duties.

Here the words that decline have similar declinations, those that don't have similar endings.14

Punning occurs when a slight change of sound or spelling produces similar words with dissimilar meanings. There are several techniques, including weakening or contracting a given letter, for example:

That man who acts so high and mighty was a slave before he became a Slav.*[15]

or the reverse:

For all their betting, they take a beating.

The effect can also be achieved by lengthening a given vowel, as in:

The song of the swan distracted the swain.*[16]

or by shortening the vowel:

He seems eager for office, but I wonder: does he really prefer the Cūria to Curia?[17]

or by adding letters:

He must train himself to restrain himself.

or subtracting:

Had he looked for friends instead of fiends,[18] he'd still be alive today.*

by transposing letters:

Would you rather trust a knave or a vain man?

or by changing them:

Carefully choose whom you chase.

These are puns or word-plays that depend on a slight change of letters or lengthening of vowels or transposition or something else of this sort.

There are other word plays in which the words are not so

similar yet not really dissimilar, of which the following is an example:

> Why I come, who I am, whom I condemn, whom I commend, what I demand you will soon find out.

There's a certain similarity among the words, not as complete as in the prior examples, but worth employing on occasion.
Here's another example of the same sort:

> Let's make sure the refined old men don't think they'll be confined.

This play shows a greater similarity than the one immediately preceding, but less than the earlier ones, because here some letters are added and others at the same time removed.
A third kind involves changing the case[19] of one or more nouns. An example with one noun:

> Alexander the Macedonian devoted his mind to virtue from childhood onward. Alexander's virtues are known and praised throughout the world. It's Alexander everyone fears, while loving him deeply. If to Alexander a longer life had been granted, Macedonian weapons would have flown across the ocean.

Here the change of cases applies to a single noun (Alexander). Changing the cases across several nouns produces a word play of the following sort:

> Tiberius Gracchus, though he administered the republic, was prevented from living longer in the republic due to an undeserved death. To Gaius Gracchus a similar doom was assigned, which tore a man most beloved by the republic from its very bosom. Against Saturninus, betrayed by his trust in evildoers, the perfidious crime of murder was directed. O Drusus, how your blood spattered the walls of your home and the countenance of your father! And from Sulpicius, to whom they just before had conceded all, they now took the right not only to live, but even to be buried!

These last three figures, the one based on similar case endings, the other on similar word endings, the third on various sorts of puns, should be used only rarely in an actual speech since they don't seem possible without a great deal of time and effort. Endeavours of this sort are better suited to amusement than to actual practice. As a result, the credibility, seriousness and austerity of the speaker are diminished if these devices are used in quick succession. They can reduce the speaker's authority because they are charming and amusing rather than dignified and beautiful. Devices that are grand and beautiful are pleasing over a long stretch, but those that are clever and jingling soon become grating, and give offence to hearing, which is the most sensitive of the senses. Therefore, if we use these devices frequently, we seem to be entertaining ourselves with schoolboy exercises, but if we intersperse them here and there throughout, their scattered use brightens the entire speech.

Subjectio, or rhetorical question and answer, occurs when we ask our adversaries – or ourselves – what could possibly be said for them or against us. We then supply what should or should not be said, what will help us or hurt them, as follows:

> I ask, then, how the defendant acquired his wealth. A substantial family legacy? But his father's goods were sold. An inheritance from someone else? But that's impossible: he was disinherited by all his near and dear. Did he win a judgement in a court case? Not only did no such thing occur, he even lost a fortune in a judicial wager. Well, then, if he wasn't enriched by any of these means, he either grows gold at home, or he acquired his wealth illegally.

Another example:

> Often have I observed, gentlemen of the jury, that many defendants seek protection from some honorable deed or association of theirs that not even their enemies can impeach. This defendant can do nothing of the sort! Can he seek refuge in the virtue of his father? No, you convicted that man of a capital crime. What about his own manner of life? What life? What honour? For you all see how he has carried on even in your presence. Perhaps he

will list all of his relatives, so that they can move you to pity?
No, he doesn't have any. Will he introduce friends? There's no
one who wouldn't be ashamed to be called his friend.

or

So I imagine that you accused your enemy, whom you considered guilty, openly in a court of law. Not so, for you killed him
although there was no conviction. Did you fear the laws that
forbid such conduct? On the contrary, you didn't think any such
had been written. When he reminded you of your longstanding
friendship, were you moved? Not in the least, instead you killed
him with all the more gusto. When his sons grovelled at your
feet, were you then touched by pity? No, instead, out of cruelty,
you even kept them from burying him.

This figure is quite energetic and impressive. When our question indicates what should have happened, our answer shows
that it didn't. Thus the indignation attached to the affair is
easily intensified. The same figure can be used in reference to
our own behaviour, for example:

For what could I do, surrounded as I was by so many Gauls?
Was I to fight? But that would have entailed advancing with a
small band of men. Besides, our position was very unfavourable.
Remain in camp? But there was no reason to expect assistance,
and we lacked the wherewithal to stay alive. Abandon camp?
But we were under siege! Sacrifice the lives of the soldiers? But I
was well aware that I had enrolled them on condition of preserving them safe and sound for their country and their families, if
at all possible. Should I have rejected the enemy's terms? Surely
it's more honourable to preserve troops than baggage.

Supplying answers in this manner makes it seem as if nothing
was to be done except what actually was done.
   Gradation or climax (ladder) is the figure in which the
speaker only proceeds to the next word after he has advanced
stepwise to the preceding one. Here's an example:

What hope of liberty remains, if what they want is permitted, and what is permitted is possible, and what is possible, they dare, and what they dare, they actually do, and what they do troubles you not in the least?

or

I didn't believe it without advising it. I didn't advise it without beginning at once to do it. I didn't begin to do it without finishing it. I didn't finish it without approving what I had finished.

or

In the case of Africanus, effort produced virtue, virtue produced glory, glory produced – rivals!

or

Rule of Greece was in the hands of the Athenians. The Athenians were under the control of the Spartans. The Spartans had succumbed to the Thebans. The Thebans were defeated by the Macedonians, who to the rule of Greece in a short time annexed Asia, which they had defeated in war.

There's a certain charm in the quick repetition of each preceding word, which is characteristic of this figure. Definition is a figure that communicates in a clear and concise manner the distinctive properties of an entity, for example:

The majesty of the republic encompasses the dignity and grandeur of the state.

Here's another example:

This is not fiscal restraint, but greed; for fiscal restraint is the careful conservation of your own resources, greed the unjust pursuit of another's.

or

> This is not courage, but rashness; for courage is disregard for
> labour and risk, with an expectation of compensatory benefit,
> whereas rashness is submission to danger, like a gladiator, with-
> out any concern for the pain to be endured.

This figure is useful because it expresses the entire force and
significance of a subject with great clarity and explains it
briefly, so that it seems no further words are needed, nor could
it be expressed more briefly.

Transition is the figure that concisely summarizes what has
been said and briefly explains what is to follow, for example:

> That's how he behaved towards his country. Now see what he
> was like with his parents.

or

> There you have my generosity towards him. Now hear how he
> returned the favour.

This figure has two advantages: it reminds the listener of what
has been said and prepares him for what is to come.

Correction involves taking back what has been said and
replacing it with something more appropriate, as in this
example:

> But if he had asked his hosts, or even merely hinted, he could
> easily have received what he wanted.

or

> For after they had conquered – and at the same time been con-
> quered, for how am I to call it a victory when it did more harm
> than good to the victors?

or

O envy, companion of virtue – how you follow good men, and often even harass them!

The listener is affected by this figure. For the expression in ordinary words seems rather bland, but when followed by the correction of the orator, it invites lively delivery. Still, someone might ask, 'Would it not then be preferable to use the best and choicest word from the outset, especially when writing?' There are times when it isn't preferable, that is, when the change of wording will reveal that the matter is of such a sort that if expressed with a common word it might seem trivial, but when corrected to a more precise word, acquires greater significance. But if you had proceeded right away to the precise word, neither the idea nor the word would have received much attention.

Open concealment occurs when we say that we are passing over or don't know or aren't willing to say precisely what we are now saying, as in the following:

> If this were the right time, I would speak of your boyhood, which you devoted to every sort of immodest behaviour. But I leave it to the side. And I pass over the reports of the tribunes concerning your poor attendance at military training. And that big fine you paid to Lucius Labeo isn't worth mentioning. So I have nothing to say about these matters, but return to the issue of this trial.

or:

> I don't discuss the money you took from our allies. I don't concern myself with all the cities, kingdoms and households you defrauded. I skip over all your thefts and robberies.

This figure is useful for indirectly drawing attention to a helpful point that isn't strictly relevant, or would be long or embarrassing or complicated to explain, or easy to refute. It's better to generate suspicion indirectly than to make a direct claim that could be refuted.

Disjunction occurs when each of two or more statements is brought to a conclusion with a distinct verb, for example:

Look how each city suffered at the hands of the Roman people:
Numantia – destroyed! Carthage – obliterated! Corinth –
demolished! Fregellae – ruined! Not at all did the physical
strength of Numantia help, the military knowledge of Carthage
assist, the cunning of the Corinthians preserve, the shared language and customs of Fregellae protect.

or

Through disease beauty fades, through old age it dies.

In this example both clauses, in the prior example each of
several clauses, ends with a distinct verb.
    Conjoining occurs when expressions are held together by a
verb placed between them:

Beauty from disease withers, or from age.

Adjoining occurs when expressions are held together by a verb
placed not between them but before or after. Before:

Withers beauty from disease or age.

or after:

Beauty from disease or age withers.

Disjunction creates a charming effect, and so we use it sparingly
so as not to overdo it. Conjunction produces concision, and so
is to be used more often. These three ornaments are of a single
type.
    Reduplication is repetition of one or more words for the
sake of emphasis or in an appeal to pity, for example:

Chaos, Gaius Gracchus![20] Domestic and civil chaos is what you
foment.

or

Were you not moved when his mother fell at your feet? Were you not moved?

or

Do you really dare to come into our midst, you traitor? Yes, I say, traitor! Do you really dare to come into our midst?

The repetition of the word has a strong effect on the listener and inflicts a serious wound on the opposing side, as if a weapon were repeatedly piercing the same organ.

Interpretatio or restatement involves not repeating the same word but substituting for one word another that has the same meaning, for example:

The republic you thoroughly destroyed, the state you completely ruined.

or

You assaulted your father, you laid hands on your parent.

It goes without saying that the emotions of the listener will be stirred up when the gravity of the original expression is deepened by restatement.

Commutation occurs when two contrasting ideas are arranged in criss-cross order, in such a way that the second, though contrasting, proceeds directly from the first, for example:

You must eat to live, not live to eat.[21]

or

I avoid writing poetry because I can't write the kind I like, and don't like the kind I can.[22]

or

> What can be said about him isn't being said, what is being said
> can't be said.

or

> A poem should be a speaking painting, a painting a silent poem.[23]

or

> If you're a fool you should say nothing. If you say nothing, it
> doesn't mean you're a fool.

One can't deny that it turns out nicely when in communicating
contrasting content the words are also transposed. I have
appended additional examples[24] of this figure, which is difficult to construct, so that it will be clear that when it is well
understood it can be devised with greater ease.

Surrender or concession is when we indicate in our speech
that we are submitting the entire matter to the will of another,
as follows:

> Since, now that all of my goods have been snatched away, only
> soul and body remain to me, these things too, which are all that
> remain of my prior abundance, I submit to you and your author-
> ity. May you use and abuse me however you deem fit. Order
> what you will with impunity. Speak and I will obey.

Although this figure can be used elsewhere, it is especially suitable for arousing pity.

Indecision is when the orator appears to ask which of two or
more is the best choice, as follows:

> On that occasion the republic suffered due to the stupidity of the
> consuls, or if it must be said, their malice. Or both.

or

Did you really dare to speak, you of all people, a man most – but what epithet can I use that matches your character?

Process of elimination occurs when, having listed every possible explanation for something, we eliminate all but one, which we insist upon. For example:

Now that it is established that 'your' estate is actually mine, then you must demonstrate either that you took possession of it when it was empty, or made it yours through use, or bought it, or obtained it as an inheritance. But you can't have taken possession of it when it was empty, because I was there! And even now you haven't made it yours through use. There's no evidence of a sale. And since I'm still alive you can't have received my property as an inheritance. The only remaining explanation is that you forcibly expelled me from my land!

This figure is of greatest use for arguments involving inference from facts. But unlike many other figures, we can't just use it when we feel like it, but only if the nature of the affair provides the opportunity.

Disconnection (asyndeton)[25] is an expression broken into distinct parts due to the omission of intervening conjunctions, as follows:

Be kind to your father, spare your relations, do favours for your friends, obey the laws.

or

Provide a full defence, refuse nothing, hand your slaves over for interrogation, make every effort to find the truth.

This type of expression has a great deal of energy and produces brevity.

Cutting off (aposiopesis) is when a saying is left incomplete, for example:

> The contest between you and me is not an equal one, because the Roman people consider me – no, I won't say it, I don't want to seem arrogant. You, on the other hand, they have often regarded as a disgrace!

or

> Do you dare to speak this way? You who recently at another man's home – no, I can't say it. I won't disgrace myself by describing your own disgraceful behaviour.

Here, an unspoken suspicion is made more shocking than a clear and open account.

Conclusion, or wrapping up, pins down the logical consequence of what has been said or done previously by means of a short argument, as follows:

> Now if the oracle said that the Greeks could not take Troy without the arrows of Philoctetes, and these arrows served no purpose but to kill Paris, then killing Paris was the same as taking Troy.

There remain ten additional figures of language that I have not scattered at random but separated from the preceding list, because they belong together in the same category. Their common characteristic is that in them language departs from the ordinary force of words and is gracefully applied to another meaning.

First of these figures is nominatio (onomatopoeia). It invites us, when a term is lacking or not really suitable, to supply it through imitation or signification: imitation, as when our ancestors spoke of roaring, mooing, murmuring or hissing; signification or pointing, as in the expression:

> After he attacked the republic there was a crack-up among the leading men.

This figure is to be used sparingly. We don't want to weary the listener with novelty. But if you use it well and on occasion, not only will it not offend, it will even improve your style.

Pronomination (antonomasia) involves using an alternative expression for something that cannot be identified by name, for example, if someone speaking about the Gracchi[26] should say:

But the grandsons of Africanus were not of this sort.

Or again if someone speaking of his adversary were to say:

Observe, judges, how Mr Swordswinger here has treated me.

With this figure we can, whether praising or blaming, stylishly employ an epithet derived from a person's physical or mental characteristics, or even extraneous matters, instead of a proper name.

Denomination (metonymy) consists of deriving an expression from something related, allowing the matter to be understood without use of the precise term. The new term can be taken from something greater than the target term, for example by saying 'Capitoline' when referring to the Tarpeian Rock.[27] It can be created by replacing the invention with the inventor, for example Liber instead of wine, Ceres instead of grain; or by substituting the instrument for its user, for example if in speaking of the Macedonians someone says, 'Not so quickly did the sarisae get control of Greece', or of the Gauls, 'Not so easily was the mataris[28] driven out of Italy.' It can also be attained by substituting cause for effect, for example if, in trying to show that a person did something in war, we say, 'Mars forced you to act this way', or by substituting effect for cause, for example calling an art 'indolent', because it makes people indolent, or cold weather 'sluggish', because it causes sluggishness, or in referring to contents by naming the container, for example:

Italy cannot be bested in warfare, nor Greece in intellectual endeavour.

Here, instead of Greek people and Italian people, the places that contain them are named. We can also refer to a container by naming its contents, for example saying gold or silver or ivory while meaning wealth. It's more difficult to list all of these denominations one by one than actually to create them, for normal usage, not just of poets and orators, but even everyday speech, is full of such expressions.

Periphrasis entails speaking of something simple in a roundabout manner, for example:

The foresight of Scipio smashed the resources of Carthage.

For here, if we weren't seeking to adorn our speech, we would simply say 'Scipio' and 'Carthage'.

Transgression (hyperbaton) refers to changing the word order through reversal or transposition. As an example of reversal:

I am convinced the immortal gods gave you this on account of virtue – yours.[29]

of transposition:

Fortune prevailed against you, unreliable as always. Chance removed the means of living well, every single one.[30]

A transposition of this sort, provided it doesn't create obscurity, will be very useful in constructing periods, which I discussed above. In such constructions we ought to create a more or less poetic rhythm, so that the period can be brought to a close in a resolved and polished style.

Surpassing (hyperbole) consists of going beyond the truth for the sake of maximizing or minimizing something. It can be used independently or in conjunction with comparison. Independently:

As long as we keep the peace in our own city, we will extend our power from the rising to the setting of the sun.

Hyperbole in conjunction with comparison can express similarity or superiority.

As an example of similarity:

His body was white as snow, his face as hot as fire.

of superiority:

> His words flowed sweeter than honey.

or of the same type:

> His weapons flashed more brightly than the rays of the sun.

Intellection (synecdoche) occurs when an entire entity is to be recognized from a part or a part from the whole. A whole from a part as follows:

> Did not the wedding flutes remind you of his marriage?

For the entirety of the marriage ritual is inferred from a single indicator, flutes.

Part from whole, for example if someone in speaking to a person wearing expensive clothing or jewellery should say:

> You display your riches and boast of your abundant wealth.

Sometimes from one many are understood:

> The Spaniard came to the aid of the Carthaginian, as did the monstrous Transalpinian, and in Italy more than one wearer of the toga felt the same way.

And from several one can be understood:

> Dire disaster struck his chests with grief, panting from the depths of his lungs[31] he gasped with dread.

For in the first example many Spaniards and Gauls and togate citizens are to be understood, in the second just one chest and one lung. There the number is diminished for the sake of elegance; here it is increased to create a sense of seriousness.

Misuse (catachresis) entails (mis)using a similar and closely related term instead of the correct and precise one, for example:

The power of a human being is short.

He is sparing in height.

His strategy is protracted.

The speech was heavy.

A shrunken conversation.

Here it is easy to understand how closely related words have been transferred to different entities through a technique of misapplication.

Translatio or metaphor occurs when a word is transferred from one referent to another, with similarity seeming to make the transfer possible and correct. It is employed for the sake of putting something before the eyes, for example:

Due to this upheaval Italy awoke in sudden terror.

or for the sake of brevity:

The recent arrival of the army quickly extinguished the state.

or to avoid obscenity:

His mother enjoys marriage every day.

for the sake of amplifying:

No sorrow or calamity could fill his hatred or satisfy his wicked cruelty.

or diminishing:

He proclaims that he was of enormous assistance because in their difficulty he had wished them well.

or just to make our speech more polished:

At some point the plans of the republic, which have dried up from the malice of enemies, will be refreshed by the virtue of outstanding men.

It's said that a metaphor should be modest, so that it makes a considered transition to a similar topic, rather than seeming to rush recklessly and eagerly, without any selectivity, to something that isn't similar at all.

Permutation[32] is a way of saying one thing literally but meaning something else. It takes three forms: similarity, argument, contrast. It takes the form of similarity when many metaphors of a similar type are used in succession:

> For when dogs start to act like wolves, to whom can we entrust the protection of our flocks?

It takes the form of argument, when similarity of person, place or thing is introduced for the sake of augmenting or diminishing, for example if someone should call Drusus[33]

> the faded glory of the Gracchi.

It takes the form of contrast when for example by way of ridicule we call a spendthrift man 'cheap' and 'miserly'. And in both the last type, based on contrast, and the first, based on similarity, we can also develop argument. For example, through similarity:

> What says the king, our Agamemnon, or, seeing how cruel he is, our Atreus?[34]

From contrast, if we should call an impious man who beat his father 'Aeneas', or a wanton adulterer 'Hippolytus'.[35]

Figures of Thought

This is pretty much everything to be said about figures of speech. Now let's turn to figures of thought.

Distribution involves assigning certain specific matters to multiple distinct persons or things, for example:

> If you cherish the reputation of the senate, you must reject this man. For he has always harshly assaulted the senate. If you want the equestrian rank to be held in high regard in your city, then you must choose to punish him severely; otherwise his shameful behaviour will be a blot upon an honourable class of men. If you have parents, show them through your punishment of this man that you will not tolerate impiety. If you have children, set an example of the penalty imposed by your state on people of this sort.

or

> The job of the senate is to help the state by giving advice. The job of the magistrate is to execute the will of the senate with energy and attention to detail. The job of the people is to select and approve with its votes the best policies and most appropriate leaders.

or

> The duty of the accuser is to bring charges. Of the defender to explain and refute. Of the witness to state what he knows and has heard. Of the presiding judge to keep everyone else to his assigned task. Therefore, Lucius Cassius, if you allow a witness, apart from saying what he knows and has heard, to draw inferences and develop arguments, you confuse the right of the accuser with that of the witness, you endorse the misconduct of a biased witness, and you force the defendant to defend himself twice.[36]

This is a helpful device, for it expresses a great deal briefly and in assigning specific responsibilities clearly defines many things at once.

It's called licence or outspokenness when in speaking before those we ought to respect or fear we nonetheless insist upon our own right to speak out because we seem to be telling the truth in criticizing them or those they love. Here is an example:

Are you surprised, fellow citizens, that your explanation is rejected by everyone? That no one takes your side, that no one stands up in your defence? Don't be surprised, recognize that you are to blame. Why shouldn't everyone shun and avoid this situation? Remember your past defenders, place before your eyes their services to you, consider how it turned out for them. Then recall how thanks to your negligence (for I must speak frankly) and total lack of effort, all of them were slaughtered right before your eyes, while their enemies, thanks to your votes, achieved the highest rank.

or

On what basis, gentlemen, did you hesitate to pass judgement or agree to grant this wicked man a second trial? Wasn't it an open and shut case? Didn't all the witnesses confirm his guilt? Wasn't his defence a feeble joke? Were you afraid that if you condemned him at a first hearing you would be considered cruel? In avoiding an improbable accusation, you opened yourself up to a charge of cowardice. Despite the extraordinary public and private disasters, with even greater ones impending, you just sit and yawn. By day you wait for night, by night you wait for day. Every day brings news of another painful calamity: do you still dawdle in dealing with the cause of these disasters, raise him up for the destruction of the republic, keep him as long as possible in our city?

If it seems a little too acrimonious, this figure can be modified with certain mitigating expressions, for example something like the following can be introduced:

Here I look to your courage, I long for your wisdom, I feel the loss of your usual good sense.

That way any bad feeling caused by frank speech can be countered with praise. The praise diminishes the audience's anger and annoyance, while the frankness prevents any misunderstanding. As in friendship, so in public speaking, frankness, at the right moment, can have a major impact. It keeps the audience from making a mistake and presents the speaker as an ally of both the audience and the truth.

There is a certain shrewder version of frankness of speech which occurs either when we criticize an audience in a way that they want to be criticized or when we say we are afraid of how an audience will take something which we know they will take very well, but insist that we will speak out anyway in the interests of truth. Here are examples of both.

Of the first:

> My fellow citizens, you are too simple and easy-going, too trusting in each and every person. You think that everyone will struggle to keep his promises to you! But you are mistaken, detained by false hope due to your own naivety. You have chosen to seek from others what you could have taken for yourselves.

Of the second:

> Yes, gentlemen, I was indeed friendly with that man, but as to that friendship, although I'm afraid of how you're going to take this, still I must say it, you have deprived me of it. How's that? Because in order to earn your approval, I have chosen to treat your attacker as my enemy rather than my friend.

Thus this figure, which is called frankness, takes two forms, as I have shown. It can be acrimonious, in which case it can be tempered with praise so as not to seem too harsh. Or it can take the form of pretence, which I described second, and which has no need of mitigation as its candour is not real and in fact fits the mindset of the listener.

Understatement (litotes) is reduction or attenuation of a claim to distinction in nature, fortune or effort on our part or that of our client. We use it in order to avoid the appearance of arrogant boasting. For example:

> Now by rights, gentlemen, I can say that through effort and discipline I have become not unknowledgeable of military affairs.

If the speaker had said 'the most knowledgeable', even if it were true, he would seem arrogant. But as it is, what he has said is sufficient for avoiding resentment while securing approval.

Here is another example:

> Did he become a criminal out of greed or necessity? Greed? But he was very helpful to his friends, which is a sign of generosity, the opposite of greed. Necessity? But his father left him an inheritance – I don't mean to exaggerate – that was hardly what we would call small.

This way we avoid saying 'big' or 'enormous'. We use this figure when speaking of great advantages enjoyed by ourselves or those we defend – the sorts of things that spark envy in life and opposition in oratory, if you discuss them thoughtlessly. Therefore just as we avoid envy in life by moderating our behaviour, we avoid opposition or hostility in speaking through careful consideration.

It's called vivid description when we present a clear, detailed and sober account of a possible outcome:

> But if, gentlemen, by your decision you free him, immediately, like a lion released from its cage or some other dreadful beast when its chains have been removed, he will fly here and there across the forum, whetting his appetite for the possessions of every one of you, charging at friend and foe alike, familiar or not, ruining the reputation of some, threatening the civil status of others, breaking up homes and households, undermining the foundations of the state. Therefore, gentlemen, drive him out of the city, free everyone from fear, take heed of your own safety. Trust me, gentlemen, if you release him unpunished, you set a wild and vicious beast upon yourselves.

Another example:

> For if you impose a heavy penalty on the defendant, judges, with a single judgement you will have ended many lives. His aged father, all of whose hope is placed in the young man, will have no

reason to go on living. His small children, deprived of their father's protection, will be exposed to the ridicule and disrespect of their father's enemies; his entire household will collapse from this undeserved calamity. But his enemies, having attained a bloody reward for the cruellest sort of victory, will rejoice in the sufferings of his people. Their arrogance will become evident in word and deed.

Another:

My fellow citizens, you all understand the terrible things that happen when a city is captured. Those who bore arms against the attackers are immediately executed in the cruellest way possible. Of the rest, those whose age and strength allow them to perform labour are carried off into slavery; those who cannot work are killed. At one and the same time a house will be set afire by the enemy and those whom nature or choice have united in intimacy and goodwill are torn apart from one another. Some children are snatched from the laps of their parents, others killed in their embrace, still others sexually assaulted at their parents' feet. Gentlemen, there is no speaker capable of conveying the reality of the situation in words or communicating the magnitude of the disaster in a speech.

This figure can stir indignation or pity by clearly and concisely expressing potential outcomes in their entirety.

Division entails separating one point from another, with an explanation supplied for each.

What's the point in reproaching you? If you're a good person, you don't deserve it; if not, you won't be affected by what I say.

or

Why should I speak about my own accomplishments? If you remember them, I will bore you. If you have forgotten them, what can I possibly accomplish with words when my deeds have had no impact?

or

> There are two things that can motivate a man to seek profit through shameful means. These are poverty and greed. We became familiar with your greed at the time of your falling-out with your brother. And we see now your poverty and need. So how can you insist that you had no motive for this crime?

The difference between division as a figure and division as the third part of a speech, following narration (which I discussed in book one), is as follows. Division as part of a speech outlines the topics to be treated in the rest of the speech. The division discussed here pertains to the matter immediately under consideration and breaks it down into two or three points for elaboration.

Accumulation involves gathering all of the dispersed aspects of a case into a single passage, to make the speech more impressive or incisive or to highlight the number of charges.

> Is there any vice of which this criminal is free? What basis is there for wanting to exonerate him? He betrays his own chastity, plots against that of others. He is lustful, out of control, nasty, arrogant. He's disrespectful of his parents, ungrateful to his friends, hostile to his relatives. He abuses his superiors, treats his peers with disdain, is cruel to those below him. In short, no one can stand him.

Of a similar sort is the kind of crowding together (frequentatio) that is so useful in conjectural cases. Accusations which when spoken separately can seem weak and trivial, if gathered together in one passage, can make the case seem clear rather than dubious. For example:

> Gentlemen of the jury: don't consider my arguments individually, but take them as a unified whole. If the defendant profited from the victim's death, if his lifestyle is of the most shameful sort, his spirit most avaricious, his family property greatly reduced, and if the crime benefited no one but him, and if no one else had equal

opportunity to commit the crime, and for him there were no more opportune means than the ones used; if he neglected nothing that was essential for the crime and did nothing that was not; and if he sought the most favourable place, the ideal occasion and the most opportune moment for committing the crime, and if he spent the longest period of time in completing the crime and did so with great hope of completing it unnoticed; and if in addition before the murder he was seen in the very place where it occurred, by himself, and shortly thereafter during the commission of the crime the voice of the victim was heard; and if after the murder, in the dead of night, as we established, the defendant returned to his home, and on the following day spoke about the murder in shaky and uncertain terms: if all of this has been confirmed either by free testimony or information obtained under torture, and is supported by the opinion of the common people, which must be true, as it arises from the facts; your task, gentlemen, is to assemble sure knowledge, not mere suspicion, on the basis of all of these considerations taken together. For while one or another of these facts may have raised suspicion just by chance, the fact that all of them from beginning to end apply to him is no coincidence but proof of his guilt.

This figure is very helpful. In a case based on inference it is almost always necessary and in other cases and speeches it is often worth employing.

Refining consists of revisiting a topic while appearing to say something different about it. This happens in two ways: we can repeat the point or elaborate on it. Even if we repeat the point, we express it differently, since our aim is to embellish the argument not bludgeon the listener. This alteration can take the form of words, delivery or approach.

Alteration will be verbal when, having made a point, we make it again using other words with the same meaning. For example:

No danger is so great that a wise man would think it to be avoided if the well-being of the country is at stake. When the eternal safety of the state is at issue, no person of good sense will consider fleeing even a danger to his life if he can benefit the republic. He will always make the decision to enter mortal danger if it is for the sake of the country.

Alteration entails a change of delivery if we speak first in a conversational style, then with great ferocity, then in one or another vocal register and with different gestures. While altering the words somewhat we alter the delivery dramatically. This sort of change can't really be demonstrated in writing, but it's easy to imagine, so no example is necessary.

The third type of alteration is in approach. We might express our meaning in dialogue form or through emotional arousal. Dialogue – which I will discuss more fully later in its place, now only briefly, as sufficient for this heading – consists of speech adapted to the rank of a specific person, as follows (for simplicity's sake, I continue with the same theme as above):

> Every wise man will believe that it is necessary to put oneself at risk for the sake of the republic. Often he will address himself as follows: 'I was born not for myself alone, but even more so for my country. Let me pay the debt I owe to fate for my life by giving it for the well-being of the country. For the country nourished me. Safely and honourably it led me to my present age. It fortified my own capacity for judgement with good laws, outstanding customs and the best possible education. How can I possibly repay it for all that I have received?' Because he speaks this way so often to himself, at a time of danger to the republic he will avoid no danger to himself.

The same topic can be approached as an occasion for stirring emotions. We present ourselves as emotionally affected while we seek to affect our listeners. For example:

> Who is possessed of such limited power of thought, whose spirit is constrained to such narrow pathways of resentment, that he does not praise this man most eagerly and judge him most wise, a man who for the safety of the country, for the security of the city, for the prosperity of the republic zealously accepts and freely submits himself to great and terrible

danger? My desire to give this man sufficient praise is much greater than my ability. And I am certain that all of you share this sentiment.

In short, we can achieve an altered presentation of the same topic through three means: words, delivery, approach, with approach taking two forms, dialogue and emotional appeal.

But when we elaborate or talk around the point, we use many different types of alteration. For example, in presenting a simple point, we might append a reason, then repeat the point either with or without reasons, then consider the contrary (all of which I have discussed under figures of speech), or add a simile or example (about which there will be more to say), then a conclusion (which I discussed in the second book, showing how to bring arguments to a conclusion; in this book we explained the figure of speech also known as conclusion). A refinement of this sort, which consists of multiple figures of speech and thought, can thus be quite elaborate. What follows is a treatment in seven parts – using the same subject matter as in the preceding example to help you understand how easily, thanks to rhetorical training, a simple point can be developed in multiple ways.

A wise man will avoid no danger if it is to the benefit of the republic. This is because often, if he will have elected not to perish for the sake of the republic, he will end up perishing along with it. Also, because all good things have been received from one's country, no inconvenience for the sake of the country is considered too serious. Therefore, those who avoid undertaking a risk for the sake of the republic act like fools. They cannot avoid a negative outcome, and besides they will be exposed as ingrates to the state. But those who expose themselves to danger while confronting danger to the country are considered wise: they repay the honour that they owe to the republic, and they prefer to die for the many rather than with the many. And so it is grossly unfair, when it comes to the life that you received from nature and retained thanks to your country, for you to return it when nature demands but not to do so when your country asks. And although you have the opportunity to die on behalf of your country with the highest degree of virtue and honour, you prefer to live in shame and cowardice. And although you are willing to undergo risk for your friends and parents and other relations, for the republic, which embraces all of these as well as the most sacred name of fatherland, you are not willing to put yourself in danger.

Thus, just as we must condemn a man who on a voyage puts his own safety ahead of that of the ship, so we must speak out against one who in the crisis of the republic considers his own rather than the communal well-being. Indeed, from the breakup of a ship, many have escaped unharmed, from the shipwreck of the country, no one can swim off safely. Decius understood this well, for it's said that he devoted himself to the gods of the Underworld and for the sake of his legions rushed into the midst of the enemy.[37] He sacrificed his life, yet he did not lose it. He bought something secure at a cheap price, something magnificent for a small outlay. He gave his life, he received his country. He gave up his life's breath, he acquired glory, which, being passed down from of old, daily shines more brightly. The value of accepting danger for the sake of the republic is evident on the basis of reason, and has been confirmed by examples. Surely those who accept any risk for the sake of their country deserve to be considered wise.

Refinement, then, is achieved in the ways just indicated. I have felt the need to elaborate on this topic both because it improves our presentation when we argue a case, and because it is a very effective exercise for developing the capacity for eloquence. It will be helpful to practise the different means of refinement outside the judicial context, and in the course of actual speeches to put them to use when we are amplifying our argument, as explained in the second book.

Dwelling on the point consists of taking our time over and even returning to the strongest argument, on which the case as a whole hinges. This is a very useful technique, especially suited to a good orator. For the audience is rendered incapable of turning its attention from the strongest point. It isn't possible to append a suitable example, since this topic isn't really separate from the rest of the case, like a limb from a body, but rather is like blood suffusing the whole of a speech.

Contrast is the bringing together of opposites. As I explained earlier, it can be a figure of speech, for example:

To enemies you are conciliatory, to friends unforgiving.

or a figure of thought:

You lament his losses, he rejoices in the blow to the republic. You fear for your fortunes, and for this reason he alone has confidence in his.

The difference between these two types of contrast is that one consists of words placed in close succession, in the other contrasting ideas are expressed comparatively.

Similitude is an expression that transfers a comparable element from a dissimilar topic. It is used as embellishment, as a means of proof, for the sake of clarity or to create vividness. And it is achieved through four methods as well: contrast, negation, parallel, brevity. Different methods are adapted to different goals.

For the sake of embellishment and through contrast, as follows:

Unlike in the palaestra,[38] where the person who receives the flaming torch runs more swiftly in the relay than the one who passes it along, the new general who takes command of the army is not better than the one who sets it down, for an exhausted runner passes the torch to one who is fresh, but an experienced general transmits command to one who is inexperienced.

The point is clear enough even without a similitude, and could be expressed as follows:

It's said that good generals take command of armies from better ones.

But a similitude is incorporated for the sake of embellishment and to give the speech a certain dignity. Here it was expressed through contrast. For a similitude is expressed through contrast when we deny the resemblance between our subject and something else.

A similitude can be used as a negation and for the sake of proving a point, as follows:

> An untamed horse, however well designed by nature, is not suited to the tasks expected of horses; just so, an uneducated man, however talented, cannot attain virtue.

The assertion that a man cannot attain virtue without education comes to seem closer to the truth when it is understood that not even an untrained horse is of much use as a horse. The comparison aims at proving a point, and is established through negation – as the word 'not' near the beginning of the passage makes clear.

A similitude is used for the sake of clarity – and expressed concisely – in the following:

> In a friendship, as in a foot race, you train not just to reach the finish line, but to push yourself beyond it.

This similitude exposes the faulty reasoning of those who criticize others for keeping a promise to support a friend's children even after his death. A runner must build such momentum that he is carried beyond the finish line; a friend must have so much goodwill that in his commitment to the friendship he goes beyond anything his friend could be aware of. This similitude is also expressed in a brief manner. For topic is not separated from topic, as in other instances, but the two are linked and expressed together.

A similitude is used for the sake of vividness, and in the form of a parallel, as follows:

> Think of a cithara[39] player who steps forward dressed in his finery – palla trimmed in gold, purple chlamys[40] embroidered with various colours, golden crown brightened with shining jewels. He holds a cithara adorned with gold and set off with ivory. His beauty, physique and pose assert his dignity.

If, having aroused the audience's expectation in this way, suddenly, when all are silent, he emits a shrieking voice accompanied by the most embarrassing contortions of his body, the greater the expectation generated by his appearance, the greater the derision and contempt as he is thrown off the stage. So too, if a person who occupies an elevated position thanks to fortune and is supplied with great wealth, abounding in the gifts of fortune and all the advantages of nature, is nonetheless completely lacking in virtue and the arts (which are the teachers of virtue), the more plentiful, brilliant and inspiring his gifts, the greater the derision and contempt as he is driven from every gathering of good men.

This figure brings the matter before the eyes of all, embellishing both sides of the comparison by expressing in parallel manner the ineptitude of one party and the indolence of the other. With similitudes it's important to make sure that when we introduce the target of the comparison, we use language adapted to the resemblance, as in the following:

Just as swallows make their appearance in springtime, when all danger of frost has passed . . .

And here, on the basis of resemblance but by means of metaphor, using the same words:

so too false friends make their appearance in calm times, but as soon as they see our fortunes grow cold, they fly away.

It's easy to find similitudes if we keep before our eyes all manner of things, animate and inanimate, mute and articulate, wild and tame, on earth, in the sky, in the sea, artificial, accidental, natural, familiar and unfamiliar, and from their midst track down similitude, such as can embellish or instruct or clarify or place before the eyes. For there needn't be resemblance between the totality of the items compared, but just with respect to the point of comparison.

An example is a presentation of some past deed or saying with specification by name of the author or agent. It serves the same functions as similitude. It makes the matter under discussion more ornate when it is employed for no reason except to make a good impression. It makes the matter easier to understand when it is used to clarify something that is a little obscure; more persuasive when it makes what is said seem likely to be true; and more vivid when it describes something in detail, almost as if you could touch it with your hand. I would have supplied an instance of each type, but I have already defined it in my discussion of refinement and explained its functions in my discussion of similitude. I would rather not write less than necessary for understanding or more than necessary once a topic has been understood.

Image-formation is comparison of one figure with another, with attention to similarity. This can be used for purposes of praise or blame.

For praise, as follows:

> He entered battle with a body like that of a powerful bull, his lunge like that of a ferocious lion.

For blame, that is to induce hatred, as follows:

> That man, who daily slithers through the forum like a hooded snake, with curved fangs, venomous glare and rasping breath, looking this way and that, trying to find someone, anyone whom he can infect with the evil content of his jaws, smearing it with his mouth, injecting it with his teeth, spattering it about with his tongue.

To induce envy or resentment, as follows:

> That fellow, who boasts of his riches, shrieks and carries on like a castrated priest from Phrygia[41] or an oracle-monger, all the while loaded and burdened down with gold.

To induce contempt, as follows:

> That fellow is just like a snail who retreats into hiding and keeps still, while he is being carried off, house included, to be devoured in his entirety.

Portraying is when physical appearance is fashioned and expressed in words, to the point of being recognized, as in the following:

> I'm talking about the man with the red face, the one who's short, stooped, with white and somewhat curly hair, greyish eyes, a big welt on his chin – just in case any of you can remember him.

This figure is useful for designating an individual and appealing if it is brief and precise.

Characterization is when a person's character is delineated by specific indicators, like markers assigned to a type. For example, if you wish to describe someone who is not necessarily rich, but likes to act as if he has money to burn:

> The fellow who thought it was a big deal to be called rich, see now, judges, how he surveys us. Doesn't he seem to be saying: 'I'd gladly give you all a little something, if only you didn't bore me so much.' He props his chin on his left hand and imagines he is blinding us all with the brilliance of his jewellery and the gleam of his gold. When he spots his one and only slave – I know him, although I don't think you do – he calls him first by one name, then by another and still another. 'You there, Sannio,' he says, 'come and see to it that these barbarians don't make a mess of things.' He wants the ignorant who are within earshot to think he is selecting one slave from among many. And he tells him, in a whisper, to arrange the dining couches at home, to beg his uncle to let the Aethiopian accompany him to the baths, to station the Asturian before the door, or ready some other flimsy prop for his fake glory. Then he exclaims, so all can hear: 'Make sure all the money is counted by nightfall, if that's possible.' The slave, who knows his master's ways, responds, 'You'd better send more slaves along, if you want it all counted today.' 'All right then,' he says, 'take Libanus and Sosia with you.' 'Of course.'

Then by chance guests arrive, men he had invited while on his grand tour overseas. The gentleman is no doubt troubled by this development, yet still he does not cease from his mischief. 'You do well to visit,' he says, 'but you should have gone straight to my house.' They reply, 'We would have done so, if we knew where it was.' 'But you could have asked anyone! Still, come along with me.' They follow him. His conversation consists entirely of boasting and bragging. When asked about the crops in the fields, he explains that it's impossible to go and check them out because the villas have burned down, nor does he dare even now to rebuild. 'Yet on my Tusculan estate, I have begun the crazy project of building on the same foundations.' While talking this way, he approaches some house or other where a dining club was scheduled to meet that day. He enters with his guests, on the basis of his familiarity with the owner.

'This is where I live,' he says. He inspects the silver, which had been set out, and checks the coverings on the dining couches. He approves. The slave approaches, he says – audibly – that the master is on his way back, in case he would like to leave. 'Is that so?' he says. 'Let us go, my friends, my brother returns from Falernum. I will meet him on the way. Do please come back at the tenth hour.'

The guests go on their way. He hurries home. As ordered, they return at the tenth hour. They ask for him, they discover whose house it really is, and realizing they'd been tricked, head to an inn. The next day they see the man. They complain and demand an explanation. He says that they had been misled by the similarity of the two places, and had missed his house by an entire street. To the detriment of his own health he had waited for them well into the night.

To his slave Sannio he had given the task of securing vessels, coverings and additional slaves. The clever little fellow had with some effort managed everything beautifully. And so our fellow leads his guests to his home. He says he's lent his biggest house to a friend for a wedding celebration. Then the slave reports that the silver is being called for. The one who had provided it had grown fearful. 'Away with you,' he says, 'I lent him my house, my staff. Does he want my silver as well? Well, even though I

have guests, let him have it, we will enjoy the Samian ware.'[42]
Why bother reporting what he does next? The man's character
is such that the pretence he creates in a single day through bra-
vado and boasting I could scarcely recount in a year of normal
talking.

Character sketches of this sort, which provide descriptions
consistent with the nature of a given person, offer a great deal
of pleasure. They put before the eyes the entirety of a character
type, whether of a braggart, as in our example, or of someone
who is jealous, puffed-up, greedy, a social climber, a lover, a
spendthrift, a thief, a professional informer: the driving passion of each type can be hauled up for scrutiny with this sort
of characterization.

Dialogue consists of assigning to a given person a type of
speech that suits his standing, for example:

> When the city was overflowing with soldiers and everyone out
> of fear was staying indoors, this man comes forward in his mili-
> tary cloak, armed with a sword and spear, accompanied by
> three youths in similar get-up. Suddenly he bursts into a house,
> and demands in a booming voice, 'Where is the rich man who
> owns this house? Why isn't he here before me? Why are you all
> keeping quiet?'
>
> Everyone else stayed silent, struck dumb with fear, while the
> wife of the unfortunate homeowner threw herself at our fel-
> low's feet: 'I beg you, by all that is dearest to you in life, have
> mercy on us, do not destroy those who are already destroyed,
> show restraint in your good fortune. We too were once fortu-
> nate. You, too, are only human.' 'Why don't you hand him over
> and stop hurting my ears with your pleas? He's not going to get
> away.' Meanwhile the master is informed of this monster's
> arrival and told how he is loudly threatening death. As soon as
> he has heard, he says to Gorgias, his children's attendant: 'Gor-
> gias, please, hide the children, protect them, lead them safely
> to adolescence.' Scarcely had he spoken when the other man
> appears and says, 'Are you still here, fool? Hasn't my voice
> frightened you to death? Now satisfy my hatred and anger with

your blood.' But the master of the house responds courageously: 'I was afraid that I had been defeated. But now I understand: you have no intention of combating me in court, where defeat is disgraceful and victory most beautiful. You only wish to kill. So be it, I will die, but I will not be vanquished.'

'How eloquent you are at the last moment of your life! You see I have you in my control. Do you not wish to beg for your life?' Then the wife speaks: 'No! He is begging and beseeching! Please, take pity – and you, by the gods, embrace him. He is your master. He has conquered you – now conquer your pride.' 'Cease to speak words unworthy of me, wife. Be silent and tend to your own affairs. And as for you, go ahead, put an end to my life – and by my death deprive yourself of any hope of living well.' The intruder pushed the wailing wife aside and as the homeowner started to say something or other, no doubt worthy of his virtue, he plunged the sword into his side.

In this example each character has been given language fitting his or her status, as should happen with this figure of thought.

There are also hypothetical dialogues, such as the following:

What do we imagine they will say if you decide the case that way? Won't they speak as follows?

Then supply their speech.

Personification consists of inventing a conversation with an absent person as if he were present, or letting a mute or bodiless entity speak out, giving it appropriate shape and speech, or even action, as follows:

But if this unconquered city should speak, would it not speak as follows? 'I, a city adorned with multiple trophies, enriched by unconditional triumphs, abounding in glorious victories, now, citizens, am assaulted by your seditious behaviour! Perfidious Carthage, powerful Numantia, brilliant Corinth – none of these could bring me to my knees. Am I now to be trampled and ground to bits by you pathetic nonentities?'

or

> But if that famous Lucius Brutus[43] should now return to life and
> appear here before you, would he not speak as follows? 'I ban-
> ished kings: you welcome tyrants. I brought forth liberty: you
> are unwilling to preserve it. I risked my life to liberate our coun-
> try: you have no interest in being free, even when there is no risk
> involved.'

Personification of this sort can be used of many entities, even
mute and inanimate ones. It is especially useful in creating
emphasis and generating pity.

Implication suggests more than it actually says. It can be
generated through exaggeration, ambiguity, logical consequence, self-interruption (aposiopesis) and similitude. Here's
an example constructed by exaggeration, with more being said
than is really true in order to heighten the suspicion:

> This man from so massive a patrimony so soon possesses not
> even a clay pot for acquiring fire.

Through ambiguity when a word can be understood in two or
more senses, but is taken as the speaker wishes: for example, if
one were to say of a man who has received many legacies:

> Look out, you who see so much.[44]

Just as ambiguities are to be avoided if they make our speech
obscure, so too they are to be sought if they produce the right sort
of implication. These can be found easily if we are familiar with
and pay attention to the double and multiple meanings of words.

Implication through logical consequence comes about when
we describe something that proceeds from something else,
making the entire subject suspect. For example, if you say to
the son of a fish-seller:

> Be quiet, you, whose father wiped his nose on his arm.

Through breaking off if we begin to say something, then stop ourselves, leaving plenty of suspicion on the basis of what we have already said, for example:

> A handsome young gentleman at a stranger's house – I'd rather not say more.

Through similitude, when we make a comparison without additional comment, letting our meaning speak for itself, for example:

> Saturninus, do not rely so heavily on the support of the people: the Gracchi are still unavenged.[45]

This figure is quite elegant and yet dignified. It allows the listener to draw an inference while the speaker stays silent.

Brevity means saying something in the absolute minimum number of words, for example:

> On his way he captured Lemnos, next stationed a guard at Thasos, then destroyed the Bithynian city, then returned to the Hellespont, where he immediately took control of Abydos.

or

> Recently consul, he was then first man in the state. He goes to Asia. He's named public enemy and exile. He becomes commander-in-chief and finally consul for the seventh time.[46]

Brevity allows us to say much in few words. It is to be used often, either when there is no need for a long speech or time does not allow us to dally.

We call it visualization when something is expressed in words in such a way that it seems to take place before our eyes. This can be accomplished if we include what happened before or after or during the event itself or if we do not back away from subsequent or surrounding circumstances, as follows:

As soon as Gracchus[47] sees that the people are wavering in fear
that he will change his mind due to the decree of the senate, he
calls for a public debate. Our villain, meanwhile, raging with
criminal intent, flies from the temple of Jupiter. Sweating, eyes
ablaze, hair on end, toga all twisted, with numerous henchmen
he hurries forth. The herald calls for silence for the speaker. But
our villain, out of control, presses his heel on a bench and snaps
off its leg, ordering the others to do the same. Just as Gracchus
begins the invocation to the gods, they all press forwards and
rush towards him from different directions. From among the
people a single voice cries out: 'Run, Tiberius! Run! Don't you
see? Turn around and look!' Then the fickle crowd, suddenly
terrified, takes flight.

But he, foaming at the mouth with crime, exhaling cruelty
from deep in his chest, twists his arm, and with Gracchus uncertain what is going on, yet not moving from his place, he strikes
his temple. Gracchus, abandoning none of his innate virtue,
falls in silence. The other, splattered with the pitiable blood of a
most courageous man, as if he had accomplished a glorious
deed, looks around, and joyously extending his criminal hand
to his well-wishers, returns to the temple of Jupiter.

This figure enriches the subject under discussion and creates
an appeal to pity, especially in narratives of such a sort. It gives
substance to the whole affair and places it before the eyes of
the audience.

All the means of adorning style I have now carefully assembled. If you practise them diligently, Herennius, you will make
your style impressive, dignified and appealing. You will speak
like a true orator and the argument you have developed will
not be presented naked and unadorned in a vulgar manner.

MEMORY

Ancient speakers were expected to deliver their remarks from memory with at most a few notes as prompts. To aid in this process, the schools of rhetoric transmitted a number of memory-systems. Most famous of these is the system of places and images, which is clearly described in the Rhetoric to Herennius. *Although the system is referred to in a number of ancient and medieval treatises, the first-century* CE *professor of rhetoric Quintilian expresses doubt as to its practical efficacy and describes alternative exercises for strengthening the memory. Whatever means were used, it seems clear that ancient speakers were expected to have exceptionally strong verbal, visual and conceptual memories, at least by contemporary standards. It's also clear that the widespread availability of writing did not diminish the social and cultural importance attached to memory. Indeed, for Quintilian, writing is a means for strengthening, rather than replacing, memory.*

Rhetoric to Herennius

3.28–40

Backgrounds and Images

Now let me turn to memory, the treasure-house of all we have discovered and the guardian of every part of rhetoric.

Whether memory can be artificial,[1] or proceeds entirely from nature, we will discuss at a more appropriate time. For now I will take for granted that art and instruction are of great value in this area, and speak accordingly. I am satisfied that there is an art of memory – why I think so I will explain elsewhere. For now let me explain what memory is.

There are, then, two types of memory, one natural, the other artificial, that is, produced by art. Natural memory is embedded in our minds and comes into being together with thought. Artificial memory is memory improved by practice and systematic instruction. But, as with everything else, natural talent at its best resembles what is provided by instruction, while art strengthens and enhances the advantages of nature. So in this case, if someone is endowed with an outstanding natural memory, it closely resembles the artificial, while the artificial retains and amplifies the advantages of nature through methodical instruction. Therefore natural memory is to be strengthened by instruction in order to become extraordinary, and the type of memory that is supplied by instruction requires natural talent. It is neither more nor less true here than in the other arts that teaching thrives on talent, and nature thrives on instruction. The training offered here will be useful to those of you who already possess a good memory by nature, as you will understand presently. And even if those who are naturally gifted have no need of our instruction, it would still be right to offer it as an aid to those who have received less from nature.

So let me speak of artificial memory. Artificial memory consists of places or backgrounds and images. By places we mean distinct locales, either natural or manmade, that are modest in size, complete in themselves and somehow striking, so that we can easily grasp and embrace them in our natural memory. A place might be a building, a space between columns, a corner, an arch or anything of the sort. An image is a figure, mark or replica of whatever we wish to remember. For example, if we wish to remember a horse, a lion and an eagle, we will place images of them in specific places. Just as those who know letters can write down what is dictated to them and recite what they have written, so too those who have studied mnemonics can situate in places the things they have heard and having extracted them, recite from memory. The places are like wax-tablets or sheets of papyrus, the images are the letters, the arrangement of the images is like script, and delivery is like reading. Thus, if we want to remember many things, we must prepare for ourselves many places so that we can deposit many images. It is also necessary to have the places in an order or sequence. Otherwise the randomness of the arrangement will make it impossible for us to follow the images forwards or backwards from our chosen starting point and keep us from speaking out what has been deposited in the places. For example, if we see numerous acquaintances standing in order it makes no difference whether we recite their names starting from the beginning, the end or the middle of the line. The same will be true of places that have been put in order: wherever we start, in whichever direction we choose to proceed, reminded by the images we will be able to speak out what we have entrusted to the places. This is why I recommend arranging places in a distinct order.

We will have to study the selected places thoroughly, so that they remain with us always. Images, like letters, are wiped away when we no longer need them, but places, like wax, should remain. In order not to be mistaken about the number of places, we should make note of every fifth one. For example in the fifth we might set a golden hand, in the tenth a man named Decimus[2] – it will be easy to do likewise for every fifth place. It will be more useful to set our places in a deserted region, as opposed to a busy one, because the crowd of people walking back and forth will confuse and weaken the marks of the images, whereas solitude will keep their shapes precise. Moreover, we should prepare places that differ from one another in type and form, so that they will be distinctly visible. If we select a series of intercolumnar spaces, confusion arising from their similarity will keep us from remembering what belongs in each place. The places should be of moderate height and width, if too large the images will seem vague, if too narrow, it becomes difficult to insert the images. The places must not be too bright or too dark so that the images aren't obscured by shadows and don't produce a glare from their brightness. The interval between places should also be modest, roughly thirty feet. Just like eyesight, thought is weakened if you move the object too far or near.

It's easy enough for a person of broad experience to prepare many suitable places. And if someone thinks he can't find enough that are suitable, then he can invent as many as he wishes. For cognition is able to embrace any region, and in it construct and arrange the setting that constitutes a place. Thus if we are not satisfied with the available supply of places we can construct a region in our imagination and provide a useful distribution of distinct places.

About places this is enough. Let us now discuss images. Because images must resemble real entities, for every real entity we must select an image. Thus likenesses can be based on entities themselves or their associated words. Likenesses based on entities are formed when we supply images that encapsulate the object or activity. Likenesses based on words are established when the memory of each proper and common noun is fixed in an image.

Often we encompass our record of an entire affair in a single notation or image. For example, let's say a prosecutor argues that the victim was poisoned by the defendant, that the motive of the crime was inheritance, and that there were many witnesses and accessories to the crime. If in order to facilitate our defence we wish to remember these claims first and foremost, then we will fashion an image of the entire affair in the first place or locale. If we know what the alleged victim looked like, we will fashion an image of him lying ill in his bed; if we aren't familiar with him, then we can use an image of another invalid, but not someone of low rank, so that he will come to mind quickly. And we will place the defendant at his bedside with a cup in his right hand, tablets in the left, and hanging from his fourth finger the testicles of a ram.[3] In this way we have a record of the witnesses, will and victim of poisoning. We can place the other charges sequentially in places, and whenever we wish to recall something, we can easily seek it in memory by attending to the disposition of shapes and noting the images.

When we intend to use images to convey the likenesses of words, we take on a greater task requiring greater ingenuity. We should do this as follows:

> Now the royal sons of Atreus prepare the homecoming.
> (*Iam domum itionem reges Atridae parant*)

If we want to remember this verse, it will be useful to put in the first location Domitius[4] lifting his hands to the heavens while being lashed by the Marcii Reges:[5] that will cover the section *iam domum itionem reges*. In the second place will be the actors Aesop and Cimber[6] dressed to perform the roles of Agamemnon and Menelaus in the *Iphigenia* – this will do for the words *Atridae parant*.[7] In this way all of the words will be depicted. But this arrangement of images is only successful if we use our notation to stimulate the natural memory, which entails running through the target verse two or three times to ourselves before representing the words with images. In this way instruction will assist nature. For each on its own is less reliable than the two combined, although methodical instruction is, by itself, much the stronger of the two. I wouldn't hesitate to explain this except that I'm worried that if I depart from my proposed outline, the clear and concise nature of my teaching will be undermined.

Some images are strong, sharp and serviceable as reminders, while others are weak, feeble and scarcely able to stimulate recollection. We must consider the basis for this distinction, and with such knowledge in mind, determine what type of images to seek and what type to avoid. Actually, nature itself tells us what to do. For if in everyday life we see objects that are small, familiar and always at hand, we tend not to remember them, because the mind is not being affected by anything new or remarkable. But if we see something that is especially shameful, immoral, unfamiliar, grand, incredible or ridiculous, we generally keep it in mind. We often forget what is immediately present to our eyes or ears. We often remember especially well things that happened in childhood. There can be no other reason for this than that familiar items easily slip from memory while what is unusual or new remains for a longer time. No one is surprised by the rising of the sun, its movement across the sky or its setting, because these things happen every day. Eclipses are noticed because they happen infrequently; and solar eclipses are more noteworthy than lunar because the latter are more frequent. Thus nature is not aroused by a commonplace object or event, but it is stirred up by something new and distinctive. Art should imitate nature, finding what nature desires and pursuing what nature displays. Nothing is discovered by nature last or by art first. So too, beginnings proceed from inborn talent, but learning produces outcomes.

We must develop images, then, of the type that will remain in memory for a long time. This will happen if we pick images that are as distinctive as possible, not vague or overly complex, but engaging in some activity; if they are especially beautiful or ugly; if we dress some of them in crowns or purple robes, to make the likeness move distinct, or depict some as bloody or filthy or smeared with red, to make the form more striking, or if we make the images somehow comical, for this too facilitates memory. Things we easily remember when they are real are not hard to remember when they are depictions that have been carefully designed. But it will be necessary again and again to pass through the original places quickly in order to keep the images fresh.

I know that most Greeks who have written about memory have drawn up lists of images corresponding to words, so that the learner can have them at the ready and not waste energy in seeking them out. I disapprove of this method for a number of reasons. First because it is ridiculous to gather images for, say, a thousand words, when there are countless words in existence. How effective can this be, if in practice we are required to remember any of an infinite supply of words? Second, why would we deprive anyone of the opportunity to take the initiative, but instead supply him with anything he seeks without his having to seek it?[8] Moreover, different people are affected by different resemblances. Often if we say that one shape resembles another, not everyone agrees, because it looks different to different viewers. So too with images: what to us seems carefully matched, to another is hardly noticeable. Thus it's really best for each of us to supply our own images. Finally, it is up to the instructor to explain how to seek an appropriate image, and to offer one or two examples, but hardly an example for everything, for the purposes of clarification. For example, when I teach how to develop an introduction to a speech, I present a method, but don't write out a thousand introductions! I think the same procedure applies with images.

Now just in case you are of the opinion that remembering words is too difficult or not very useful, and are content with remembering content, thinking it easier and more productive, you need to be reminded of why I do not disapprove of remembering words. I believe that people who would like to perform easier tasks without toil or trouble should exercise first on more difficult tasks. What's more, I don't propose memorization of words to help us recite poetry, but instead want this exercise to strengthen memory of content, which is in fact more useful. From the difficult practice of verbatim memory we can effortlessly make a transition to the other kind.

Still, just as in every other discipline, instruction is ineffective without the utmost practice, so too with mnemonics, teaching has little effect unless it is reinforced with industry, study, effort and attention. In order to assure that you have as many places as possible and that they are as well adapted to precepts as possible it will be useful to practise placing images on a daily basis. Although we are sometimes distracted from other studies, nothing can be allowed to interfere with memory exercises. There is never a time when we aren't trying to commit something to memory, least of all when we are engrossed in some important business. Ease of recollection is a useful skill, and as you know, the greater the benefit to be obtained, the greater the effort it's worth investing. You yourself will be able to make the right evaluation once you recognize its utility. It's not my intent to preach further on this topic. I don't want to seem uncertain of your commitment or to have spoken less than the subject requires.

Quintilian
Oratorical Instruction
11.2.23–51

Other Techniques of Memory

I don't deny that such techniques are useful in some circumstances, for example if it's necessary to recall a sequence of items in the order in which they were heard. Those who employ these techniques will set the items in the places they have learned previously, a table, say, in the entry-hall, a platform in the atrium and all the rest, then read them off from where they have placed them. The procedure may also be helpful to those who, after an auction, recall what they have sold and to whom, with the clerks checking against their notebooks. (It's said that Hortensius[9] could do just this.) But the same technique is less useful for memorizing a continuous oration. Thoughts don't supply images the way objects do, but they require invention of a new sign. Still, a particular place may remind us of them, for example the locale in which a given conversation was held.

But how can a connected series of words be grasped using this method? Never mind that some words cannot be represented by likenesses, for example conjunctions. Even assuming that we could provide definite images for everything, like scribes using shorthand, and had an infinite supply, enough to express every word in the five speeches of the second action against Verres,[10] and that we can recall all of them, as if they had been placed in a safe-deposit box, won't the flow of our speech be hampered by this double process of remembering? How can words flow as linked units if for each word we must seek out a unique form? So let Charmadas and the Metrodorus of Scepsis[11] I just mentioned, both of whom used this system, according to Cicero, keep it for themselves. We shall pass along a simpler approach.

If a speech of some length is to be memorized, it will be helpful to learn it part by part. For memory struggles under too great a burden. And the parts must not be too short; otherwise their large number will cut the memory to bits. I'm not going to specify a particular length – that will be determined by the boundaries of the passage, unless it happens to be very long, in which case it too will need to be divided. Still, boundaries must be set so that frequent and continuous practice can preserve the order of the words (which is the most difficult thing), and further repetition can unite the parts that have been memorized. In the case of passages that are difficult to remember, it will be helpful to associate symbols or markers that can serve as reminders and prompt recollection. For no one is so inept as to be ignorant of the symbol he has assigned to each locale. Even if a person is a little slow in this regard, he can use the device of attaching appropriate symbols to the ideas that otherwise slip away. For example, as I mentioned above, an anchor if he needs to speak about a ship, a spear if the topic is a battle.

Symbols are very effective, and one idea can proceed from another, as when we move a ring or tie something to it to remind ourselves of why we did so. Even more useful is to lead the memory from one item to something it resembles. For example, in the case of names, if we need to remember someone named Fabius, we associate him with the famous Fabius the Delayer,[12] who can't be forgotten, or to a friend with the same name. This is even easier in the case of Aper (Boar), Ursus (Bear), Naso (Nose) or Crispus (Curly), since we can recall the etymology of the names. Origin also helps in remembering derived names, like Cicero, Verrius or Aurelius.[13] But enough of this.

A technique that will be helpful for everyone is to learn a speech from the tablets on which you composed it. The orator will track down his recollection by following certain signs, and as if with his eyes he will see not just the pages but even the lines, and he will sometimes speak as if he were reading. If there is a deletion or addition or alteration there are certain marks that keep us from going astray. This procedure bears some resemblance to the technique I discussed earlier, but, based on my experience, it is simpler and more effective.

QUINTILIAN *ORATORICAL INSTRUCTION* 11.2.23-51

To memorize the speech in silence would be best (for I have been asked about this), were it not that other thoughts often occur as if to a mind at ease. Because of this, the mind should be prompted by the voice, and memory assisted by the double effort of speaking and hearing. But the voice should be low, almost a whisper. The person who learns his speech by listening to someone else read it is hampered in that sight is a keener sense than sound; but he's helped in that after he's listened to the speech once or twice he can test his memory and try to keep up with the person who is reading it aloud.

More generally we should test ourselves from time to time, for continuous reading passes over passages that are harder and easier to recall at an equal pace. In testing whether we remember something or not, our focus improves and we waste less time on passages we already know. Only passages that have escaped memory are repeated, to be shored up with frequent repetition, although they tend to stick in the mind precisely because they had once slipped out.

Learning by heart and writing have this in common: they both benefit when health is good, food has been thoroughly digested and the mind is free of other thoughts. In recalling what we have written and retaining what we think, pretty much the only things that matter (not counting practice, which is the most important) are division and composition. If you make the proper division, you cannot go wrong about the sequence of things. For there is a particular correct order in both the distribution of questions or issues and in their development, that is, first, second and so on. The entire sequence will be so cohesive that any addition or omission will be obvious. Aren't we told that Scaevola, in a game of twelve rows,[14] in which he had moved a pebble first and still been defeated, while he headed back to his farm, recalled the sequence of the entire game, and being reminded of where he had gone wrong, went back to the person he had been playing against, who admitted that it had happened just as he remembered? Will order be less important in a speech, especially when it's entirely determined by our judgement, than when a rival participates equally?

A well-composed speech will lead memory according to its sequence. Just as we learn verse more easily than prose, we learn tightly structured prose more readily than loose or random. Even passages that appear to have been uttered extemporaneously can be recalled verbatim. I've managed this, although there's nothing special about my memory, on occasions when someone who was worthy of the honour interrupted one of my declamations and asked me to repeat something. There are witnesses still alive who can verify that I am not lying.

Still, if anyone asks what I consider the single most effective memory technique, I answer: practise, practise, practise. Learn much by heart, think up much and, if possible, do so every day, which will be most effective. Nothing benefits as much from attention, or declines as much from neglect. From the outset boys should be memorizing as much as possible; and whoever, regardless of age, wishes to improve the memory will swallow their initial distaste at regurgitating what they have written and read and chewing the same old cud. The task will go more easily if we begin with just a little and memorize only as much as does not repel us, then increase the amount by a verse each day, an addition of labour that we will barely notice, until at last we can absorb an unlimited amount. We should start with poetry, proceed to oratory and finally attempt writings that are loose in rhythm and far removed from everyday speech, like those of the legal specialists. For training should be more difficult than what we are training for, as with athletes who practise while carrying lead weights, even though their hands will be empty and bare in the actual contest. Nor should I fail to mention that slow minds are least reliable when it comes to recent memories, as will be obvious from everyday experience.

There's no apparent reason for the remarkable fact that even a single night will greatly improve memory – perhaps it's the break from labour that had made it grow tired, perhaps recollection (which is the strongest aspect of memory) ripens and strengthens. Things that could not be recalled on the spot are reassembled on the following day, and time, which is generally considered a cause of forgetfulness, actually strengthens memory. Memories acquired quickly disappear just as quickly. They depart as if, having accomplished their present duty, they have no obligation to the future. It's not really a surprise that memories that have been implanted in the mind over a long period of time are more likely to stay put.

Given the differences in natural talent that I've referred to, we might ask whether a speech should be memorized word for word, or whether it's sufficient to recall the force and order of things to be discussed. Without a doubt there is no universally applicable answer to this question. For if the memory is reliable and there is plenty of time, I would rather not let a single syllable escape. Otherwise there would be no point in writing. This precision is especially to be sought for in boys and their memories should be trained in this habit. We must not grow accustomed to making excuses for ourselves!

For the same reason I think it's a mistake for the boy to be prompted or to look at his notebook, which provides an excuse for inattention. Nor will he recognize that he hasn't learned it well enough if he's never afraid of losing track of something. This is how delivery gets interrupted, and the speech becomes hesitant and irregular. It's as if the speaker is still learning his speech; he loses all the charm of what he has carefully written by making it obvious that he has in fact written it. Memory, on the other hand, creates a reputation for a quick wit. We will seem to have invented what we are saying right then and there, instead of transporting it from home. This will be a big advantage for the orator as well as his case. For a judge admires more and fears less what he does not imagine to have been prepared against him. In courtroom pleading we must take special care that what we have composed so brilliantly we present as flowing naturally and that we sometimes seem to be thinking out and hesitating over the very words we have brought with us.

So the best course of action is clear to all. But if our memory happens by nature to be a little dull or time is insufficient, it will be useless to bind ourselves to each and every word. Forgetting even one of them can prompt an unattractive hesitation or even silence. It's safer by far to hold in mind the facts of the case and allow ourselves to speak without constraint. All of us are reluctant to let go of a word we have carefully selected, and it's difficult to find another when we are searching for the one we wrote. But even this is no compensation for a weak memory, unless the speaker has developed the capacity for talking off the cuff. If he can't do either,[15] I would urge him to give up the work of a pleader and if he has any talent for literary arts, turn to writing. But this is a rare type of incapacity.

Be that as it may, there are numerous examples of the power of memory, whether natural or cultivated. Take Themistocles, who is said to have spoken Persian exceptionally well after only a year; or Mithradates, who is said to have known twenty-two languages, as many as the nations he commanded; or Crassus the Rich, who, when he was in charge of Asia, understood five dialects of Greek, so that whatever the language of the petition, he responded in the same; or Cyrus,[16] who is believed to have known by heart the names of all of his soldiers. Why, it's said of Theodectes[17] that however many verses he heard just once, he could repeat them immediately. People used to say that there are some alive today who can perform the same feat, but I've never had the opportunity to be present. Well, this much we can rely on: whoever believes such things can hope to achieve them.

DELIVERY

Oral performance was key to an orator's success. Performance, or delivery, included vocal projection and modulation, bodily comportment, dress and gesture. Quintilian's Oratorical Instruction is an especially rich source of information on the performance of speeches. He gives many specific, positive suggestions for strengthening the voice, making a positive physical impression and using gesture effectively. In the first selection below, he considers all of the ways in which the orator can make the conclusion, or peroration, of his speech effective, including dramatic delivery, the use of props and the careful orchestration of the behaviour of other people involved in the case. As always, Quintilian is concerned with both what can go right and what can go wrong.

In the second selection, he gives guidance on the orator's conduct during the course of the altercation. This was the brief period allotted to direct, back-and-forth argument between the opposing speakers in a case and required a very different set of skills than the delivery of a speech composed ahead of time. In the final selections on delivery, Quintilian describes many of the mistaken, even ridiculous, uses of voice and gesture he has encountered during his years in the courtroom. Perhaps more than any other passages on ancient rhetoric, these selections from Quintilian give a sense of the everyday life of the working orator.

Quintilian
Oratorical Instruction
6.1.9–52

Appeals to the Emotions

Both parties appeal to the emotions, but to different ones, with the defence using emotion more frequently and more intensely. The prosecution has to rouse the judges, the defence must soothe them – although even the accuser sometimes seeks tears of pity for the victim he avenges, and the defendant at times must vehemently protest against outrageous slander or conspiracy. Thus it's convenient to treat strategies for rousing and soothing, respectively. Techniques are similar to what I discussed in connection with the proem, although here, in the peroration, we have freer rein.

At the beginning of a speech we are more sparing in our attempt to sway the judges, since it's enough to set out on our course, and the entire speech remains. In the epilogue, on the other hand, we have to consider the judge's state of mind as he proceeds to deliberate, and we no longer have an opportunity to speak or hold arguments in reserve.

So both sides have the common task of winning the judge to their point of view and turning him against their adversary, rousing and settling his feelings. A brief rule can be given as follows for either side: the orator should examine all of the strengths of his case, and, having determined which, in reality or as presented, provoke envy, favour, dislike or pity, emphasize those that would affect him the most if he were judge. But it will be safer to consider this topic in detail.

In my discussion of the exordium I have already described factors that incline the judge towards the accuser. Certain considerations, which it is sufficient to outline at the beginning of a speech, must be treated in full in the peroration, especially if the accused is a violent, unpopular or dangerous sort, or if conviction will bring glory to the judges and acquittal damage their reputations.

For example, Calvus spoke especially well against Vatinius,[1] when he said 'you judges all know that bribery was committed, and everybody else knows that you know.' In his *Speeches against Verres*,[2] Cicero went so far as to argue that the bad reputation of the courts could be corrected by condemning the defendant (which is one of the methods mentioned earlier). If you are going to summon fear for the same purpose, better here than in the proem. I have already shared my thoughts on this matter in another book.

It's possible to rouse envy, hatred and anger more freely in the summation. The defendant's influence makes the judge resentful, his disgraceful conduct rouses hatred and his hostility to the proceedings rouses anger, that is, if he is aggressive, arrogant or indifferent, which can be sensed not only from his deeds or words but from his facial expression, dress and overall manner. When I was young the prosecutor of Cossutianus Capito[3] was held in high regard for having spoken, in Greek, to this effect: 'You are reluctant to show fear even of Caesar.'

For the accuser, it's most important to make the crime seem especially atrocious and, if possible, exceptionally pitiable. Its atrocious character can arise from the act itself, the perpetrator, the victim, the intent, occasion, place or manner, all of which lend themselves to an infinite range of treatments.

Let's say we are prosecuting a case of assault. First we speak about the deed itself, then if the victim was old, young, a magistrate, respectable, a good citizen, also if he was struck by someone vile and contemptible or in contrast by someone with too much power or by one who was especially obliged not to do so. Did it happen on a feast day or during a period when the courts were being severe in punishing this type of crime or at a time when the community was in turmoil? Did it happen at a theatre? a temple? a meeting of the assembly?

Resentment is more intense if the crime wasn't committed

by mistake or in a moment of anger, or if the anger was un-
justified, for example the victim was helping his father or
defending himself or running for office against the assailant,
or if it appears that the assailant had intended to do something
even worse. The manner of a crime is especially indicative of
its atrocious nature, for example, if the act was done deliberately or with intent to insult the victim, as when Demosthenes
seeks to rouse resentment against Medias by describing where
on his body he was struck, the expression on his assailant's
face and his own costume on the occasion of the crime.[4]

Or, consider a prosecution for murder. Was it committed
with a sword? fire? poison? one wound or many? immediately,
or after tormenting the victim with anticipation? – all highly
relevant considerations. The accuser will often make use of
an appeal to pity by lamenting the misfortune of the one he
avenges or the loss suffered by children and parents. He can
stir the judges with an image of the future, describing what
awaits those who have filed complaints about violence and
wrongdoing if they don't gain justice: exile from the city, loss
of property or whatever else an opponent will force them to
endure.

But more often the prosecutor's task is to keep the judge
from pitying the defendant and to incite him to do his duty
courageously. You must anticipate what the opposition might
say or do. For it makes judges more scrupulous about their
responsibility and deprives the defence of any advantage if the
latter are forced to restate arguments that have already been
addressed by the prosecution and have thus lost their surprise
value. For example, Messalla, in his prosecution of Aufidia,
warned Servius Sulpicius not to mention the danger faced by
the signatories or by the defendant herself.[5] So too, Aeschines
predicted the arguments Demosthenes would use in making a
defence.[6] Occasionally it will be necessary to tell the judges
how they should respond to defence petitions. This is a type of
recapitulation or reminder.

In support of the defendant, one can cite personal dignity
and valour, the scars of war, and the nobility and deeds of
ancestors. This last point Cicero and Asinius raised, almost as

if in competition, with the one defending the elder Scaurus, the other defending the younger.[7] It's also helpful to explain the motivation behind the case, for example if the defendant seems to have roused enmity on account of an honourable deed, especially an act of generosity, decency or compassion. It will make his position seem more in line with justice if he can be shown merely to seek from the judges what he has granted to others. Reference can be made to the interests of the state, the renown of the judges, the precedent to be set by the decision and the memory of posterity.

Still, an appeal to pity has the greatest effect. It inclines the judges in your direction and all but forces them to reveal their feelings through their tears. Pity will be sought on the basis of prior or current sufferings of the defendant or the sufferings that await him if condemned. These can be made to seem twice as bad if we discuss his past and potential future status. It's also worthwhile to call attention to the age and sex of the accused, to his loved ones, namely children, parents and close relations, all of which can be handled in various ways. Sometimes the speaker will emphasize his own close relationship to the defendant, for example Cicero in his speech *For Milo*:[8]

> O wretched me! O unlucky you! You, Milo, were able to restore me to the country by appealing to these men right here. Will I not be able to retain you in this country by appealing to them as well?

This approach is particularly useful if, as was then the case, the accused is not in a position to beg on his own behalf. For who could stand it if Milo beseeched the court for his own acquittal, given his admission that he had indeed, albeit out of necessity, killed a man of noble rank? And so Cicero sought the favour of the judges by emphasizing Milo's distinction, and did the weeping for him.

Especially useful in such circumstances are prosopopoeiae, or speeches impersonating others, of the sort an advocate might put in the mouth of a client. The bare facts can stir emotion, but when we speak in the voice of others, their personalities intensify the effect. It is as if the judge is encountering the voice and feeling not of someone lamenting another's fate, but of the wretches themselves whose silent appearance alone would summon tears. And although it is very moving for a defendant to utter his own laments, it can be even more effective for those laments to be uttered by an impersonator, just as an actor is more effective in stirring emotions when he performs a fictional role on stage than when he speaks in his own person. For example, Cicero, who composed no entreaties for Milo, but instead commended him to the judges for his distinguished character, indirectly supplied him with words befitting the lament of a courageous man, saying:

In vain all my labours! My false hopes! My useless plans![9]

An appeal to pity should never be lengthy. Not without reason do we say that nothing dries faster than tears. Time lessens real sorrows; no wonder the semblance of suffering that we fashion in speaking disappears so quickly. If we drag out our lament, the listener grows tired of the tears, takes a mental break and resumes the more intellectual approach which the emotional assault had curtailed. We must not let the effect fizzle out, but should instead abandon the emotion just when we have made it most intense. Nor are we to expect that anyone will weep for long over another's troubles. In this portion of a speech, then, more than anywhere else, our eloquence must swell, because any expression that does not augment the earlier effect seems to detract from it, and emotion that grows weak easily vanishes.

Action is as important as speech when it comes to summoning tears. This is why defence counsel routinely have their clients appear dirty and ungroomed, along with their children and parents, while the prosecution will display a sword smeared with gore, bone-fragments plucked from wounds, blood-drenched clothing, unbandaged wounds and battered bodies stripped bare. The effect of such displays is enormous as they all but guide the minds of men into the event itself, as when the bloody toga of Julius Caesar[10] carried at the head of his funeral procession stirred the Roman people to a frenzy. Everybody knew that he had been killed and that his corpse had been placed on the bier. But the robe drenched with blood made the image of the crime so vivid that it seemed not that Caesar had been killed, but that he was being killed right then and there.

Still, I wouldn't recommend a practice that I have read of and even witnessed, in which the actual crime is depicted on a placard or canvas with the intent of angering the judge at its atrocity. How childish an orator must be to think that a drawing will speak more effectively than his eloquence! On the other hand, I know for a fact that mourning clothes and squalor, on the defendant and his relatives, have been advantageous, and that prayers of entreaty have saved the day. Appealing to the judges by all that is near and dear to them, especially if the defendant too has a wife and children, will be useful, and calling upon the gods gives the appearance of a clean conscience. Falling on the ground and grasping the knees of the judges can also make a difference, unless the status and prior life of the defendant keep him from doing so. Some deeds must be defended as boldly as they were committed, although there must be a reasonable basis for our insistence. Otherwise overconfidence might cause resentment.

Cicero gives an excellent example of such techniques in his defence of Lucius Murena against very distinguished accusers.[11] He persuaded the court that nothing was more advantageous in the then-current state of affairs than that both consuls (including Murena) take office on the first of January. Of course there is no need for such an argument nowadays, when the safety of the state relies on the attention and protection of a single leader and can hardly be imperilled by the outcome of any given trial.

I have spoken about prosecutors and defendants because appeals to emotion are especially important in public trials. But perorations of both sorts are employed in private cases as well, with one side depending on a point-by-point summary of evidence, and the other depending on tears, at least if the status or reputation of the litigant is at risk. To play the tragedian in a minor dispute is like dressing a baby in the mask and boots of Hercules!

Here is another warning: it makes a great difference, in my judgement, how the client adapts himself to the speaker during the epilogue. Sometimes it is the client's inexperience, stiffness, clumsy or awkward behaviour that spoils the effect, so the speaker must take extra precautions. Believe it or not, I have even seen clients undermining their patrons by showing no expression or changing seats at an inappropriate moment or by some action or expression that sparks laughter, even when the presentation is taking a turn for the dramatic.

Once a patron transferred a little girl, who was said to be the sister of his opponent (for this was the subject of litigation), to the opposite benches, as if he would leave her on her brother's lap. But the brother, whom I had warned in advance, had left the room. The patron, an eloquent man on other occasions, was rendered speechless by the unexpected turn of events, and carried the infant back to his side, quite awkwardly.

Another orator thought it would be of great benefit to the defendant to display the image of her husband, but it only caused repeated laughter. For the men who were assigned the task of presenting the portrait, not knowing what an epilogue was, kept uncovering the image whenever the speaker looked in their direction. Being a wax impression taken from an old man's cadaver, it was hideous, and its repeated display ruined the effect of the rest of the oration. What happened to Glyco, whose cognomen was Spiridion, is also well known. When he asked a little boy he had led into court why he was crying, the boy answered: because my tutor is pinching me. But nothing is more instructive about the perils of a peroration than the story Cicero tells about the Caepasii.[12]

Still, even unexpected events can be handled by a speaker who finds it easy to adapt his performance. Those who stick to the script either grow silent during these incidents or say things that are very often untrue. Hence 'he extends his suppliant hands to your knees' or 'the wretch clings to his children' or 'he cries "look at me"' even though nothing of the sort is happening.

This kind of mistake is the fault of the schools, where we freely make things up, and whatever we want is taken as a given. Reality doesn't work this way. When a young pleader challenged Cassius,[13] 'Why do you glare at me with angry countenance, Severus?', the latter brilliantly responded, 'I was doing nothing of the sort, but if that's what you've written, take a look', and scowled at him as theatrically as he could.

Something especially to keep in mind: never try to summon tears unless you intend to use the full force of your talent. As effective as an appeal to pity can be when it succeeds, it leaves the audience cold when it fails. A weak speaker would be better off letting the judges figure things out on their own. For the appearance, voice and expression of the defendant too often become a source of amusement to men they are intended to sway. The speaker must take careful stock of his abilities and recognize how great a burden he would be assuming. There is no middle ground here: the performance is met with tears – or laughter.

Of course, the task of the epilogue includes dispelling pity as well as summoning it. We can lead back to justice the judges who have been moved to tears, sometimes through a steady explanation, sometimes with a clever quip, for example 'Give the boy some bread so he stops crying.' Or, as counsel said to a heavyset litigant, whose adversary, again a boy, had been carried about among the judges by his own advocate, 'What am I supposed to do? I can't hoist you!'

But there's no need for clowning. Thus, I don't approve of that once-distinguished orator who, when his opponent had brought forth some little boys during his epilogue, scattered dice among them, which they began to fight over. Their lack of awareness of the seriousness of their situation could just as easily have aroused the audience's pity. Also mistaken was the speaker who, when the prosecution had displayed the bloody sword that was said to be the murder weapon, immediately, as if in terror, hurried from the benches and, when summoned to speak, peaked out from the audience with his head partly covered and asked whether 'that fellow with the sword' had gone away. He got a laugh, but still looked ridiculous.

Theatrical effects of this sort can be diminished by eloquence. Cicero provides a good example when he speaks very gravely about the portrait of Saturninus in defence of Rabirius[14] or in his defence of Varenus[15] uses many witticisms to counter the appearance in court of a young man whose wound kept being unbandaged.

Epilogues can be of a gentler sort, for example, when we ingratiate ourselves with an adversary who happens to be a person worthy of great respect, or when we offer some friendly advice or encourage reconciliation. Passienus handled this well when he represented his own wife Domitia in a suit to recover money from her brother Ahenobarbus.[16] For when he had spoken at length about their relationship, he went on to discuss their fortunes, which were both enormous, saying: 'There is nothing either of you needs less than what you are arguing about.'

Appeals to emotion, even if they seem characteristic of the proem or the peroration, where indeed they do occur most frequently, nevertheless are sometimes welcome in other sections, provided they are brief and much is kept in reserve. But in the conclusion, if ever, it is permitted to draw on all the sources of eloquence. For if we have spoken well so far, we will have the goodwill of the judges, and, having steered clear of the rocky shoals, can unfurl all our sails. Because the chief task of the epilogue is amplification, it is perfectly acceptable to deploy grand and elevated words and thoughts. It's time to stir up the whole theatre, so to speak, now that we've reached the point at which the tragic and comic playwrights of old would command the audience 'applaud!'[17]

Quintilian
Oratorical Instruction
6.4.1–22

Conducting an Altercation

It might seem better to consider the principles of altercation[18] after covering everything pertaining to continuous oratory, since it takes place last in order [in a legal proceeding]. But altercation exclusively entails invention, making no use of organization and little of stylistic ornament, and not requiring anything special in the way of memory or delivery. And so I think it will not be out of sequence to discuss prior to the second of the five parts of rhetoric something that depends entirely on the first.

Other writers have omitted altercation entirely, perhaps on the grounds that it is covered by the rest of their instruction. For altercation consists of either attack or defence, about which no more needs to be said here, since whatever produces proof in a continuous speech does so as well in a brief and discontinuous engagement. We don't say different things in an altercation, we just say them in a different manner, through question and response, a topic that was also covered in our discussion of witnesses. Nevertheless, since we have undertaken a work designed to be rather broad and no one can be called a perfect orator without this skill, let us devote some attention to this distinctive task as well, which is sometimes the chief factor determining victory. For in cases involving general quality, where the question is whether an act was right or wrong, continuous oratory is most important, with a speech usually being sufficient for addressing issues of definition or the determination of facts by artificial proof. In other cases (the most common type), which are decided by inartificial or mixed proofs, it is during the altercation that the conflict is most acute and speakers clash in close combat.

In the altercation our strongest points must be impressed on the judge's memory; we must sustain all that we have committed to in our speech while refuting the false claims of our opponents. This is when the judge pays closest attention. A number of mediocre speakers have rightly earned renown as advocates thanks to their success in altercation. Others, in contrast, thinking they have done justice to their clients with a showy display of declamation, abandon the courtroom with their entourage of admirers and leave the decisive battle to inexperienced and often low-status colleagues. As a result, in private suits you may well see one advocate present the case, another defend it. If responsibilities are to be divided, surely the latter is the more important, and it is an embarrassment to the art of speaking if lesser men are of greater use to clients. In public cases, to be sure, the proclamation of the herald acknowledges the altercator in addition to the other speakers.

Altercation requires above all a quick and supple intelligence, and an assertive presence. There is no time to think. You must speak at once, and respond almost before your opponent has delivered his blow. On every issue the advocate must know his case not just in detail, but inside and out; in altercation it is especially important to have complete awareness of every person, circumstance, time and place. Otherwise the altercator will often have to remain silent or accept the promptings of others – who frequently, out of eagerness to say something, make foolish suggestions. And so it often happens that we are embarrassed by our trust in another's stupidity. Nor do these prompters always speak privately: some turn the altercation into an open brawl. A whole host of people, infuriated, might cry out so that the judge hears something inadvisable and ends up learning that something damaging to the case is being covered up right before he is to make his decision.

And so the skilled debater must avoid the mistake of growing angry; no emotion is a greater obstacle to clear thinking or more likely to carry the speaker beyond the case at hand or induce him to give – and therefore receive – verbal abuse.

Sometimes it even incites him against the judges. Restraint and occasionally even meekness are preferable. Refuting the statements of opponents is not the only strategy. They can be treated with contempt, made light of, even ridiculed. No occasion offers greater opportunity for wit and charm. Of course, this only applies if the case is being conducted in an orderly and professional manner. If the opposition is stirring things up, then we must be bold and courageously stand up to their shameless conduct.

For there are some speakers so brazen that they raise a great outcry and interrupt other speakers and throw everything into confusion. It will be necessary not just to avoid imitating them, but even to repel their onslaughts and crush their insolence by repeatedly calling on the judges or presiding magistrates to enforce the order of speaking. The task of the altercator isn't suited to a retiring personality or one that is overly yielding; too often we make the mistake of describing as decent conduct what is really just weakness.

The most effective quality in altercation is acumen (keenness of insight). This does not arise from art (for nature cannot be taught), but it can be improved by art. Above all we keep before our eyes the issue in question and our desired outcome. When we do so, we will not drift into wrangling nor waste our allotted time in insults, and we will be quite happy if our opponent does just that.

Preparation for every occasion entails careful anticipation of possible assertions by the opposition and possible responses on our part. An additional technique consists of suddenly producing in altercation arguments that had been concealed in the set speech. This is similar to a surprise attack or incursion made from ambush. This is only to be attempted when there is no immediate response available to the opposition, even if they could so reply, given time. For it's best to advance reliable arguments right away in the actual pleading, so that they can be restated often and at length.

It hardly seems necessary to explain that the altercator should never be merely frantic or loud in debate, or joke around like an ignoramus. Reckless behaviour might throw an opponent off

his game, but it offends the judge. It's also harmful to battle too
long over points you cannot win. When a point must be con-
ceded, it's best to do so promptly. If there are many issues of
dispute, you'll seem more plausible on the others. If there's only
one, a frank admission often yields a milder punishment. Ten-
acious defence of a mistake, especially one that's been caught, is
a further mistake.

While the battle is underway, it takes a great deal of skill
and strategy to draw out an adversary who is making a mistake and get him to continue his error for as long as possible,
to the point where he becomes overconfident in his expectation
of success. For this reason it's a good idea to keep some arguments under wraps. Our opponent may press on, staking the
whole case on what he imagines to be a weakness on our side,
thus in the end making our proofs seem even more compelling
thanks to his demands for them. It can even be useful to yield
a point that the adversary thinks is to his advantage, if by
grasping one advantage he is forced to yield something even
better. Or set up two alternatives, either one of which hurts his
case. This is more effective in altercation than in a speech,
since in the latter we end up responding to ourselves, while in
the former we trap the opponent in a kind of admission.

A keen advocate will closely observe which arguments influence the judge, and which he rejects. This can often be ascertained
by some expression or remark or other action on his part. It's
then necessary to press on with the promising points and to
retreat as gently as possible from those that are of no assistance.
Doctors follow a similar course of action, as they continue or
abandon treatments once they observe that the patient is accepting or rejecting them.

Sometimes, if a point can't be developed easily, it's good to
introduce a separate topic and, if possible, divert the judge's
attention to it. What else can you do, if you can't come up with
a response, but find something to which your opponent also
can't respond?

In general, as I have said, altercation requires the same treatment as cross-examination, the difference being that altercation
is a contest between advocates, cross-examination a struggle

between witness and advocate. Practice in altercation is much easier. It can be very useful to adopt some subject, real or fictitious, with a fellow student, and to take the different roles in an altercation. This can even be done with questions of a simpler type. I want an advocate also to recognize that the proper order for presenting proofs to a judge is the same as with arguments: the strongest should be placed first and last. Those placed first prepare a judge to believe, while those placed last guide him to decide in our favour.

Quintilian
Oratorical Instruction
11.3.51–60

Voice and Breath

The voice must not be strained beyond its natural capacity. Strain can make it choke up or become less clear or even make that sound the Greeks call 'rooster song'.

We must not speak in a jumbled rush, thereby destroying clarity and emotional impact, not to mention sometimes even depriving individual words of their full enunciation. The opposite of this, also a vice, is excessive slowness. It betrays a certain difficulty in knowing what to say, and causes the listener's attention to wander. It also wastes the time on the water clock, which is no small thing. Our speech should be fluent, not rushed; deliberate, not delayed.

We mustn't take a breath so often that we chop a thought into pieces, nor extend a breath so long that it fails us. The gasp produced by the loss of breath is unattractive; we sound like a man held too long under water, we inhale for too long and at the wrong time, as if by necessity rather than choice. When about to deliver a lengthy period, we should gather our breath, briefly and quietly, so as not to make it obvious. Elsewhere it will be best to inhale at the natural breaks in the discourse.

Breath must be trained if we are to hold it as long as possible. With this in mind, Demosthenes used to recite as many continuous verses of poetry as he could while climbing a hill. To improve his enunciation, he would practise speaking at home while manoeuvring pebbles under his tongue. Sometimes our breathing capacity may be adequate for full and clear expression, yet unreliable when pressed, or tremulous, like bodies that appear sound but lack sinew. The Greeks call this phenomenon 'quavering'.

There are some speakers who, due to missing teeth, do not so much take breaths as suck them in, complete with slurping sound. Others breathe so often and with such internal ruckus that they sound like yoked oxen struggling beneath their load.

Some even make a show of this style, as if they are burdened by the abundance of their ideas and a greater force of eloquence stirs within them than can possibly be emitted through their throats. With others there seems to be a violent struggle between mouth and words. Although not strictly vices of the voice, a number of other faults can be cited here since they happen through the voice, namely excessive coughing and spitting, hacking up phlegm from the depths of the lungs, spewing saliva on those close by and talking while breathing through the nose.

But I could more easily endure any one of these faults than the practice of chanting, which is now so popular in both courtrooms and schools. I can't decide whether it is more harmful or disgusting. What could be less appropriate for an orator than the kind of vocal modulation that is heard on stage or resembles the carryings-on of drunkards and party-goers? What could be more contrary to the goal of summoning emotions, such as sorrow, anger, indignation or pity, than not just abandoning the very feelings to be induced in the judge, but destroying the sanctity of court with the wantonness of the Lycians and Carians?[19] For Cicero reported that speakers from Lycia and Caria all but sang their perorations[20] – and we have abandoned even their somewhat austere mode of singing!

To put it succinctly: who on earth sings in a trial – never mind one for murder or sacrilege or parricide, but even one dealing with numbers or accounts? And if such behaviour is acceptable, there's no reason we shouldn't assist the vocal fireworks with lyres or flutes, or even, by Hercules, cymbals, which are especially suited to this hideous practice.

Yet we put up with such behaviour willingly. No one finds his own singing unpleasant, and it's less trouble than actually pleading. And there are some who, in line with other aspects of their lives, are seduced by the pleasure of always hearing something that soothes their ears. Well, what of it? you might ask. Doesn't Cicero himself say that there is a 'hint of song' in oratory?[21] Doesn't song originate in nature? A little later I will explain when and to what extent music, or – what many refuse to understand – a 'hint' of song, is acceptable.

Quintilian
Oratorical Instruction
11.3.117–36

Bad Uses of Gesture

Next to be considered are the mistakes that even experienced speakers make while gesturing. Many writers mention a gesture for demanding a cup, threatening a flogging, or indicating the number five hundred that involves bending the thumb, but I have never seen it used, even by peasants.

I do know that the following occur often. A speaker exposes his flank by thrusting his arm; or he keeps his hand within the fold of his toga; or he stretches it out as far as possible, or raises it to the roof, or swings his arm so often over his left shoulder that he ends up beating his back, endangering anyone standing behind him, or he swings the left arm in a circle, or with a quick jab of the hand assaults bystanders, or flaps both elbows against his sides. With others the hand is sluggish or trembles or hacks like a saw, or they bend their fingers and drag them down the side of the head or flip the same hand on its back and push it upwards towards the heavens. There is another gesture in which the head is bent on to the right shoulder, the arm extended from the ear, the hand stretched out with the thumb pointing upwards. This gesture is a favourite of those who boast that they speak with 'rousing force' or 'uplifted hand'.

We might as well add those who hurl flashing epigrams from their fingertips, or make denunciations with 'uplifted hand', or (which isn't necessarily bad in itself) rise up on tiptoe when pleased with themselves. They turn the action into a fault when they simultaneously hold one or two fingers erect, or arrange their hands as if they were carrying something.

Then there are the faults that arise not from nature but from nerves: struggling with lips that refuse to open; grunting as if something is stuck in the throat when memory or mind is failing us; flaring our nostrils; parading about without finishing a thought; and stopping suddenly to demand applause with our silence. To recount all such failings would take almost for ever. Everyone has his own special faults.

Take care not to let the chest or stomach protrude. It exposes the posterior, and all such bending is repulsive. Let your flanks share in your gesture. The movement of the whole body is what makes a difference, so much so that Cicero thinks that it, rather than the hands, is the basis of oratorical performance. As he says in his *Orator*:

> No flicking of the fingers, or using them to mark the time; the orator moves with his whole torso, bending and stretching in a manly manner.[22]

Striking the thigh, which Cleon[23] is said to have introduced at Athens, is now a familiar practice, used to indicate indignation and rouse the listener. Cicero noted its absence in Calidius: 'no smacking of the forehead, no striking of the thigh'.[24] Although, if I may, I disagree about the forehead, for even clapping hands and pounding the chest are theatrical tricks.

It will also occasionally be appropriate to tap the chest with the fingertips of a hollowed hand, for example if we address ourselves, or offer encouragement, complaint or pity. But if we do so, it will not be unbecoming also to pull the toga back a little. With respect to feet, we need to pay attention to our stance and gait. To stand with the right foot extended, thus projecting the same hand and foot, is not a good look.

Sometimes it's acceptable to lean forwards on to the right foot, as long as we don't in so doing twist the chest. Even then, the gesture is more that of a comic actor than of an orator. It's a mistake when putting our weight on the left foot to elevate the right, or position it on tiptoe. To place the legs far apart is ugly if we are standing still and virtually obscene if we are moving. Taking an occasional step forward is acceptable, provided it is deliberate, short and steady. The same is true for walking during the delays created by applause, although Cicero says that pacing should be rare and of no long duration.[25] Running about, or what Domitius Afer called Manlius Sura's 'hyperactivity',[26] is completely ridiculous. Flavius Verginius displayed his wit when he asked a rival professor how many miles he had declaimed.[27]

I understand that it is sometimes said that we should, when walking, never turn our backs on the judges, but instead move diagonally while continuing to look at the panel. Although this recommendation can't be followed in private cases, the possible distance to be traversed is quite short, and we won't show our back for any real length of time. Nevertheless, it is sometimes acceptable to step backwards gradually. Of course some speakers jump backwards, which is out and out ridiculous.

Stamping the foot, as Cicero indicates,[28] can be advantageous at the start or finish of a lively passage; but doing so repeatedly is silly and of no appeal to the judge. It's also unattractive to sway left and right while placing weight on one foot or the other. Above all avoid effeminate movement, of the sort Cicero faulted in Titius,[29] after whom the 'Titian' dance is named. I also advise against frequent, vigorous rocking from side to side, something Julius made fun of in the elder Curio,[30] when he asked who it was that was speaking from a rowing boat. So too, Sicinius, who, when Curio's colleague Octavius[31] was sitting nearby, bandaged up and reeking of ointments, and Curio himself was bouncing about as usual, said to Octavius, 'You'll never be able to thank your colleague sufficiently – without him, you'd be eaten alive by flies!'

Some speakers jerk their shoulders, a fault Demosthenes is said to have corrected by speaking on a narrow platform with a spear suspended just above his shoulder. If in the heat of the argument he made this mistake, he was reminded by bumping into the spear. Talking while walking is only called for if, in the course of a public trial with many judges, we wish to impress our points on them one by one.

Some speakers will toss the toga over the shoulder and use the right hand to pull the fold up to the waist, gesturing with the left as they walk and talk. This is not to be tolerated. It's even objectionable to pull the left hand back while protruding the right. I'm reminded of a foolish practice I must not forget to mention: some speakers use the interruptions caused by applause to whisper in a colleague's ear or crack a joke or signal to clerks, as if to recommend a reward for those expressing their support.

It's fine to lean towards the judge while explaining something, especially if the point is a little obscure. But it's rude and aggressive to tower over an advocate seated at the opposing bench. As for leaning backwards and letting yourself be propped up by the members of your entourage, it's quite affected, unless the speaker is justifiably worn out. The same goes for being prompted out loud or openly reading our text as if we'd forgotten something.

All of these mannerisms weaken the force of our eloquence, chill the emotions and make the judge think we have too little regard for him. To cross over to the opposing bench is disrespectful, and Cassius Severus was quite clever to insist that a barrier be placed between him and an opponent who kept doing so. And even if heading to the other side might cause a stir, returning to one's own inevitably dampens the mood.

Much of what I've explained will need to be adapted if speaking before a tribunal. The speaker's face must be directed upwards in order to see his addressee, and gestures must likewise be directed upwards. Other adjustments will occur without my having to mention them. So too when speaking while seated, as in minor disputes. The same forcefulness in delivery is not possible, and some movements that might otherwise seem faulty become necessary. For example, if an advocate is seated to the left of the judge, he must extend his right foot, while if he is seated to the right, many gestures will have to be from right to left in order to be directed towards the judge. I have even seen some speakers getting up at the ends of periods and some even walking about a bit. I leave it to them to decide whether such behaviour is appropriate. When they act thus, they can't be described as pleading while seated.

Drinking (and even eating) while pleading used to be a

common custom, and is still practised by some. My orator will do nothing of the sort. If a person can't for that reason fulfil the obligations of the speaker, then it isn't such a bad thing for him to stop pleading altogether, and certainly better than revealing his contempt for his profession and his audience.

Quintilian
Oratorical Instruction
11.3.157–60

Getting Started

Even when we turn to the judge and the praetor has given us permission to speak, we should not burst out talking right away, but take a brief pause for reflection. Caution on the part of the one about to speak pleases the audience, and allows the judge time to compose himself.

Homer teaches this through the example of Ulysses, whom he describes as standing still with eyes fixed on the ground and sceptre held steady before he releases his storm of eloquence.[32] During this pause, there are certain 'delaying tactics', as actors call them, that are not inappropriate, such as stroking our head, looking at our hands, snapping our fingers, feigning a struggle, revealing anxiety with a sigh or whatever suits us better. These tactics can be continued for a longer period if the judge is not yet paying attention.

Our stance should be upright, our feet placed parallel and a little apart, or perhaps the left one set forwards just a bit. The knees should be unbent but not stiff, the shoulders relaxed, our facial expression serious, not mournful or blank or apathetic. The arms should be at a slight distance from our sides, the left hand placed as I have explained above,[33] the right, as we are about to begin, extended beyond the fold of the toga in as modest a gesture as possible, as if waiting for the signal to commence.

The following are all mistakes: looking at the ceiling, rubbing the face to give it a rude appearance, jutting the head forwards insolently, knitting the eyebrows to look fiercer, unnaturally pushing the hair back from the forehead for shock value; also (a common practice of the Greeks) feigning thought by twitching fingers or lips, coughing loudly, jutting one foot far forwards, clutching part of the toga with the left hand, standing with legs spread apart, or stiff, or bent backwards, or stooping, or hunching our shoulders like wrestlers.

RHETORIC AND
COGNITION

Implicit in much ancient teaching on rhetoric is a particular understanding of the operations of the human mind. Unlike philosophers, who tended to regard thought as intrinsic to the individual thinker, rhetoricians were interested in the interaction between internal thought processes and external realities, including the objects of the world and the opinions and preconceptions of others. In calling rhetoric an art, rhetoricians suggested that the validity of rhetorical propositions was determined by their demonstrable impact on the minds and actions of others, rather than measured in terms of abstract principles of truth and falsehood. Rhetoricians' interest in the interconnectedness of cognitive processes helps to explain their focus on externalized or artificial memory (discussed elsewhere in this book), their view of the underlying unity of all artistic styles (explained here by Crassus in Cicero, On the Orator*), their application of a theory of ornament to multiple arts and their admiration for types of speaking that prompted a listener to visualize the people and actions being represented in language (discussed here by Quintilian). Generally speaking, ancient rhetoric seems to come closer to recent models of thought as embodied, externalized and enactive, than to traditional models that emphasize internal representations.*

Cicero
On the Orator
3.19–37

Embodied Cognition

Crassus is speaking.

Your influence and friendship, as well as Antonius'[1] fluency,
deprive me of the freedom to say no, although I would have
very good reason for doing so. In distributing the topics for
our discussion, he took responsibility for explaining the content of an oration, while leaving it to me to explain how a
speech is to be enriched. He divided what cannot be separated,
for inasmuch as every speech consists of content and language,
language has no basis without content, and content is imper-
ceptible without language.

Men of old,[2] having embraced more with their minds, seem
to me also to have seen much more than our mind's eye can
observe. They stated that all reality, above and below, is a single
entity, held together by a single natural pattern of harmonious
interaction; for there is no class of entity which, plucked from
everything else, can stand on its own, or without which everything else can retain its ongoing power of existence.

But if this seems to be too grand an explanation for human
perception or cognition to grasp, there is also a true saying of
Plato[3] (surely familiar to you, Catulus),[4] to the effect that all the
teaching of the free and humane arts is held together by a single
bond of association; when we perceive the explanatory power
of reason, whereby causes and consequences come to be known,
we find a marvellous unity and harmony of all branches of
learning. And if this explanation, too, seems too lofty for us
earth-bound beings, surely we ought to know and grasp the one

presented earlier, which we have embraced, which we profess, which we have acknowledged as our own. For eloquence is a single entity, into whatever shores and regions of discussion it is carried, as I insisted yesterday and as Antonius indicated at several points in the conversation this morning.

Whether we talk of the nature of the heavens and earth or divine and human power, whether from a position of inferiority or equality or superiority, whether we seek to stir men to action, to teach them, to deter them, to rile them or calm them, set them on fire or soothe them, whether we speak to a few or many, among foreigners or our own people or with ourselves, good speaking is distributed into channels, not drawn from different sources, and wherever it proceeds, is accompanied by the same procedures of adornment.

But these days we are flooded with the opinions, not only of the common people, but also of those who, despite a veneer of education, are unable to grasp the totality of the subject and thus find it easier to handle it by picking it apart, separating words from thoughts or body from mind, which is the death of both. Therefore I will not discuss more than has been asked of me, but merely state in brief that polished language is impossible unless thought is also being expressed, and that no thought can be clear and impressive without clear and impressive language.

Before I try to touch upon the various means by which, in my view, discourse is polished and made radiant, I will state briefly my view of oratory as a totality. As I see it, there is no natural category that does not contain within it numerous dissimilar objects, which nonetheless deserve similar respect. For example, many sounds perceived with our ears delight us, even though they are so varied that the one you just heard seems most charming. Our eyes take in innumerable captivating delights that please a single sense in diverse manners. And different objects of delight gratify the remaining senses, so much so that it is difficult to decide which is the most agreeable.

And what is true of natural entities is also applicable to the arts: there is a single art of sculpture, in which Myro, Polyclitus and Lysippus[5] excelled, despite differing from one another; a single art and discipline of painting, in which the very different painters Zeuxis, Aglaophon and Apelles[6] excelled, without any one of them seeming to be deficient in his art. And if all this is both remarkable and true where non-verbal arts are concerned, how much more remarkable when it comes to language and oratory? Although the same thoughts and words may be employed, speeches can have very great differences, without it being the case that some speakers are to be derided. Rather, those who deserve praise should be praised, despite a difference in style.

The validity of this observation is clear from poetry, which is closest in nature to oratory. How greatly Ennius, Pacuvius and Accius[7] differ among themselves, or Aeschylus, Sophocles and Euripides[8] among the Greeks – yet virtually the same degree of respect is attributed to all, despite their difference in style. Consider examples from our area of inquiry: Isocrates was charming, Lysias subtle, Hyperides sharp-witted, Aeschines sonorous, Demosthenes[9] forceful. Which of them was not outstanding? Yet which was similar to anyone but himself? Africanus was authoritative, Laelius gentle, Galba a little rough, Carbo[10] fluent, even tuneful. Which of these was not a leading orator of days gone by? Yet each was a leader in his own style.

Still, why do I look to the past, when it's possible to find examples among those alive and present right here? What has ever been more pleasing to our ears than a speech of Catulus?[11] His eloquence is so pure that it seems as though he's the only person who speaks Latin; so serious, yet humane and charming, with a dignity all his own. What else can I say? When listening to him I always think that to add or change or take away anything would only make the speech worse. And what about our friend Caesar?[12] Hasn't he introduced a new style of oration and manner of speaking that is almost unique? Who besides him has treated tragic affairs with a comic touch, sad topics in an easy-going style, severe matters light-heartedly, the business of the court with the charm of a play? In his speeches humour coexists with seriousness, and his witticisms never diminish the gravity of the issue. And here in our midst also are two orators of almost the same age, Sulpicius and Cotta.[13] What a difference between them! How distinctive the excellence of each! Cotta is accurate and precise, explicating his subject matter in appropriate and well-suited language. He sticks to the case always, and once he has keenly determined what needs to be proven, fixes his mind and speech on it, omitting all other arguments. Sulpicius, in contrast, with his ferocious intelligence, full and booming voice, remarkable combination of physical energy and dignified movement, and abundance of serious expressions, seems by nature uniquely equipped for public speaking.

To turn now to the two of us, since we are so often compared that it's almost as if we were being called to court in the judgements of men. What could be more dissimilar than my way of speaking and that of Antonius? Although he is an orator without a superior, I am frequently paired with him by way of comparison, despite my dissatisfaction with myself. You're familiar with the style of Antonius, are you not? He is bold, vehement, energetic in delivery, his speeches fortified on every side, keen, acute, precise, with each point given due attention. He is generous in making concessions, energetic in pursuing any advantage; he intimidates, he implores, he uses every type of style without causing the audience to feel overwhelmed.

As for me, whatever my status as an orator, although all of you hold me in some esteem, I am still quite different in my style from Antonius. Whether it's good or not isn't for me to say; after all, we know ourselves least of all and have the hardest time with self-assessment. Still, the difference between Antonius and me is apparent in my limited reliance on movement, that is, my tendency to finish my speech standing just where I started; also in the great effort I make in selecting vocabulary, due to my fear that if my speech is a little too old-fashioned it might not seem worthy of the undisturbed attention of the audience.

But if such differences and distinguishing characteristics are apparent among those of us here present, with quality decided on ability and not choice of style – indeed every performance that is perfect in its own way deserves praise – well, what do you think would happen if we took into consideration all orators from every locale and every era? Don't you think we'd find almost as many styles as there are speakers?

On the basis of what I've just said, it might seem to some that if there are almost innumerable types of speaking, different in appearance but in their own kind praiseworthy, then styles that are so different can't be fashioned on the basis of shared teachings and a single type of instruction. In fact, this isn't the case, and it's necessary for instructors to observe very carefully the natural inclination of each student. We are well aware that impressive students of very different types can and do emerge from the same classroom, as long as the teacher adjusts instruction to the natural inclination of each.

Leaving aside the other arts, we find an excellent instance of this principle in Isocrates' remark that as teacher he used spurs on Ephorus and reins on Theopompus:[14] in other words, he repressed the bold language of the one and tried to fire up the shy hesitation of the other. He didn't make them turn out the same, but added to the one and filed down the other in order to make them conform to their respective natures.

Well, I've said all this by way of introduction so that if not everything I propose is to your preference or style, you will understand that I am describing the style that I approve the most.

Quintilian
Oratorical Instruction
8.3.61–81 and 9.2.40–44

Visualization

The ornate[15] is something beyond what is clear and correct. It entails grasping what you want to say, expressing it and making it seem more brilliant, what you might call embellishment. As a result, we must include among ornaments visualization, which I mentioned in the section on narrative. It is more a making visible or present than simple clarity, since the latter presents the content, while visualization somehow thrusts it forwards.

Now, it's a great virtue to set forth our subject matter clearly and in such a way that it seems to be seen. For a speech will not have sufficient impact nor will it be fully authoritative, as it should, if it can only affect the ears, and the judge only has confidence in the matters he adjudicates as they are narrated, rather than as they are presented or displayed to the eyes of the mind.

Because this topic has been treated in various ways, I won't divide it into the sort of bits and pieces, the number of which is increased by some out of pure ostentation, but I will touch on the essentials. There is one sort of 'making visible' in which a full picture of events is, in a manner of speaking, painted with words. 'There stood on his toes at once upright each contestant'[16] and so on. The words make the appearance of the boxers starting their match as clear to us as it would have been to the spectators.

Cicero excels at this sort of thing, as at everything else. When reading in his *Speeches against Verres*,

> on the shore stood the praetor of the Roman people, dressed in
> slippers, purple cloak and ankle-length tunic, propped up on his
> pathetic female companion,[17]

is there anyone so incapable of visualization as not to see the
people, the place, their outfits? Indeed, do we not add our own
details on the basis of what we have been told? For my part, I
seem to see the faces and eyes and disgusting kissing and
petting of the two figures, as well as the silent embarrassment
of the people approaching them.

Sometimes the appearance we try to express depends on
lengthier description, as in this next example, also from Cicero
(for on his own he can provide an example of every type of
embellishment). In a description of a sumptuous banquet,[18] he
writes:

> I see some entering, others leaving, some tottering from wine,
> some yawning from yesterday's drink. The floor is filthy, smeared
> with wine, covered with wilting wreaths and leftover fish-bones.

What more would anyone who had entered the scene catch
sight of?

Pity for captured cities can be intensified in the same way.
Without doubt the mere assertion that a city has been stormed
implies all that happens in such a situation, but like a short
dispatch, it fails to touch the emotions. But if you make per-
ceptible everything included in the single word 'downfall', then
there will appear flames rushing through houses and temples,
the crash of falling buildings, the single sound arising from the
cries of many, the attempted escape of some, others halted by
the final embrace of their loved ones, the wailing of infants and
women and old men maliciously preserved by fate for that
awful day. Next will come the pillage of goods both sacred and
profane, the plunderers' loot and their footsteps as they hurry
to find even more, each prisoner in chains and driven before
his captor, the mother struggling to keep her babe and the
victors' fighting among themselves over the choicest booty.
Although, as I have noted, all of these events are implied by the

one word 'downfall', it is less effective to say everything than to say each thing.

What we say will be vivid as long as it resembles the truth, and it will even be acceptable to invent details of the sort that typically occur. Clarity is also achieved by mentioning circumstances arising from the actual events, for example:

Chill horror strikes my limbs, my blood congeals from fear.[19]

Also

Trembling mothers pressed babies to their breasts.[20]

It's actually quite easy to attain the most powerful of oratorical effects: observe, then follow nature. All eloquence concerns the activities of life, each listener relates what he hears to himself, and the mind most readily accepts what it recognizes as true.

Similes have been found to be especially illuminating. Some are placed among arguments for the sake of proof, others composed for the purpose of conveying an image of events, which is relevant here. For example:

like a dark cloud of ravenous wolves,[21]

or

like a bird skimming the surface of the sea, near beaches, near fish-filled reefs.[22]

With this type of expression we must be especially careful that the referent of the simile is itself neither obscure nor unfamiliar. What is presented for the sake of clarifying something must be clearer than what it clarifies. Therefore, while we allow poets examples like this:

as when Apollo abandons Lycia and the streams of Xanthus or visits maternal Delos,[23]

the same will not suit an orator, as it explains the obvious by
means of the obscure.

But the type of simile we described when discussing arguments also adorns a speech, rendering it elevated, lively,
delightful, marvellous. The more distant the source of the likeness, the greater the surprise and sense of novelty it produces.
Similes like the following are commonplace and useful only for
conveying a sense of the speaker's reliability: 'As the soil is
improved by cultivation, so the mind by education' or 'As doctors amputate limbs made useless by disease, so dangerous
miscreants, even if related by blood, are to be cut away.'[24]

More elevated is the following from Cicero's *Speech in
Defence of Archias*:

> Rocks and deserts respond to a voice, monstrous beasts often
> turn and stop at the sound of song[25]

and so on.

To be sure, some speakers, with the wantonness characteristic of declamation, have corrupted this style, making false
comparisons or failing to apply them to the relevant object.
Both errors occur in the following, which were repeated every-
where when I was a young man:

> The sources of great rivers can still be sailed.

and

> Healthy trees bear fruit as soon as they are planted.

In every comparison, either the resemblance precedes and the
object follows, or vice versa. Yet sometimes they are freely placed
at a distance, and sometimes – which is by far the best – the object
and the image are interconnected in a kind of reciprocal comparison, called antapodosis. Thus, the resemblance precedes in the
previously cited example, 'like a dark cloud of ravenous wolves...'
It follows in the first book of *Georgics*, when after the long lament over civil and external wars, we find the following:

as when the chariots, released from the holding cells, rush lap upon lap, and the charioteer, vainly pulling the reins, is carried instead by the horses, who ignore all attempts at restraint.[26]

But these lack reciprocal comparison, which places before the eyes items on both sides of the relationship and makes them all equally vivid. I find many outstanding examples in Virgil, but it is preferable to cite oratory. Cicero in his *Speech in Defence of Murena*, says:

> As they say of Greek musicians that those who cannot handle the lyre take up the flute, so we see among Romans that those who cannot become orators step down to the law.[27]

In the same speech another example is almost poetic in spirit, but with its reciprocal representation is well suited to oratorical embellishment:

> For just as storms, though often preceded by some signal in the sky, also often arise unpredictably and without any evident cause, so too in the storms that pass through electoral assemblies, sometimes it's clear how they started, sometimes they seem to be stirred up for no apparent reason.[28]

There are short examples as well:

> wandering through the woods like wild beasts

or this from Cicero's speech against Clodius:[29]

> he fled from court like a naked man from fire.

Similar sayings can occur to anyone from everyday speech. They have the virtue not only of putting things clearly before the eyes, but of doing so quickly and concisely.

[. . .]

The figure called 'placing before the eyes' comes about when, in addition to describing an event we demonstrate how it took place, not all at once, but part by part. In the previous book we considered this procedure under the heading 'making visible' or 'visualization'. Celsus[30] also gave this name to the figure; others call it hypotyposis when a certain shape of events is expressed in words in such a way that the events seem to be seen rather than heard. For example:

> Our villain, burning with crime and madness, came into the forum, his eyes ablaze, his entire face flashing with cruelty.[31]

We form an image not just of what has been done or is being done, but even what will happen or will have happened. Cicero handles this well in his *Speech in Defence of Milo*, explaining what Clodius would have done had he obtained the praetorship.[32] Earlier speakers were more cautious when using this transfer of time, properly called metastasis, in vivid description, for they would preface it with something like 'imagine you are looking at . . .' or, as Cicero put it, 'what you didn't see with your eyes you can observe in your minds'.[33] Modern speakers, especially declaimers, are bolder in creating mental pictures, doing so with real excitement. For example, there is the controversy discussed by Seneca in which a father, under the guidance of one son, finds the other committing adultery with his stepmother, both of whom he kills:

> Lead, I follow. Grasp this aged hand and thrust it where you will.

And a little later:

> 'See,' he says, 'what for so long you have failed to believe. I do not see, night and thick fog block my view.'[34]

This figure is a little too obvious. It seems to perform the event rather than recount it. Some assign the same term to clear and revelatory description of places, others call the latter topographia.

RHETORICAL ORNAMENT

The theory of ornament is one of the subtlest, yet most influential aspects of ancient rhetorical teaching. Although ornament sometimes refers to supplementary adornment, more generally it describes the outcome of a process of making language (or any substance) special. Ornamented speech sounds different from everyday speech, just as a well-designed building looks and feels different from mere functional construction. In Crassus' account, from Cicero, On the Orator, ornament serves to differentiate rhetoric from philosophy in that it reunites thought and language, truth and beauty, knowledge and wisdom. Ornament is also closely associated with the principle of decorum, which specifies that there are ways of speaking appropriate to circumstances, speakers and even sections of a speech. Observing the principle of decorum situates rhetorical output in the physical continuum that unites all aspects of the universe. Although ornament and decorum may seem to be features of linguistic style, they are not exclusively so, for one can speak of decorous delivery or arrangement and, as Crassus illustrates at some length, the cadences and rhythms of a speech are important aspects of ornamentation. Perhaps not surprisingly, discussions of ornament in On the Orator and other works of Cicero became important touchstones for later theorists of other arts, including architecture, painting and music.

Cicero
On the Orator
3.52–8, 91–125, 132–43, 148–230

Antonius has just praised Crassus for his account of pure and clear diction. Crassus now turns to the more difficult topic of ornament or stylistic polish.

'Well, Antony, the two topics I have just run through – or all but passed over! – namely, speaking Latin and speaking clearly – are easy enough. The remaining topics are big, complicated, varied and serious. Admiration of talent and praise of eloquence depend on them entirely. No one was ever admired as an orator just for speaking Latin correctly; if he didn't, people would laugh at him and deny that he was a cultivated person, much less an orator. Nobody ever praised a speaker on the grounds that his listeners understood what he was saying; no, we despise him if he can't even do that.

'What kind of speaker thrills his listeners? At whom do they gaze in awe or shout approval? What speaker do people regard as a god among mortals? Why, the one who speaks in a distinctive yet straightforward manner, whose speeches are rich and brilliant in thought and language, who achieves in his orations a certain rhythm and measure: in short, the one who speaks ornately. And if he moderates all of this in accordance with the importance of the issue under consideration and principals in the case, then I say that he deserves praises for speaking in an appropriate and suitable manner.

'Antonius stated that he had never encountered speakers of this sort, and that they alone would deserve to be called eloquent. So if you take my advice you will scorn and laugh at all those rhetoricians, as they are now called, who think they have embraced the entire range of oratory, when they can't even understand the role they have assumed or the content of their own teaching. For the true orator will have investigated, heard, read, debated, discussed and generally immersed himself in every aspect of human life, since that is his business and his subject matter.

'Eloquence, you see, is one of the greatest virtues.[1] Although all virtues are equal in value, they can differ in beauty and distinction. This is the case with eloquence, which, having acquired a knowledge of its subject, explains in language the contents of the mind so that it can impel listeners in whatever direction it presses them. The greater its power, the greater the need for it to be wedded to the utmost integrity and good sense. If we grant facility in speaking to those who want nothing to do with virtue, then rather than creating orators we give weapons to madmen.

'This system of thought, expression and speech the Greeks of old called wisdom. It accounts for men like Lycurgus, Pittacus and Solon,[2] or Romans of a similar sort, such as Coruncanius, Fabricius, Cato and Scipio,[3] who, although perhaps lacking education, had energy and purpose like the Greeks. Still others had a share of practical wisdom, but pursued peace and quiet, following a different plan of life, such as Pythagoras, Democritus and Anaxagoras.[4] Instead of governing communities they focused entirely on acquiring knowledge. Due to the tranquillity of their lifestyle and the inherent appeal of knowledge, which is uniquely pleasing to human beings, they have attracted more followers than is in the best interests of public governance.

'And so, as men of high intellectual ability turned to the pursuit of knowledge in itself, due to their abundance of free time, even very learned individuals, abounding in leisure and excessive creativity, decided to devote attention, inquiry and investigation to more topics than were really essential. For in the past the same sort of instruction taught proper conduct and excellent speech. The teachers weren't split into two camps, rather the same ones were preceptors of living and of speaking, for example Phoenix in Homer, who says that he was assigned by Peleus to accompany his young son Achilles to war, in order to make him both a speaker of words and a doer of deeds.[5]

'But just as men who are accustomed to strenuous daily labour turn to handball or dice or dominoes or even dream up some new form of amusement when the weather keeps them from work, so too, when potential civic leaders are kept from their work by current events or choose to take a holiday, they turn, some to poets, others to geometers, still others to musicians. Some, like the dialecticians, have even created a new type of study and entertainment and end up devoting their entire lives to the so-called "arts" that were created in order to shape the minds of boys in the direction of culture and virtue.

[. . .]

'What's the point of this long-winded presentation of mine? The two remaining aspects of brightening and elevating discourse, speaking ornately and speaking appropriately, have the task of making an oration as pleasant as possible, influential over the thoughts and feelings of the audience, and fortified with the greatest range of information. Yet the ordinary tools of wrangling and dispute, derived as they are from commonplace notions, are weak and inadequate for these ends. And even the lessons that the so-called professors of rhetoric transmit don't amount to anything much more valuable. What we require instead is a full complement of resources that have been carefully selected, gathered from every possible source, acquired and adopted, as you, Caesar, will have to do in the coming year.[6] And as I did, labouring during my aedileship due to my conviction that I couldn't do the Roman people justice by employing cheap and low-quality materials.

'It's easy to explain the selection and ordering of words and creation of satisfying rhythms. In fact, it can be done through practice alone without systematic instruction. There's an abundance of resources, which, because the Greeks have not kept them to themselves, our own youth have in essence unlearned while learning; and – heaven forfend! – in the last couple of years Latin teachers of rhetoric have appeared on the scene, although as censor I issued an edict banishing them, not because

I didn't want the skills of our young men to be sharpened, as I'm told some people have been saying, but, to the contrary, because I didn't want their wits to be dulled or their impudence strengthened.[7]

'For among the Greeks, whatever sort they were, I recognized that apart from exercises in talking they did possess a certain learning and knowledge worthy of cultivation; whereas these new teachers, as far as I could tell, couldn't teach anything except audacity! And that's certainly to be avoided even when joined with good practices. So, since this was the one lesson they transmitted and their school was a training ground in shamelessness, I decided that it was up to me as censor to keep them from doing more damage.

'But my decree does not lead me to abandon hope of treating the matters under discussion in polished Latin, for both our language and the nature of this business allow the excellent traditional wisdom of the Greeks to be transferred to our own usage. It requires learned men, such as we have up to this point been lacking; but when they exist, they will surpass even the Greeks.

'Speech becomes ornate in the first place through its style, a certain colour and flavour of its own. For to be serious, appealing, learned, generous, admirable, polished and endowed with just enough feeling isn't a characteristic of individual parts but of the body as a whole. Moreover, when a speech is to be decorated with flowers of language and thought, they shouldn't be spread evenly across the whole, but distributed and arranged as brilliant highlights. So it's necessary to select a style of speech that keeps the interest of the listeners and brings them pleasure, only not too much. For I doubt that at this point you expect me to warn you not to speak in a weak, unpolished, vulgar or obsolete style. Your talent and your stage of life demand something more from me.

'For it's difficult to explain why the very things that most please and stimulate our senses upon first being encountered also alienate us the soonest, due to a certain disgust and sense of excess. How much more florid with beautiful and varied colours are new paintings as opposed to old!

Yet even if they captivate us at first glance, they fail to please for very long, while older paintings, despite their rough and out-of-date appearance, still retain our attention. In music, trills and falsetto singing are softer and more delicate than sure and steady notes. Yet not just austere critics, but even the general multitude shout them down if they occur too frequently.

'The same point applies to the remaining senses: perfumes fashioned to be supremely sweet and keen are less pleasing over time than moderate ones, and the scent of earth is appreciated more than that of saffron. In touch there is a limit to the appreciation of softness and smoothness. Even taste, the most pleasure-seeking of all the senses, the one most sensitive to refinement, quickly spurns and spits out anything that is sweet and only sweet. Who could enjoy a sweet drink or sweet food for very long? In either case, what pleases the senses in moderation quickly becomes cloying.

'Thus in every instance, disgust is very close to great pleasure, with the result that there is no reason to be surprised that where language is concerned, whether in poetry or oratory, a style judged to be harmonious, crisp, polished and charming, if pursued without relief or remission or any variety at all, although decked out in brilliant colours, can't provide continual pleasure. We are annoyed even more quickly with the curlicues and dyes of the orator or poet because with other senses it is nature rather than the mind that is repelled, whereas with writing and speaking smeared-on vices are recognized not just by the ears but by the judgement of the mind as well. Even though we often hear "bravo", I'd rather not hear "how pretty! how charming!" very often – although I wouldn't mind hearing "couldn't be better" on a regular basis. Features that attract wonder and praise should retreat into the background from time to time, so that the highlights can be even more distinctive.

'When Roscius[8] delivers the following verse, he never uses the range of gesture of which he's capable:

The wise man seeks honour as a prize for virtue, not as prey.[9]

Instead he tosses it off so that in delivering the next line he can prance, stare and gape with wonder:

But what do I see? One girt with steel holds the sacred seats.

Or to take another example:

What protection am I to seek?

How gently, how softly, with what restraint, for he proceeds to sing

O father, O country, O house of Priam![10]

Which he couldn't deliver with such force if he had exhausted himself on the preceding utterance.

'Nor did actors recognize this principle before poets and composers of musical accompaniment, both of whom lower the tone, then elevate it, perform some parts vibrato, others staccato.

'So we want our orator to be polished and charming – how could it be otherwise? – but his charm should be austere and solid, not sweet and superficial. The precepts of ornamentation can be applied even by the worst sort of speaker. As I said before, first prepare an abundance of material, as Antonius explained, then shape it according to the texture and style of the speech, brightening it with figures of language, varying it with figures of thought. The greatest achievement of eloquence is to amplify and adorn the subject matter, which comes about not just through adding and elevating, but also through refining and removing.

'Amplification is desirable in all the lines of argument that Antonius has described as suited to making a speech believable, whether we explain something or win support or rile our listeners. But it matters most with respect to the last – stirring emotion – for this is the achievement most particular to the orator. It's especially important when it comes to praise and blame, topics that Antonius took up recently, having set them to the side in our first conversation. For nothing is better suited to amplifying an oration than the ability to use each of these to the fullest extent.

'Next in importance are the topics[11] which, although they
ought to be natural to legal arguments and bound to their very
sinews, are nonetheless, due their universal treatment, called
commonplaces by rhetoricians of old. One set of these supplies
an amplified attack on vices and sins, such as cannot and is
not ordinarily contradicted: for example, denunciation of the
embezzler, the traitor, the parricide. Of course the charge must
be proven, or the denunciation is pointless.

'A different set of commonplaces aims at mitigation or pity;
still others provide in a general way for copious analysis on
either side of a disputed issue. This last approach is now considered the special concern of the two schools of philosophy I
discussed earlier;[12] but among our predecessors it was practised by anybody who sought to speak in court with a certain
richness and formality. And indeed we should have the means
of speaking on either side when the discussion concerns virtue,
duty, fairness, dignity, advantage, honour, disgrace, reward,
punishment and like matters. But now we have been driven
from our vast estate into a small and contested space, and
although we protect others, we can scarcely safeguard our
own property. So, despite the indignity of it all, let us borrow
what we need from the very people who have broken into our
paternal home.

'There's a group of philosophers, now named Peripatetics or
Academics after a small part of their city,[13] who at one time,
on account of their impressive knowledge of the most important matters, were identified as political philosophers by the
Greeks and thus given a name derived from public affairs in
general. According to these teachers, all public speaking falls
into one of two categories. Either it concerns a limited controversy pertaining to specific events and agents, for example,
should we Romans rescue our captives from the Carthaginians
by returning theirs? Or it concerns a topic of universal applicability: what in general should be the rule concerning prisoners
of war? They call the first type of discussion a hypothesis or
controversy and restrict it to three categories – lawsuit, policy
debate or laudations. The other, open-ended type they call a
"consultatio" or thesis.

'Rhetoricians, too, make this distinction in their instruc-tion, seeming to borrow it from philosophy rather than reclaiming it as their own, whether by law or force. They do retain their hold on the first category, namely topics specified by occasion, place and person, but only barely, for I hear that "controversies" are popular among the followers of Philo,[14] who has a great reputation in the Academy; the latter they identify in their teaching as belonging to the orator, but neglect its importance, nature, subdivisions and types. Frankly, they'd be better off dropping the subject rather than treating it so tentatively, since their reticence ends up seeming due to ignor-ance rather than to conscious choice.

'At any rate, every issue is open to the same techniques of investigation and analysis, whether it's of a general sort or one of the specific topics that are treated in political life and the courtroom. All have as their goal either knowledge or action.

'For example, knowledge is the goal when we ask whether virtue is to be pursued for its own sake or because it is advan-tageous; and a plan of action is at stake when we ask whether a wise man ought to involve himself in politics.

'Now there are three means of coming to know something, namely inference from facts, definition and what I call deduction. We seek the presence of something through inference, for example, whether wisdom exists within the human race; defi-nition explains the particular force or function of a thing, for example if we ask what wisdom is. And deduction is applied when we consider the application of a principle, for example whether it is ever permissible for a good man to tell a lie.

'With respect to inference, four types have been identified: whether something exists, for example, does human justice exist by nature or is it just a matter of convention; what is the origin of a given thing, for example, of laws or constitutions; or the reason for something, for example, if we ask why the most learned men disagree about the most important matters; or about the possibility of change, for example, whether a per-son's virtue can diminish or even change into vice.

'Disputes over definition occur either with respect to the general sense of a thing, for example, whether justice consists of the interests of the majority; or its properties, for example, is eloquence a unique possession of the orator or can others practise it; or its distribution into parts, for example, if we consider whether there are three types of preferables, goods of the body, goods of the mind and external goods; or its distinguishing characteristics, for example, how to recognize a miser, a rebel, or a braggart.

'Under deduction or application are placed two main types of inquiry: a simple dispute, for example whether glory is to be pursued or not; or a comparative evaluation, such as whether praise or wealth is preferable. The simple type takes three forms: is something to be sought or avoided, for example, should one seek offices, is poverty to be shunned; questions concerning right and wrong, for example, is it right to take revenge for injuries by a close relation; and questions concerning what is honourable or shameful, for example, is it honourable to commit suicide for the sake of glory?

'Comparison has two subsets: one, when we ask whether things are the same or different, for example, fear and reverence, a king and a tyrant, a flatterer and a friend; the other, when we consider which of two is better, for example, would a wise man rather have the praise of the best men or of the populace as a whole? These are pretty much all of the types of disputes over knowledge that have been listed by scholars.

'As for discussions concerning a course of action, they involve either disagreements about obligation, that is determining what is right and what needs to be done, a field that encompasses the entire range of virtues and vices; or the summoning, settling or elimination of some emotion – a field that includes exhortation, reproach, consolation, commiseration, in short anything that impels, or, if the situation demands, mitigates any kind of feeling.

'Now that I have laid out these types and modes of discussion, it doesn't really matter if there's some difference between my list and that of Antonius. We presented the same components, but arranged and distributed them differently. Let me now go ahead and return to my appointed task. For all arguments pertaining to whatever category of inquiry are to be derived from the topics explained by Antonius, with different topics better suited to different categories. There's no point in talking about this, not because it would take a long time but because the matter is perfectly clear. The most ornate speeches, in short, are those that range most widely and turn from the private and unique case at hand to explain the general issue, so that the audience is able to make its decision about individual defendants, charges and disputes with full awareness of the general principle at stake.

'This is the training that Antonius has been urging on you younger men. He wants you to leave behind narrow debates on trivial points and to get you to embrace the full force and richness of deliberation. What he has in mind can't be accomplished with a few pamphlets, as the writers on rhetoric think, or during a morning walk or afternoon conversation on a Tusculan estate. It isn't just a matter of developing or sharpening one's ability to speak. The mind, too, must be filled with a rich abundance of ideas about topics of the greatest importance.

'If we are truly orators, that is, if we deserve to take a leading role in the disputes and trials of citizens and in public deliberations, then learning and wisdom, endangered as they are, which men of leisure have seized upon while we have been preoccupied, in fact belong to us. Others merely ridicule the orator, as Socrates does in the *Gorgias*, or teach something or other about the art of the orator in a few short books they presume to call "rhetorical" – as if the very topics they discuss, such as justice, duty, the instruction and guidance of citizens, the conduct of life and nature itself, are not proprietary to rhetoricians.

'Because such knowledge isn't available elsewhere, let's take it back from the people who stole it from us. And let's make sure that we transfer it to the public realm where it belongs, and which it protects. And let's not devote every moment to learning what they have to teach. Once we are familiar with the sources (which if we can't understand quickly we will never understand), whenever there is need we will draw on them as the situation demands. For human insight is not so keen that we can automatically recognize these things without guidance.

On the other hand, they're not so obscure that an intelligent person can't understand them, once he has observed closely.

'Thus the orator should be free to explore such a vast terrain as he wishes, in confidence that wherever he takes a stand he has a right to be. All the resources for eloquence are his for the taking. Richness of understanding yields richness of language. If the content of a speech is impressive, the accompanying language will automatically be so too. Only see to it that the speaker or writer receives a liberal education in boyhood, burns with excitement for his studies and is assisted by nature; and that in practising on general or unlimited issues he selects the most sophisticated writers and speakers to study and imitate. He will hardly need teachers to explain how to arrange and enrich his language, so easily does nature itself, when provided with an abundance of matter, arrive at ornamented oratory – but only with practice.'

Catulus praises Crassus for his wide-ranging knowledge coupled with practical experience and criticizes the Greeks, who, though enthusiastic for literary and rhetorical studies, have made no new intellectual acquisitions or even preserved what has been handed down to them. Crassus then continues:

'Other arts in addition to eloquence have been reduced in value as a result of division and separation into individual parts. Do you really suppose that in the time of Hippocrates of Cos,[15] some doctors specialized in sickness, others in wounds, still others in eyes? Or that Euclid and Archimedes, Damon and Aristoxenus, or Aristophanes and Callimachus[16] treated their respective branches of geometry, music and literature as so distinctive that none embraced a general outlook, but instead each took for himself a little piece to work over in detail?

'I heard repeatedly from my father and my father-in-law that any Roman with intellectual ambition would seek to embrace all the knowledge then available at Rome. They told me about Sextus Aelius; and in our day we have seen Manius Manilius[17] walk across the forum, quite impressively sharing his insight with all of his fellow citizens. People would approach men like these whether they were out walking or sitting at home in order to consult them not just about civil law but about betrothing their daughters, buying an estate, cultivating a field, in short any type of business or responsibility.

'This was the sort of wisdom that characterized the famous Publius Crassus of yore, or Tiberius Coruncanius, or my son-in-law's great-grandfather, the extraordinarily astute Scipio,[18] all of whom also held the office of pontifex maximus.[19] They were consulted about every type of affair, whether religious or secular. They shared their trustworthy advice in the senate, among the people, in the lawsuits of friends, both at home and while in military service.

'What did Cato[20] lack besides the hyper-refined contemporary learning we have imported from across the sea? Because he studied legal theory, did he therefore refrain from trying cases? Or, given his ability to argue a case, did he neglect the science of law? He worked hard and excelled in both domains. Was he reticent to participate in public affairs because he was successful in private business? No one was more effective in addressing the common people, no one better as a senator; and he was easily the best general. There was no knowledge available in our state at that time that he didn't investigate, master and even commit to writing.

'Today, in contrast, most men set out to acquire public office all but naked and unarmed, lacking the equipment provided by experience and knowledge of affairs. But if some individual happens to stand out from the crowd, if he shows some distinction, perhaps in courage or other military traits (which are all but obsolete today!), or knowledge of the law (although hardly of the whole law, since no one studies pontifical law), or eloquence (meaning a raucous torrent of words), he certainly won't acknowledge the kinship and unity of all the liberal arts, indeed of the virtues themselves.

'But to come back to the Greeks, whom we cannot avoid,

particularly in this sort of discussion (for we look to our own people for virtue, to the Greeks for learning): it's said that at one time there existed seven individuals who were considered, and indeed called, "sages". All of them, except for Thales the Milesian,[21] were leaders of their respective cities. Who from that era is said to have been more learned, whose eloquence better fortified with knowledge of literature, than Peisistratus?[22] He is said to have been the first to put the previously disorganized books of Homer into the order we now follow. He didn't act in the interests of his people, but he was so eloquent that he stood out as a leading figure in literature and learning.

'What about Pericles?[23] He was such an effective orator that although he spoke rather forcefully against the opinion of the Athenians concerning the security of their state, the very fact that he opposed popular leaders made him popular and agreeable to all. Even when the comic playwrights maligned him (which was then legal in Athens), they acknowledged that his speeches were so compelling that the arrows he released stayed fixed in the minds of his listeners. Yet it was no "declaimer" who taught him how to keep barking until time ran out, but, so we hear, Anaxagoras of Clazomenae,[24] a man knowledgeable about the most demanding subjects. Thanks to the learning, good sense and eloquence he acquired, Pericles was the leading man at Athens for some forty years, in both domestic and military affairs.

'What of Critias or Alcibiades?[25] Although unreliable where their fellow citizens were concerned, they were surely learned and eloquent – and weren't they trained in Socratic eristics? Who prepared Dio the Syracusan[26] in every field of learning? Was it not Plato? One and the same teacher of eloquence and virtue encouraged, instructed and armed him for the liberation of his country. Did Plato instruct Dio in arts any different from those Isocrates taught the heroic Timotheus, son of the famous general Conon,[27] and himself a leading general and most learned human being? What about Lysis the Pythagorean, teacher of Epaminondas of Thebes,[28] who was quite possibly the greatest man in all of Greece? Or Xenophon teacher of

Agesilaus?[29] Or Philolaus, who taught Archytas of Tarentum?[30] Or Pythagoras himself, who taught the entire Greek region of Italy, once called "great"?[31]

'This is not mere opinion on my part. For I see that there was a single type of education that addressed every subject worthy of an educated man and of anyone hoping to succeed in public affairs. Those who received it, provided they had the talent to put it to use and actually engaged in public speaking (assuming there was no natural impediment), were recognized for their eloquence. Thus Aristotle himself, when he saw Isocrates basking in the glory of his students once he had changed the topic of his treatises from legal and civil affairs to mere elegance of style, immediately altered his own pedagogical approach, citing a verse attributed to Philoctetes, albeit with a minor change. For Philoctetes said that it was shameful for him to remain silent yet allow barbarians to speak; Aristotle that it was shameful to let Isocrates speak.[32] This witticism didn't escape the notice of the very wise king Philip, who summoned Aristotle as teacher for his son,[33] who was to acquire from him guidance in conduct as well as speech.

'Now, if anyone wants to give the title of orator to a philosopher who transmits to us a richness of knowledge and of language, it's fine with me. So too, if you'd prefer to give the title of philosopher to an orator who unites wisdom and eloquence, I won't object to that either. Just make sure we agree that neither an inarticulate man, with knowledge he can't share by speaking, nor an ignorant one, who chatters on without knowing the facts, deserves our respect – although if we have to choose between them, better tongue-tied good sense than eloquent nonsense.

'But if we're after the best type of all, then the prize belongs to the learned orator. If it's granted that he is also a philosopher, then the controversy comes to an end. But if a distinction is necessary, then the philosophers are inferior. The ideal orator possesses the knowledge of philosophers, but the domain of philosophers does not necessarily include eloquence. And although they're disdainful of it, it can only complement their own art.'

Having said these things, Crassus was silent for a while, as were all the rest.

In the subsequent paragraphs, Cotta gently observes that Crassus has still not fully explained what he means by elegance and appropriateness of style. Sulpicius echoes the complaint, with greater vigour, after admitting that he has no use for Crassus' views on the relationship between knowledge and eloquence. Seemingly unfazed, Crassus resumes his discussion of ornament, without recanting his deeper account of the inseparability of knowledge and eloquence, or matter and form.

Crassus answered:
'What you're asking about, Sulpicius, has been widely discussed and is even familiar to you. Honestly, who *hasn't* spoken or written about this topic? But I'll go ahead and humour you by briefly outlining what I know – although I recommend consulting the writers who discovered these refinements.

'Every speech consists of words, which need to be considered first as individual entities, then in combination. There is a certain type of polish that comes from individual words, another from their arrangement. The words we employ are either appropriate and specific to the things they describe, almost as if they had come into being along with them; or they are transferred and placed, as it were, in a foreign context; or we invent them.

'In selecting appropriate words, the orator should avoid colloquialisms or clichéd expressions and instead use impressive language that is rich and resonant. Even among appropriate words, discrimination, based on judgement by ear, is still necessary. This capacity will improve with practice in speaking. The common observation, such as "he has a good vocabulary", or "his choice of words is terrible", even coming from those who aren't experts, is less a product of art than of a certain innate sensibility. Success in this area depends less on avoiding mistakes, important as that is, than on using a good, rich vocabulary. This is the base and foundation.

'How the orator builds artistically on this foundation is the next point to consider. In selecting individual words, the orator has in effect three resources for embellishing his style: rare words, new words and words used metaphorically.

'Rare or unfamiliar words are those that are archaic or have dropped from everyday usage. They are more readily available to poets than to public speakers, yet if used sparingly provide a certain poetic dignity even in an oration. I wouldn't hesitate to say, with Caelius,[34] "how unseasonably the Carthaginian came to Italy" or to use the words progeny, scion, prognosticate or appellation,[35] or, as you like to say, Catulus, "I reckoned not" or "I opined",[36] or many other words which, when used correctly, give a speech a certain archaic grandeur.

'New words are those invented by a speaker, either by combination, for example "then fear outspits all wisdom from my soul" or "surely you do not prefer the tongue-twisty malice of this man . . ." (for you see that "tongue-twisty" and "outspit" are formed by combining words); or, as often happens, from scratch, for example "that derelict oldster", "birthifying gods" or "curven with their load of berries".

'Metaphorical language is widespread. Necessity, due to lack and constraint, created it, pleasure and delight have made it popular. Much as clothing was invented first to ward off cold, but then to adorn and dignify the body, so metaphorical language had its origin in need, but became commonplace from delight. Even peasants say that "a vine is bejeweled", "the grass luxuriates", "the crops rejoice". When there is no specific word for something, another word, used metaphorically, can describe it through resemblance.

'Such metaphors constitute a type of borrowing, in which you take from elsewhere what you yourself lack. Others are a little bolder, and rather than filling a need aim to impress. It isn't really necessary for me to go through them systematically.

'Just make sure that a metaphor either clarifies meaning, as in all of the following expressions, where clarity is achieved by transferring words on the basis of similarity:

> The sea shudders,
> shadows multiply, night and cloud blind with blackness,
> flame flashes between the clouds, the sky trembles with
>   thunder,
> hail mixed with lavish rain rushes headlong,
> on every side all the winds burst free, savage whirlwinds
>   approach,
> the vast expanse is boiling.[37]

or conveys additional information about a deed or thought, for example when a character's secret intent is communicated through a double metaphor, as in the following:

> he cloaks himself in words, builds a fortress with deceit.[38]

Sometimes a metaphor is used for the sake of brevity, for example:

> if the weapon flees his hand.[39]

A single transferred term expresses the unforeseen nature of the weapon's release more concisely than an accurate description could.

'While we're on this topic, I should say that I've often wondered why people derive so much pleasure from using metaphors as opposed to precise language. If there is no unique term to describe the "foot" on a boat[40] or a contract that "binds" or "departure" from a wife, then of course we must take what we need from something else. But even when an abundance of words is available, people still enjoy metaphors, as long as they're used within reason. I suspect this is the case either because it seems ingenious to pass over the obvious and seek something from a distance, or because the listener is led to think of something additional, without losing the train of thought, which brings a great deal of delight. Or because through a single word a complete analogy is expressed, or because every successful metaphor appeals to the senses, especially sight, which is the keenest sense.

'Expressions like a "whiff of urbanity", "softness of disposition", "murmur of the sea", "sweetness of style" depend on other senses. Metaphors from sight are much sharper; they place what cannot be seen or discerned right before the mind's eye. For there is no term referring to a natural entity that can't be used in other contexts. Whatever the source of the resemblance – which can be anything – the transfer of a single word makes a style sparkle.

'The first thing to be avoided under this heading is dissimilarity: "the massive archways of heaven".[41] It's said that Ennius brought a sphere on stage, yet a sphere is nothing like an archway![42] On the other hand, in the expression:

> Live, Ulysses, while you can.
> Snatch the last ray of light with your eyes![43]

he didn't say "seek" or "take", which might imply the slowness of a person expecting to live for a long time, instead he said "snatch", just the word to pair with the preceding phrase "while you can".

'Next, see to it that the resemblance isn't far-fetched. Instead of the "Syrtis of his inheritance", I would say "shoals"; not the "Charybdis of wealth" but the "whirlpool",[44] for the mind's eye is led more easily to what we have seen than to what we have heard of.

'Because the whole point of metaphor is to have a direct impact on the senses, we need to avoid drawing the listener's attention to anything shameful. Thus, I'd rather not say that the death of Africanus "castrated" the state, or call Glaucia[45] the "dung-heap of the senate-house". The resemblance might be genuine, but in either case we are forced to think of something ugly. I reject a metaphor that is on a larger scale than what it describes, for example, "a hurricane of a party" or on a lesser scale, such as "a party of a hurricane". I also reject the transfer of a term that is narrower than the normal one would be:

> Please, what is it? Why do you decline[46] my presence?

It would be better to say "forbid", "prohibit" or "put a stop to",
since the other speaker had just said,

> Come no closer!
> My touch, even my shadow, may harm the righteous.

If you're worried that the metaphor may be a little harsh,
then soften it with an additional expression. For example, if
it seemed too much to say that at the death of Marcus Cato,
the senate was "orphaned", then one could have included, by
way of mitigation, the phrase, "so to speak". In fact, a metaphor should look a bit bashful, as if invited to a new residence
rather than breaking in by force. Still, no other manner of
speaking produces livelier language or gives greater sheen to a
speech.

'Metaphor can consist not just of a single word but of an
interconnected sequence, so that something other than what is
said can be inferred:

> I will not suffer
>   to crash against the same rock yet again, like the Achaean
>   fleet of old.

or

> How mistaken you are! For the strong rein of the law will curb
> your arrogance and impose on you the yoke of authority.[47]

As I have explained, words borrowed from one thing are transferred to another.

'This is an important ornament of style, but be careful to
avoid obscurity – for the same procedure can produce a riddle,
although the latter involves not individual words, but a continuum of discourse.

'Substitution or metonymy entails linguistic innovation, but
of a different sort. For example,

> Rugged Africa trembles with terrible tumult[48]

where "Africa" replaces "Africans". There's no neologism, as in "the sea with smashingrock waves",[49] or metaphorical transfer, as in "the sea softens";[50] rather the figure here consists of replacing one proper noun with another, as also in "cease, Rome, your enemies . . ."[51] or "The Great Fields testify." This is a reliable type of adornment and should be used frequently. Of a similar sort are expressions such as "Mars" commonly used of war, "Ceres" for grain, "Liber" for wine, "Neptune" for the sea, "curia" for the senate, "field" for assemblies, "toga" for peace, "arms" for war.

'In like manner, the name of a virtue or vice might be used in place of the people who possess them, as in:

a house invaded by extravagance

where greed has made its residence

loyalty prevailed

justice won in the end.

In each instance the alteration or replacement of a word allows the meaning to be expressed more elegantly. A related device, less ornate, but not for that reason to be passed over, entails implying a whole from a part, for example saying walls or roofs instead of buildings. Or implying a part from a whole, for example calling a single squadron of horsemen "the Roman people", or out of one we imply many, for example:

the Roman, though the affair has turned out well, trembles in his heart.[52]

or understanding one from many, for example:

now we are Roman who once were Rudine[53]

or however we manage to communicate what is meant rather than what is said.

'There is another common means of exploiting a term,

although not so elegantly as metaphor. The device is rather free, but still at times not inappropriate, as when we say that an oration is "expansive" rather than "long", or call a person's mental capacity "diminished" instead of "small". Surely you understand that the devices mentioned earlier involve not a word but a larger expression, since they arise from a series of metaphorical expressions. These latter techniques, such as exchanging words or understanding them differently, are metaphors of a particular kind.

'It follows, then, that admirable use of individual words falls into one of three categories: use of an archaic term that nonetheless fits current usage; a term either invented from scratch or created through combination, with due attention to sound and usage; or metaphor, which enlivens a speech with highlights, like stars in the night sky.

'The next topic is the sequence of words, in which two considerations are relevant: first, order or juxtaposition; second, a certain rhythm and balance. Juxtaposition requires placing words so as to avoid both a harsh clash of sounds and hiatus, or breath between words, and thus to produce a smooth transition. An author especially qualified to do so made a joke about this topic, speaking in the person of my father-in-law:[54]

> How charmingly he orders his orations:
> words squiggling like mosaic-tiles that form a curve.

Nor did he leave me alone, once he had mocked Albucius.[55]

> I have a son-in-law Crassus, in case you are rhetorically inclined.

What of it? This Crassus you ridicule by name, what did he accomplish? Evidently something better than Albucius, he implies, and I agree. But really, he was only joking with me, as he often did.

'At any rate, it is important to preserve the order of words that I'm discussing, since it produces a close-knit, coherent style with a smooth and even flow. You'll achieve this effect if you order the ends and beginnings of contiguous words without hiatus or unpleasant junctures.'

Prose Rhythm

'The next topic, which I fear Catulus will consider rather silly, is the rhythm and shape of words. The Greeks of old thought that it was acceptable to use near-verses, that is, metres, even in prose. They wanted the ends of periods to be an occasion of taking a breath and not the result of exhaustion. They said that such breaks should be distinguished not by the punctuation of copyists but through the arrangement of words and thoughts. Isocrates first made it a practice to tighten up the loose constructions of his predecessors and give pleasure to the ears, as his student Naucrates[56] writes, by means of rhythm.

'For musicians, who used to be poets as well, developed two techniques for generating pleasure, namely, verse and melody, so that by the rhythm of words and the mode or melody of the voice they could delight, rather than bore, their listeners. They then transferred these techniques of vocal modulation and the arrangement of words from poetry to eloquence, to the extent that the seriousness of oratory could accommodate them.

'The most important point here is that even though it's a mistake to create a line of poetry within a speech through the arrangement of words, nevertheless we do want groupings of words to have a rhythmical cadence, a rounding off, a sense of completion. Nothing better differentiates the orator from the ignorant and inexperienced speaker than the latter's tendency to pour out in disorderly fashion as much as he can and to take a break because he's out of breath rather than for artistic purposes. The orator, on the other hand, constrains his thought with his words by means of a loose yet binding rhythm. For once he has bound his thought with form and measure, he loosens and relaxes it through a change of order, so that his words are neither tightly constrained as if by a fixed metrical law, nor loosened so as to wander aimlessly.

'How then are we to undertake so great a task as to consider ourselves capable of attaining this power of rhythmical speech? In fact, it's not as difficult as it is important, for nothing is as soft and malleable as speech. From speech are verses fashioned, from speech irregular rhythms, from speech comes prose composed of varying patterns of many types. There isn't one lexicon for conversation, another for debate; nor one language for daily usage, another for stage and spectacle. We take up words from the common store and like softest wax mould and fashion them at our discretion. Sometimes we are vehement, sometimes subtle, sometimes in between: just so our style follows our thought, changing and adapting to please the ear or stir the soul.

'And, much to our amazement, as with so much else, so with eloquence, nature has arranged that what is most useful is also most dignified and even most beautiful.[57] We see how, for the safety and security of everything, the universe is ordered as a sphere with earth suspended in the middle of its own accord, how the sun travels around it, sinking before the midwinter constellation then gradually rising in the opposite direction; how the moon receives the light of the sun as it waxes and wanes; how the five planets accomplish the same circuit despite differences in speed and route. This arrangement is so successful that it cannot cohere if it undergoes even slight alteration; so beautiful, that nothing more attractive is even imaginable.

'Consider for a moment the form and figure of human beings or any other living creatures. You won't find anything added unless necessary; the totality of each form has been perfected, it would seem, by art not chance. What of trees? No trunks, branches, leaves exist except for the purpose of preserving their nature, yet every part is beautiful. Set nature aside and consider the arts. In a ship, the sides, hold, prow, deck, sails, sail-yards and masts are all indispensable. Yet each is so attractive that it seems to have been invented for pleasure as well as security. Columns support temples and porches, yet are as dignified as they are functional. Necessity, not beauty, fashioned the pediment of the Capitol and other temples; for when a scheme was devised for allowing water to flow from either side of the roof, the impressive appearance of a temple pediment followed from its function. Even if the Capitol were placed in the heavens, where there are no rainstorms, it would seem undignified without such a gable.

'The same is true of every aspect of eloquence, namely that

a certain sweetness and charm follow upon function and necessity. The limited nature of breath led to rhythmic cadences and pauses in the flow of language. These are so charming that even if a speaker never had to stop for breath, we wouldn't want him to proceed without interruption. What is not just possible, but even easy for our lungs, turns out to be pleasing to our ears.

'And so, while the longest group of words is that which can be reeled off in one breath, this is the standard of nature – art has another. From among the numerous possible rhythms, your Aristotle, Catulus,[58] banishes from oratory frequent use of iamb and trochee,[59] metres that naturally occur in our speeches and conversation. But the beats of these metres are too strong, and their feet too short. This is why he tells us to use heroic metre,[60] which is permissible for two feet or a bit more, provided we don't fall into actual verse or even the semblance thereof. These three feet can be used decorously at the beginning of a period. For example:

Tall twin girls were the maids of the house.

'He especially approves of the paean, which takes two forms: a long syllable followed by three shorts, as in "then give it up, next get it going, push down on it"[61] or three shorts followed by a long, as in "when they had crushed" or "the clatter of hooves".[62]

'That philosopher further recommends beginning with the first type of paean, concluding with the second. This second type, please note, is almost equivalent to a cretic, not in number of syllables but to the sense of hearing, which is a keener and more reliable judge. The cretic is composed of a long followed by a short followed by a long, as in "how to seek, where to find, when to run".[63] Fannius began a speech with this rhythm when he said "if my friends, that man's threats . . ."[64] Aristotle thinks the rhythm more suitable for clausulae, or the ends of periods, which are generally to be terminated with a long syllable.

'This topic doesn't demand such careful attention as it would in the case of poets. For them metre consists of enclosing words within verse-forms, so that nothing is shorter or longer, not even by the smallest breath, than required. Prose style is looser, not to the point of running free, but controlled without being tightly restricted. I agree with Theophrastus,[65] who thinks that polished prose should have a relaxed rather than rigid rhythm.

'As he goes on to suggest, from the metres just discussed, which form standard components of verse, a certain more extended metre emerged, namely the rather licentious and luxurious dithyramb,[66] whose cola and feet, as Theophrastus says, are diffused throughout all serious prose. And if there is variable length in all sounds and expressions, such as can be perceived and also measured out, then it's proper for this sort of metre, as long as it isn't used in a continuous sequence, to appear in prose. For if non-stop talking is considered crude and unsophisticated, it must be because nature itself has adapted ear and voice to one another. But that wouldn't be the case if rhythm weren't intrinsic to spoken language.

'In a continuous outpouring there is no rhythm. A beat, that is to say, a marking of equal or varied intervals, constitutes a rhythm. We take note of the rhythm of raindrops, which are separated by intervals, but we cannot do so with a rushing stream. And if the flow of words in prose is more fitting and more attractive when divided into joints and limbs (commata and cola) than when uninterrupted, then the so-called limbs will have to be arranged and modified. If they are too short at the end of a unit, they break up the circuit of words – what the Greeks call turnings or periods of speech. This is why later units should be equal to or longer than earlier ones, and the last equal to or, even better, longer than the first.

'These are the sorts of claims made by the philosophers you so admire, Catulus, a fact I cite so that by praising their authority I can avoid the charge of ineptitude.'

'What ineptitude are you talking about?' says Catulus. 'What could be more elegant, more subtle, than the explanation you have just delivered?'

'Be that as it may,' says Crassus, 'I worry that such guidelines may strike our listeners as too difficult to pursue, or that we might seem eager to make them appear especially challenging, since they aren't transmitted in the standard handbooks.' To which Catulus replied, 'You are mistaken, Crassus, if you think that I or anyone else here today expects from you everyday or familiar advice. You are telling us just what we want to be told, and not just to be told but to be told as you are telling it. I am absolutely certain that I speak not just for myself but for everyone present.'

'For my part,' says Antonius,[67] 'I have now found what I claimed I hadn't found in the book I wrote – an eloquent man! I held back from interrupting you, even with praise, because I don't want to lessen the time available for your remarks with even a single word of my own.'

So Crassus continued: 'We must conform our speech to this law of rhythm both in oral practice and in writing, which provides refinement and polish in this sphere as in others. Still, it isn't as big a task as it seems. We needn't apply the rigid standards of the specialists in rhythm and music. Our one goal is to make sure that our discourse doesn't just wander or stop short or extend too far. Its component parts should be articulated, its periodic structure resolved. Nor is it necessary always to employ continuous periods. Better to break the discourse into smaller units that are bound together rhythmically.

'And don't let the paean or the dactyl cause you worry either. They will occur naturally in a speech, they will present themselves without being summoned. Make it your practice in writing and in speaking to have your thoughts finish together with your words and your words be joined in long and limber rhythms, especially the dactyl, the first paean and the cretic, but let them come to an end in a varied yet clearly defined manner. For similarity is especially noted in concluding. And if the first and last feet follow this system, the ones in between can pass without notice, provided that the circuit of words is neither shorter than the ears expect nor longer than strength and breath can handle.

'In my opinion, the endings of sentences deserve more careful attention than the openings, since it is on the basis of the endings that completion and resolution are assessed. With verses, the beginning, middle and end are all noticed equally, and the line is weakened wherever the flaw. In oratory, few judge the beginnings, almost all the endings. Because they will be noticed, they must be varied, so as not to offend our judgement – or our ears. Two or three feet ought to be reserved for the ending and made noticeable (provided the preceding are not too short or clipped). These will need to be trochees or dactyls, or trochees or dactyls alternating with the second paean, which Aristotle is so fond of, or its equivalent, the cretic. Having a mix of these will keep the listeners from getting bored with repetition and keep us from seeming to have worked too hard.

'Antipater of Sidon,[68] who is such a favourite of yours, Catulus, used to utter hexameters or whole verses in other metres right on the spot. Through practice, a quick-witted man with a good memory, once he committed himself to a verse, was able to generate words automatically. How much more easily will we accomplish this in our orations, provided we train and practise.

'And no one should doubt that even an inexpert audience can notice such things, for here as elsewhere the power of nature is truly remarkable. All people, by means of a certain implicit sensibility, without any art or discipline, can differentiate what is right and wrong in artistic compositions. They manage to do so in the case of paintings and sculptures and other such works, where nature has given them fewer tools. All the more so do they display an ability to judge words, rhythms and utterances, which are rooted in a shared sensibility and naturally familiar to everyone.

'Thus everyone is affected by words that have been skilfully arranged, as well as by rhythm and delivery. For what portion of the population has a disciplined understanding of rhythm and metre? Yet the entire theatre cries out against even a small violation, such as a contraction that makes a verse too short or an extension that makes it too long. It's the same with pronunciation: whole troupes and choruses, or sometimes individual members, are booed offstage by the crowd due to a single inconsistency.

'It's remarkable how little difference there is between an expert and an amateur when it comes to judging, although the difference is great when it comes to creating. Because art took its start from nature, it would seem to accomplish little if it couldn't move and delight in a natural manner. Nothing is so naturally adapted to our feelings as rhythm and language. We are riled up, inflamed and assuaged by them; we grow relaxed and are often led to joy or grief. Their extraordinary power, well suited to song and chant, was not neglected, it seems to me, by Numa,[69] most learned king, or by our ancestors, as the use of lyres and flutes at sacred feasts and the verses of the Salian priests[70] make clear; they were held in especially high regard in archaic Greece. If only you had asked for a discourse on topics like these rather than an elementary subject like metaphor!

'At any rate, just as the common crowd notices a mistake in versification, it also recognizes when we somehow slip up in speaking. And although the audience may pardon us while not forgiving a poet, still the general silence does not mean they think what we have said is fit and perfect. Those orators of old, not to mention quite a few today, being unable to complete a rounded circuit of words (for we have only recently begun to be able or, better, to dare this task) would speak in units of three or two or even single words, although even in those early days they tried to balance their phrases and use regular pauses, as the sense of hearing requires.'

Elegance of Style

'I have now explained, to the best of my ability, the chief components of ornate speech. For I have spoken about individual words, their combinations, their rhythm and pattern. But if you insist on also hearing about the style and tone of a speech, there is the full yet rounded; the thin, yet taut and strong; and a third that is midway between the other two. Each of these three types should supply a certain colour, not like smeared-on dye, but like blood diffused throughout. Finally, this orator of ours must shape his words and thoughts so that like a fencer or a boxer he has a system not just for avoiding and delivering blows, but also for moving gracefully. Like those who handle weapons, he should use his words in a fitting and suitable manner and deploy his thoughts so as to make his speech impressive. Words and thoughts can be arranged in an almost infinite number of ways, as I know you recognize. But there's a difference between figured language and thought: if you change the words, the figure of language disappears, but a figure of thought remains whatever words you use.[71]

'Although you all compose in this way, I think it still worth recommending that an orator needs nothing, no matter how outstanding or remarkable, when it comes to individual words, but frequent metaphors, occasional neologisms, rare archaisms. In continuous discourse, as I have said, we must keep in mind the need for smooth arrangement and careful use of rhythm, while making frequent use of brilliant figures of thought and language.

'For example, delay over a single point can have a great effect, as can a vivid explanation of events, as if they were happening right before our eyes. These techniques are of value both in presenting the facts and in illuminating or amplifying what is presented. The aim is to make what is augmented seem to the audience as grand as the power of oratory permits. In contrast, there is hurried summary, the hint that more is to be understood than you have spoken, clipped brevity of speech, disparagement, even joking, as long as it follows the precepts of Caesar![72]

'Other devices include digression from the main point, a source of entertainment that is followed by a smooth return to the subject; introduction to what you are going to say, distinguishing it from what has already been said, and a return to the proposition for restatement and fitting summation of the argument. There's also exaggeration for the sake of emphasizing or belittling some point; interrogation, including rhetorical question that in effect states one's own opinion; irony or dissimulation, meaning saying one thing and meaning another, which really works its way into people's thoughts – it's also quite enjoyable when expressed in a conversational rather than polemical style; then there's hesitation, distribution and correction – before or after you have made a statement, or by denying its applicability to yourself.

'A device known as laying the groundwork prepares the way for your case; transfer puts the burden on the other side; consultation is a kind of deliberation with the audience; imitation of manners and behaviour, either in character or not, adds a great deal to a speech and works to calm people down or rile them up. Impersonation of another is a terrific way to call attention to a topic; there's also description, deliberately misleading, raising a laugh and anticipating; then two especially effective devices, simile and example; division into parts, interruption, provocation, reticence, issuing of compliments; unbridled speech for the sake of emphasis; feigned anger, invective, promise of proof, belittlement, beseeching, brief divergence from the subject (on a lesser scale than actual digression), excusemaking, apology, lashing out, praying and cursing. Such are the figures of thought by which we brighten a speech.

'As for figures of speech, we can brandish them like weapons, either to threaten and attack or to create an aesthetic effect. There can be charm as well as force in repeating a word, changing it slightly, using it at the beginning or end of successive units, or at the beginning and end of the same unit; so too with adjunction, increment and different uses of the same word, revocation of a word, words with the same endings, nominal or verbal, or balanced or parallel constructions.

'There is also stepwise progression, inversion, hyperbaton, antithesis, declination, self-correction, exclamation, contraction, use of the same noun in several cases, matching, explanation whether of a statement as a whole or individual details, deferment, a different kind of hesitation, improvisation, enumeration, a second kind of correction, local distribution, running on and breaking off, simile, answering one's own questions, metonymy, distribution of terms, order (balanced or unbalanced) and circumscription. For these are the relevant figures – and there may be more like them – that embellish a speech with thought and ideas or with verbal patterns.'

'Well,' said Cotta,[73] 'I see that you have just let them flow, pouring them out without definitions or examples, on the assumption that they are familiar to us.'

'To be honest,' replied Crassus, 'I didn't suppose anything I

said earlier was news to any of you either, but merely answered
your request. As for what I have just discussed, the position of
the sun told me I needed to be brief. It is setting quickly and
has forced me to speak almost as quickly. Still, demonstrations
and instructions on this topic are readily available. Their use,
however, is a serious matter, the most difficult in the whole
field of rhetoric.

'So then, since all topics pertaining to adornment of speech
have been noted, if not fully explored, let us consider the matter of appropriateness, or decorum, in language. This much is
surely clear: no single manner of speaking is suited to every
case or listener or speaker or occasion. Capital cases demand
one style of language, private or trivial affairs another. Deliberations, eulogies, trials, conversations, consolation, invective,
intellectual debate and narrative all expect different styles. It
makes a difference who is listening – the senate, the people as
a whole or jurors. Are they many or few in number, or just one
person; and what sort of people are they? What of the orators?
How old? What status and authority do they have? And as for
the occasion, is it a time of peace or war, is the audience in a
hurry or at leisure?

'So at this point it doesn't really seem possible to offer specific advice, except to say that we should choose a full or simple
or in-between style, in accordance with the matter at hand. It
will be permissible to use the same techniques of ornamentation, sometimes more energetically, other times in a more
restrained manner. In every instance, the ability to do what is
fitting is a matter of art and of nature; knowing what is fitting
and when is a matter of practical intelligence.

'But all of these devices are enacted through delivery. Delivery alone dominates when it comes to public speaking. Without
it even the best orator is of no account; with it, a mediocre
orator often surpasses the best. When asked what was the
most important aspect of speaking, Demosthenes[74] said delivery came in first – and second, and third. And, in my opinion,
Aeschines[75] put it even better. He had left Athens and moved
to Rhodes, due to a disgraceful failure in a trial. As the story
goes, the Rhodians asked him to read out the famous speech

against Ctesiphon[76] that he had delivered in opposition to Demosthenes. Having done so, he was asked the next day to read the opposing speech that Demosthenes had delivered in defence of Ctesiphon. When he had finished reading this one too in a beautiful and resounding voice and all were expressing admiration, he remarked: "How much more amazed you would be, if you had heard the man himself!" In this way he made clear the importance of delivery, since he believed that the same speech became something different with a change of speaker.

'What was it about Gracchus' oratory, Catulus, that caused so much discussion? You remember better than I do, since I was just a boy.

> Where in my misery am I to take myself? Where am I to turn? To the Capitol? But it is soaking with the blood of my brother. Home? To see my mother wretched, grieving and despondent?[77]

We've been told that he used his eyes and voice and gesture so effectively that even his enemies could not hold back their tears. I discuss these matters at greater length because orators, who are performers of reality, have abandoned this whole area of study, while actors, who merely imitate reality, have seized it for themselves. Without doubt in every instance reality is superior to imitation, and if reality in itself were sufficient in performance, we would have no need of art. But emotion, which has to be communicated through performance, is often so confused as to be hard to identify. As a result, it's up to the orator to eliminate uncertainty and make the emotion in question distinct and obvious.

'We can do this, inasmuch as every emotion by its very nature has a corresponding facial expression, sound and gesture. A person's body, face and voice resonate when struck by emotion, like strings on a lyre. Voices are tightened up, like strings responding to touch, high, low, quick, slow, loud, quiet, with a middle type in the midst of each pair; and there are further modifications, such as smooth or rough, quiet or loud, continuous or staccato, trilling or clipped, diminishing

or rising in crescendo. Everything of this sort can be modu-
lated through art. They are the colours available to a performer,
as to a painter, for purposes of variation.

'Anger will use one tone of voice – shrill, hasty, agitated, for
example:

> He urges me, my brother! to consign my sons, O woe!
> to my jaws.[78]

or the lines you quoted some time ago, Antonius:

> You dared to separate from yourself[79]

and

> Does no one take note? Tie him up![80]

and almost the entirety of the *Atreus*.[81]

Compassion and sorrow use another tone, wavering, full, halt-
ing, mournful:

> Where now am I to turn? What journey commence?
> To my paternal homestead? Or to the daughters of Pelias?[82]

or

> O father, O country, O house of Priam!

and the lines that follow:

> I saw everything in flames
> and Priam violently deprived of life.[83]

The performance of fear is submissive, hesitant, downcast:

> I am besieged in every manner, by sickness, exile and destitution.
> Fear has forced all insight from my soul

My mother menaces my life with terrible torture and with death.
There's no one so strong and steadfast that his blood
Would not recoil and flesh turn pale in terror at these threats.[84]

Energy is indicated by a voice that is taut, vigorous and intimidating:

> Again Thyestes dares to menace Atreus,
> again he attacks and stirs me from my sleep.
> More trouble, more evil must I conjure
> to grind and crush his own cruel heart.[85]

The voice of one in a state of pleasure is loose, gentle, soft, lively, at ease:

> But when she carried a wedding wreath
> she carried it for you. Although at first she pretended to
>   give it to another,
> she was happy to present it to you, smartly, delicately.[86]

Distress requires a low or heavy voice, without appeal to pity, steady in its pressure and volume:

> At the time when Paris joined Helen in unwed wedlock
> I was on the verge of giving birth, the tally of months complete.
> At the same time Hecuba bore her last child, Polydorus.[87]

All of these emotions should be accompanied by gesture – not the stagey kind that seeks to represent each word, but gesture that expresses the general meaning and sense, not explicitly, but through suggestion, a strong and virile movement from the core outwards as found in military exercises or the wrestling-school rather than on stage and among actors. Hand movements should not be overly precise: let the fingers follow the meaning rather than expressing it. The arm should be brandished as if a weapon of speech, the foot stamped at the beginning or end of an emphatic passage.

'But everything depends on the face, which is dominated by the eyes. The older generation showed good judgement when they withheld praise even from Roscius if he wore a mask. Performance performs the soul, the face is its image, the eyes its index. This is the one part of the body that, however numerous the movements of the soul, can express them all. And no one achieves the same effect with eyes closed. Theophrastus quotes Tauriscus[88] as saying that an actor who gazed fixedly at something while delivering his lines might as well turn his back on the audience.

'This is why it's important to keep the eyes under control. Avoid changing the appearance of the face too much so as not to look foolish or depraved. It's through the eyes that we correctly correlate speech with emotion, by straining or relaxing our gaze, staring or moving them about. Because delivery is the language of the body, it must accord closely with the mind. And nature gave us eyes for the purpose of communicating emotions, as it gave a mane, a tail and ears to horses and lions. Thus when it comes to performance the face is second in importance only to the voice, and the eyes are the leading feature of the face.

'Still, nature grants a certain power to all aspects of delivery, which is why the uneducated, the crowd, even barbarians are greatly affected by it. Words can only affect a person who shares in the same language, and clever sayings can pass right by listeners who are less than clever. But delivery, by displaying emotion, affects the emotions of all. For all people are moved by the same feelings and use the same means to recognize them in others and express them in themselves.

'But performance, especially good performance, without a doubt depends primarily on voice. It's what we should hope for most of all, and whatever kind of voice we have, we should look after it. How to care for the voice is not a topic of instruction here, although I emphasize that it must be cared for. Still, it seems relevant to our discussion to point out, as I said earlier, that often what is most useful is also, somehow or other, especially attractive. For maintaining the voice nothing is more useful than frequent modulation. Nothing is more dangerous than uninterrupted strain.

'What is more suited to our ears and to making delivery attractive than change or variation? The same Gracchus (as

you may learn, Catulus,[89] from your client Licinius, an educated man, who used to be his slave secretary), during his
speeches to the assembly, would keep hidden behind him an
expert with a little ivory flute who would quickly blow a note
to rouse him when he relaxed his voice or call him back when
he strained it.' 'Indeed I have heard just that,' said Catulus,
'and often marvelled at the man's careful practice as well as his
knowledge and learning.'

'I admired him as well,' said Crassus, 'and it saddens me
that men like him ended up doing damage to the republic;
although today such a web is being woven and such a pattern
of public life displayed to posterity, that we are eager to have
citizens [even] of the sort our fathers did not tolerate.' 'Please
drop this subject,' said Julius, 'and return to the little flute of
Gracchus, for I don't yet understand the principle of its use.'

'In every voice,' said Crassus, 'there is a certain mean, specific to the voice. It produces a pleasing effect to rise gradually
from this mean (for it is boorish to start screeching at the outset); and it's a healthy practice for strengthening the voice.
There is also an extreme of straining, which is still just below
the most acute sound, and the pipe does not allow you to go
beyond, and will call you back from this high point. Again,
there is a deepest tone, reached through stepwise lowering.
This range and run through the whole course of the voice will
protect it and add charm to delivery. But you can leave the
piper at home as long as you take the awareness inculcated by
the practice with you when you head to the forum.

'I have now explained what I could, not as I would have
liked, but as the limited time demanded. For it's a clever thing
to blame the circumstances, when you aren't able to add more,
even if you want to.'

'But you have gathered together everything,' said Catulus, 'as
far as I can tell, and done so with such brilliance that you seem
not to have borrowed from the Greeks but to be able to serve as
their instructor. I am happy to have been a participant in this
conversation with you, I only wish that my son-in-law, your
associate Hortensius,[90] had been here. I am confident that he
will excel in everything you have included in your discussion.'

'Will excel?' responded Crassus. 'I think he already excels, as I thought when he defended the cause of Africa in the senate during my consulship[91] and even more so when he recently spoke on behalf of the king of Bithynia.[92] And so you are correct, Catulus, for this young man seems to lack nothing in natural ability or in education.

'All the more reason for you, Cotta, and you, Sulpicius,[93] to stay up late and study hard. For no commonplace orator arises to succeed your generation, but one with keen intelligence, burning ambition, extraordinary training and a unique memory. Although I am a fan of his, I want him to become pre-eminent only within his own generation, for it is scarcely honourable for a man who is so much younger to surpass the two of you!

'But let us rise,' he said, 'and have some refreshment, and at least for a while relax our attention and concern from the stress of this discussion.'

THE LIFE OF THE
ORATOR

Rhetorical training and practice shaped the lives of free male citizens throughout the long history of Greek and Roman antiquity. Rhetoric became the focus of anxieties concerning status, gender and identity, even as it provided a means of upward mobility for ambitious youth. The famous, if tragic, careers of Demosthenes at Athens and Cicero at Rome provided inspiration for generations of everyday students and practitioners. In the present section, we consider three stages of the life of the orator.

First is education in grammar school, that is, training preparatory to immersion in the system of rhetoric. In offering advice on the proper conduct of such education, Quintilian gives us precious insight into the workings of such schools, their intended outcomes and the expectations placed on children whose talents were varied.

Second is Cicero's brief review of his own career as an advocate in the Roman courts, especially his rivalry with the slightly older (and recently deceased) orator Quintus Hortensius. Cicero's discussion in his dialogue called Brutus *comes near the end of a long review of the roster of Roman orators from early times to the end of the republic. It is both a eulogy and a call to action for the next generation to revive the Roman tradition of free, vigorous debate.*

The third selection consists of three brief biographies of imperial-era sophists and rhetoricians. Although rhetoric maintained its function in the courtroom and civic debate, it also became a means for the display of brilliance and wit, often in the context of entertainment. The three speakers and

intellectuals described here by the Greek biographer Philostra-
tus illustrate the range of activities in which successful students
of rhetoric might engage and the extraordinary financial,
social and political rewards they occasionally reaped.

Quintilian
Oratorical Instruction

2.1.1–2.12.12

In the Schools

The custom has taken hold, and indeed grows more common on a daily basis, whereby boys are sent to teachers of eloquence, Latin always, but even sometimes Greek, at a later age than is reasonable. There are two explanations for this development: first the teachers of rhetoric, especially on the Latin side, have abandoned their responsibilities; and second, the teachers of literature have occupied alien terrain.

For the rhetoric teachers consider it their sole responsibility to declaim and to transmit knowledge and skill at declamation, and even then treat only deliberative and judicial issues, despising the rest as unworthy of their profession. Meanwhile the teachers of literature consider it insufficient merely to take up what has been neglected (for which they really ought to be thanked), but push their way into declamations in character or on deliberative themes[1] – both of which require great expertise at speaking.

And so it happens that what used to be the first phase of rhetorical study becomes the last phase of literary study, and at the age when the student is ready for more serious subjects, he stays behind in lower school and practises rhetoric among grammarians. Most absurd of all, the boy isn't sent to the teacher of declamation until he knows how to declaim.

Let us hereby impose a limit on each profession. *Grammatice*, which in Latin is called study of letters or literature, needs to recognize its natural boundaries, for it has been carried far beyond what little is implied by its name, although its early practitioners stopped at that. Although it began as a narrow stream, it has become swollen in its expanse by assuming the powers of historians and critics. In addition to the study of correct speech, an abundant subject in itself, it has come to embrace knowledge of all the highest arts. Meanwhile rhetoric, which takes its name from public speaking, must not disparage its own obligations or rejoice that its work has been taken up by others. When it abandons its responsibility, it is all but driven from its birthright. I won't deny that at least some teachers of literature are capable of attaining sufficient knowledge to teach these other subjects as well. But when they do so, they fulfil the function of a rhetorician, not their own.

We would also like to know at what point a boy is likely to be ready for the instruction provided by a rhetorician. Here the deciding factor is not the boy's age but the extent of his achievements in his studies. And so as not to discourse at length on the appropriate time for assigning him to the rhetorician, I believe it is best specified as follows: when he is able.

But this question really depends on the preceding one. For if the task of the grammarian is in fact extended to include declamation on fictional themes, then the need for the rhetorician is postponed. If the rhetorician does not decline to teach the elementary stages of his subject, then it's desirable to have him involved in instruction as soon as the boy starts composing narratives and short exercises in praise and blame. It's well known that among our predecessors it was routine to develop eloquence through practice on general theses and familiar themes and other matters without specification of actions or persons – the kinds of issues that both real and imaginary disputes entail. Obviously, then, it's a disgrace for rhetoric today to have abandoned an area of study for which it once took primary, indeed for a long time, exclusive, responsibility.

For what aspect of the exercises I have just mentioned is not relevant to all the duties of a speaker, most especially in judicial cases? Is there no need for narration in a court of law? Indeed, it may be the most important part. Are not praise and invective frequently inserted into legal controversies? What of commonplaces, whether attacks on vice of the sort we read that Cicero composed, or treatments of general questions, of the sort published as well by Quintus Hortensius,[2] such as 'should minor points of argument carry a case' or 'for witnesses', 'against witnesses' – are they not to be found in the very heart of lawsuits?

Weapons of this sort are always kept in readiness, to be used when the case demands. Anyone who thinks they aren't relevant to oratory will believe that a statue hasn't been commenced even as its limbs are being cast. And please don't accuse me of rushing the pupil, as if I thought that a boy assigned to a rhetorician should necessarily be removed from the grammarians. Time will be allotted to them as well, nor need we fear that the boy will be overburdened by two instructors. Work that had been combined under one teacher will be separated under two, and each instructor will be better suited to his task. The Greeks still retain this practice, although it has been neglected by Latin teachers, and perhaps understandably, inasmuch as there are those who have been ready to take over the job of the rhetorician.

Therefore when the boy is sufficiently accomplished in his studies that he can undertake the first steps in rhetorical instruction, let us place him with a teacher of this art. The first point to consider is the moral character of the instructor. I address this matter at this point, not because I think it less demanding of attention where other teachers are concerned, as I have already discussed in Book 1. Rather, the age of the students makes it especially crucial to consider the matter here. For boys are undergoing puberty when transferred to these teachers, and remain with them even as young men. All the more reason to make certain that the integrity of the teacher will protect the younger ones from mistreatment and that his authority will deter the wilder sort from bad behaviour.

It isn't sufficient for the teacher to display the highest degree of self-control unless he is also able, through the strictness of his discipline, to regulate the conduct of those around him. Let him therefore adopt above all the attitude of a parent towards his students, and regard himself as assuming the role of those whose children are entrusted to him.

He must not have vices, or tolerate them. He should be

serious, but not cruel, friendly, but not easy-going, avoiding hatred in the one case, disrespect in the other. He should talk a great deal about what is good and honourable, for the more often he advises, the less often he will punish. He should avoid anger, yet not overlook mistakes that need correction, be straightfoward in his teaching, hard-working, rigorous rather than rigid.

He should respond readily to questions, and question those who offer none on their own. When praising the efforts of his students, he should be neither grudging nor effusive: the former generates distaste for labour, the latter leads to overconfidence. In revising what needs correction he will not be harsh or abusive, for many are driven from studies by teachers who correct pupils as if they hated them. He should declaim something, indeed a great deal, on a daily basis, giving his listeners something to take away with them. For although he will supply plenty of examples for imitation from readings, still the living voice, as it is called, provides greater nourishment, especially the voice of a teacher whom students, if only they have been rightly trained, come to love and revere. It's difficult to overestimate how much more freely we copy the people that we like.

By no means should boys be permitted, as they are in many schools, to jump up and dance about in support of a speaker. Audiences, even young men, must indicate their favour with restraint. That way the student will look to the judgement of the teacher, and upon receiving his approval will be confident in having spoken correctly.

The worst sort of 'positive reinforcement', as it is sometimes called, consists of reciprocal and indiscriminate applause. It is unbecoming, theatrical and foreign to the strict environment of the school. It's also a very dangerous enemy of real endeavour. For attention and labour seem superfluous when anything a boy spouts off is met with praise. The audience should pay attention to the teacher just as carefully as the speaker does. In that way they will come to recognize what is and isn't worthy of approval. Just as fluency comes about through writing, so critical judgement develops through listening.

Instead boys today are hunched forward, bracing themselves

to leap up at the end of a period, even to run about and shout with unseemly enthusiasm. And they expect the same as reward for their own declamations. They become so swollen in their sense of self-worth, so puffed up by the outcry of their peers that they hold it against a teacher who seems to praise them too little. Moreover, teachers themselves should want their speeches to be received thoughtfully and with restraint. The teacher must not speak for the judgement of students; rather, the student speaks for the judgement of the teacher. If possible, the teacher should even make note of what each student praises and how he does so, thereby deriving satisfaction from the fact that what he says well is pleasing not just to himself but also to the students who exercise good judgement.

I don't like boys to sit together with older youths. For even if the teacher in charge has the necessary learning and good character and can keep the older ones under control, still the weaker students should be kept separate from the stronger. We must be careful to avoid not just accusations of shameful conduct, but even suspicion thereof. I have thought it necessary to mention these points only briefly. I hardly consider it necessary to explain that both the teacher and his school must be free of the worst vices. And if any parent fails to steer clear of obvious misconduct when choosing a teacher for his son, he needs to understand that everything else I am saying with regard to the well-being of the young is superfluous if this responsibility is neglected.

I must not pass over in silence the opinion of those who think that boys, even when considered ready for a rhetorician, ought not to be placed under the most prominent teacher, but rather retained for a period among the lesser sort. It's as if they think that a mediocre teacher is a better teacher because easier to understand and imitate and less disdainful of the tedious aspects of elementary instruction.

I don't think it's necessary to spend much time in pointing out how much better it is to be imbued with the best instruction, or how much more difficult to be rid of faults once they have become ingrained. No need to impose a double burden on the next teacher, with the task of unteaching before teaching. This is why, as the story goes, the renowned musician Timotheus[3] demanded double fees for flute lessons from those who had prior instruction versus those who came to him untaught.

There are really two mistakes here: first, people think that inferior teachers suffice for the time being and are pleased with their willingness to put up with anything. Such lack of concern warrants correction, but could at least be tolerated if the teachers in question taught less, rather than worse. Second, and more commonly, they think that those who have reached a higher level of knowledge of the subject do not lower themselves to the lesser topics, either because they disdain to give attention to elementary matters or because they can't.

For my part, I refuse to consider anyone unwilling to do so as belonging to the ranks of teachers, and I insist that the best teacher is particularly capable of doing so, provided he is willing. First because it seems reasonable to believe that the man whose eloquence has raised him above the rest has paid closest attention to the means through which he became eloquent; second because the learned man is the one with the fullest grasp of the discipline as a whole, which makes him most effective as a teacher; finally, because no one excels in the most important aspects of an art if he lacks understanding of the basics – unless you think that Phidias[4] designed his statue of Jupiter beautifully, but others would have been better at executing the details, or that an orator is incapable of carrying on a conversation, or a famous doctor of curing a mild illness.

What, you ask? Is there not a kind of eloquence too demanding to be pursued by weak-minded boys? I imagine there is. But it will be necessary for our eloquent teacher to have good sense as well and to know something about teaching. He will submit to the pace of the learner, just as the fastest walker if he happens to be making a journey with a small child, gives him his hand, shortens his step and doesn't proceed beyond what his companion can keep up with.

And, generally speaking, matters explained by an expert are much clearer and easier to understand. For the first virtue of eloquence is perspicuity, and the lesser a person's talent, the more he tries to puff himself up, the way short men stand on tiptoe or weak men make a lot of threats. For those who are swollen and corrupt and raucous and show off in any other way I regard as suffering from an excess of weakness rather than strength. They are like bodies swollen from sickness rather than health, or like travellers who when worn out by a steady march keep turning off to the side. The weaker the speaker, the more obscure the speech.

I recognize that in the preceding book, when I was arguing in favour of education in school as opposed to home, I wrote that during the early stages pupils more readily imitate their peers, because it is easier. This may lead some to suppose that in the current discussion I am contradicting myself, which is far from being the case. A young boy's propensity to imitate his peers explains why he must be entrusted to the very best teacher, for such a man's pupils, having been better trained, will either say things not unworthy of imitation or, if they make a mistake, will be immediately corrected. The ignorant schoolmaster, on the other hand, may well approve something in error, and by his judgement lead the listeners to approve as well. Let the ideal instructor therefore be as remarkable for his knowledge of eloquence as for his moral rectitude, a person who will offer instruction in speech and action, as Phoenix[5] did, according to Homer.

Let me now turn to the preliminary pedagogical tasks of the rhetorician, postponing a little what is typically regarded as the art of rhetoric proper. To me the best way to start will be with lessons similar to what the boy has already learned in grammar school.

With respect to narration, there are three types (other than that used in actual trials): story, as found in tragedy and poems, which bears no relationship to reality; plot, which, although false, resembles reality; and history, which presents actual events. Poetic narration we have assigned to the grammarians; the teacher of rhetoric should begin with historical narration, which is more powerful because it is true.

I will explain what seems to me the best method of narration when I speak about its use in court. Here it is sufficient to note that narrative should not be dry and lifeless (for what's the point of expending so much effort on our studies if it is considered sufficient merely to point to bare and unadorned facts?), nor should it be convoluted, luxuriating in the sort of far-fetched descriptions many speakers are drawn to in imitation of the freedom of poetry. Both are serious faults, although lack of development is more harmful than excess.

For it's impossible to demand or expect perfect oratory from boys. Yet there is potential good in innate exuberance, expansive effort and a spirit that sometimes aims at more than is appropriate. In these early years, a student never offends through excess. I would prefer teachers to take care to nurse tender minds with more digestible food, and to let youngsters have their fill of more enjoyable instruction. Their plump bodies will slim down as they age, and give reason to expect strength. A child who is scrawny all over threatens to remain weak and underdeveloped.

Let the young child takes risks and exercise his imagination, and enjoy doing so, even if it what it produces isn't always deadly serious. It's easy to correct exuberance; barrenness can't be conquered, no matter how hard we try. I have least confidence in a boy whose talent is constrained by self-critique. I prefer raw material that is richer and more abundant than seems necessary. The years will melt it down, method will smooth what is rough, parts will be rubbed away by experience, provided there is something that can be chiselled and trimmed. And such metal will exist, provided we do not slice the sheet so thin that deep engraving breaks it. My view will seem less remarkable to anyone who has read the following in Cicero: 'I want creativity to express itself in the young.'[6]

Therefore one should above all else avoid a teacher who is dull and dry, especially for young boys, just as you would avoid dry soil when setting out young plants. They turn out humble and downcast, as it were, daring nothing beyond ordinary speech. They confuse skinniness with health, uncertainty with good judgement. As long as they think it sufficient to lack faults, they commit the fault of lacking virtues. Therefore, don't let their talents ripen too soon, or their juices dry up before their time; that way they will last for years and continue to improve with time.

It's also worth remembering that the innate ability of boys can actually diminish as a result of excessive criticism. They lose hope, suffer disappointment, grow to hate their studies and, worst of all, attempt nothing because they are fearful of everything. This is familiar to farmers who think that pruning should be withheld while a plant's leaves are still young, because they seem to 'shrink from the blade'[7] and are not yet able to endure scarring.

The teacher of young boys, then, should be an amicable sort, one whose corrections, which are naturally annoying, are expressed gently. He should by turns praise, tolerate and correct (always with an explanation), and even clarify the lesson by inserting something of his own. Sometimes it will be helpful for him to dictate entire themes for the boy to imitate and occasionally even love as his own. But if the composition is so deficient that it isn't worth correcting, I have found it useful to explain the theme again and have the boy write a fresh version, telling him he can do better. For nothing makes effort more enjoyable than hope. Criticism should be age-appropriate, and assignments must be set and corrected in accordance with the students' abilities. When my students would venture on something a little too free or daring, I used to say that I would praise them for the moment, but the time would come when I would not permit such writing. In that way, they could take pleasure in their talent without being misled in their assessment.

But let me return to the point from which I digressed: written narratives are to be composed with the greatest possible care. Just as at the beginning, when children are learning to speak, it is useful for them to repeat what they have heard for the sake of acquiring language, so too it is worthwhile to require them to repeat a story in reverse order from the end or to start in the middle and retell it in either direction. But this is only to be done while the child is still in the teacher's lap. It will strengthen his memory while he is capable of little more, and just beginning to associate words and things. Once students begin to recognize proper speech, spontaneous chatter, without a pause for thinking before commencing, can be left to the carnival barkers. Ignorant parents take pointless pleasure in such nonsense, and the boys themselves become contemptuous of real work and shameless in their self-presentation, making a habit of speaking badly and repeating their mistakes. Often the resulting excess of confidence has ruined even great promise. The time will come for acquiring ease in speaking, and I won't pass over the topic. Meanwhile, it is enough if the boy takes as much care and effort as his age allows to write something acceptable. Let him get used to this, making it second nature. The boy who will be able to achieve the end we have in mind, or at least come close to it, is the one who will learn to speak correctly before speaking quickly.

It's useful to join the study of narratives with the tasks of refuting or confirming them, called anaskeue and kataskeue respectively. This can be done not just with fables and stories told in poems, but even with historical accounts. For example, it might be asked 'whether it's believable that a raven landed on the head of Valerius during battle, and beat the face and eyes of the Gallic enemy with its beak and wings' – and a great deal can be said for and against. The same goes for the legend of the serpent that fathered Scipio, or the she-wolf who nursed Romulus, or Numa's Egeria.[8] For Greek history often allows a licence similar to that of poetry. One can discuss the time and place in which an event is said to have occurred, sometimes even the actors involved; even Livy[9] frequently expressed uncertainty, and historians differ among themselves.

From here little by the little the student will begin to attempt a greater challenge, namely to praise distinguished men and denounce the wicked. This assignment is useful in more than one respect. The mind is exercised due to the abundant and varied material, an ethical disposition is formed through contemplation of right and wrong, and much knowledge of affairs is acquired. When the need arises, the student will already be well prepared with examples, which are highly effective in every type of case.

Comparison is the next exercise, that is deciding which of two is better or worse. It's similar to the preceding, but requires twice as much material, and treats not just the nature of virtues and vices, but degrees as well. Still, the proper treatment of praise and blame, which is the third section of rhetoric, will be presented in its own place.[10]

Commonplaces (I mean those through which we attack bad behaviour in general rather than specific individuals, for example the adulterer, the gambler, the bully) come right out of the courtroom, and if you name a defendant, turn into accusations. Although even as general treatments, they are often given some degree of specificity, for example a blind adulterer, impoverished gambler, elderly bully. Sometimes they can be argued from the standpoint of the defence, as we might speak in favour of luxury or love, or defend a pimp or parasite not as such, but against a specific charge.

Theses derived from comparison ('which is preferable: country life or city life?' 'who deserves greater respect: a lawyer or a soldier?') are wonderfully appealing and productive as exercises in speaking, being helpful for both deliberative oratory and courtroom disputes. Cicero provides a very rich treatment of the second thesis cited above in his *Speech in Defence of Murena*.[11] Some such theses are almost exclusively deliberative in nature, for example, 'should one marry?', 'should one run for office?' These become in effect suasoriae when they involve specific individuals.

My own teachers used to prepare us for conjectural cases with a type of exercise that was both useful and enjoyable. They had us discuss and develop questions such as 'why do the Spartans depict Venus in armour?' and 'why is Cupid believed to be a boy, to have wings, and to be armed with arrows and a torch?'[12] In these exercises we would try to discover intention, which is often an issue in controversiae.[13] They can be regarded as a type of chreia, or anecdote about a character.

For certain topics, for example 'are witnesses always believable?' or 'should we trust minor arguments?', are so obviously relevant to forensic speaking that certain men well known for their civic achievements have written them down and carefully committed them to memory so that, whenever the occasion arises, they can enrich their 'extemporaneous' remarks with them, as if decorating their houses with bas-reliefs. Such a practice (for I have no intention of withholding judgement) seems an admission of great weakness on their part. For what can they find appropriate for use in cases which are always new and varied, how respond to the claims of the opposition, swiftly meet the challenges posed in debate, interrogate a witness, if they are unable to express the most commonplace sentiments relevant to almost every case without using language prepared well in advance?

Surely when they are repeating the same things in so many cases they become disgusted, as if serving cold leftovers, or ashamed that their audience has so often seen their shabby furniture, which like that of pretentious paupers is worn down from being put to so many different uses. An additional consideration: there's hardly a commonplace so common that it can be made to fit a specific context unless somehow linked to it. It must appear interwoven, not stitched on – as will happen if it is too different from the rest of the speech or if, as is often the case, it was put to use because it was available rather than needed. Some speakers extend these commonplaces at great length for the sake of the ideas they contain when in fact the ideas should arise from the context. These utterances can be impressive and useful if they arise naturally from the case, otherwise no matter how attractive, expressions of this sort, unless they lead to victory, are superfluous, even counterproductive. But I have digressed enough.

Praise or blame of laws requires more developed powers, the sort suited to virtually the most demanding tasks. Whether this exercise is more closely related to suasoriae[14] or controversiae depends on the custom and law of the individual state. Among the Greeks, a proponent of a law was called before a court, among the Romans it has been customary to speak pro and con at an assembly. Either way, the arguments are few in number and of a fairly specific type. For there are three kinds of law, sacred, public and private, a division that lends itself to use in praise, for example if an orator glorifies a decree step by step, first as a law, then as public, then as composed for the worship of deities.

Some common topics are common to every kind of law. For there can be dispute concerning the proponent of the law, as when it was argued that Publius Clodius[15] had been named tribune irregularly, or concerning the proposed law itself, taking various forms – was it promulgated within the requisite time frame? Was it proposed, or is it being proposed, on an improper day, in defiance of a veto or the auspices or anything else that might constitute a legitimate obstacle? Does it contradict any existing law?

But such considerations aren't really suitable for elementary exercises, which don't involve specified persons, occasions or cases. The rest can generally be treated as follows, whether the case is real or fictional: for the error is either in the words or in the facts. If in words, it's a question whether they are sufficiently clear or contain some ambiguity; in the facts, whether the law is internally consistent, whether it should be applied retroactively or against particular individuals. It's especially common to ask whether the law is just and whether it is useful or expedient. I am well aware that many instructors introduce subdivisions of the first category, but in my view 'justice' encompasses piety, religious scruples and all the rest.

Still, the justice of a law is not usually considered in only one respect. We might discuss the act covered by the law, asking whether it merits punishment or reward; or argue about the type of reward or punishment, objecting to one or the other as too great or too small. Expediency is sometimes intrinsic to an act, at other times specific to the context. We also often ask whether a law can be enforced. Keep in mind that laws can be criticized in their totality or in part, with examples of both to be found in well-known speeches. Nor does it escape me that some laws are not intended to apply in perpetuity, but concern particular offices or commands, such as the Manilian law, on which we have Cicero's speech.[16] But nothing can be said about such matters here, since they depend on the specifics of each case, not on any general issue.

Such were the exercises in eloquence employed by the ancients, who also adopted techniques of argumentation from the dialecticians. It is generally accepted that the Greeks initiated the practice of declaiming on fictional legal and deliberative topics around the time of Demeterius of Phalerum.[17] Whether he invented this type of exercise I have not been able to ascertain, as I acknowledged in another book of mine. Even those who insist on the point cite no satisfactory authority. Cicero is the one who tells us that Latin rhetors got their start late in the lifetime of Lucius Crassus, with Plotius being the most famous.[18]

A little later I will consider the proper use of declamation. Meanwhile, because we are discussing the rudiments of rhetorical education, I must not refrain from reminding the teacher of rhetoric how much he will assist his students' progress if he guides them in the reading of histories and speeches, following the same techniques used by the grammarians in the exposition of poetry. I have employed this practice with a few pupils who were suitable in age and whose parents believed it would be useful. Still, although at the time I thought it an ideal practice, there were two obstacles, first that tradition had established a different expectation for teaching, and second, that the students, being energetic young men, didn't need this kind of exercise, and instead just treated me as their exemplar. Still, although my discovery came somewhat late, I'm not embarrassed to recommend it to my successors. For I am now aware that this technique is used by Greek teachers, or rather their assistants, since the former are seen as having too little time to be constantly supervising individual readers.

To be sure, the preliminary reading used in this practice, which is intended to make it easier for the boys to follow the text chunk by chunk,[19] and includes the definition of uncommon words, is thought to be beneath the rhetorician. But to point out the virtues of what is being read, and if they occur, the mistakes, most definitely is part of his profession and responsibility, insofar as he promises to be a teacher of eloquence. All the more so because I am hardly asking the teacher to summon the boy to his lap and assist him in reading any book he chooses!

To me it seems easier and more productive to call for silence, then appoint one student at a time as reader, allowing them to get used to public delivery. The case for which the oration was composed should be explained (which makes it easier to understand what's being said) and everything worth noting about invention and style should be discussed, for example the means of winning the favour of the judges in the proem; the clarity, conciseness and plausibility of the narrative – and sometimes too the hidden strategy and cunning (for here the only real art is one that is apparent to no one but the artist); the foresight evident in the division of the issues; how subtle and numerous the arguments; how energetically the speaker rouses the audience, how charmingly he soothes them, the ferocity of his invective, the urbanity of his wit, how he lords it over their emotions, forces his way into their hearts, aligns their judgement with his words. As for style, point out each appropriate, choice and elevated word, the admirable use of amplification and diminution, each striking metaphor and figure of language, the smooth, polished, yet virile composition.

It can even be beneficial to consider on occasion speeches that are corrupt and faulty, yet admired due to the depravity of the critics. Have them read out loud, let the students be shown how much in them is inappropriate, obscure, bombastic, fawning, ugly, salacious or effeminate. Such speeches are praised by many, which is bad enough, but even worse, they are praised for the very features that make them depraved. For language that is direct and natural in expression is thought to contain nothing of genius, while the more distorted an expression the more we admire it as exquisite, much as some people prefer bodies that are deformed and even monstrous to those that have lost none of the advantages of normalcy. Being captivated by appearances, they think there's greater beauty in those whose hair has been plucked or depilated or curled with a curling-iron or dyed a bizarre colour than there could possibly be in uncorrupted nature. They seem to imagine that a beautiful body requires an ugly character.

The instructor must explain these things, but also ask frequent questions and test the good judgement of his students. This will keep the listeners from feeling too comfortable or letting their lessons go in one ear and out the other. At the same time they will be led to the goal of this instruction, namely to figure things out for themselves and understand on their own. For what's the point of teaching except to keep students from always needing to be taught? I dare say that this kind of exercise brings greater advantage to the learner than all the textbooks of all the specialists, which without doubt are quite helpful: but which among them can possibly cover the whole range of cases that arise on an almost daily basis?

Consider as a parallel the art of war. Although many general precepts have been passed along, still it will be more useful to know how any given general acted, whether wisely or not, in a particular action, time or place. For in just about every subject precepts are less valuable than experience. Yes, a teacher will declaim as a model for his audience. But wouldn't there be more benefit in reading Cicero or Demosthenes? If a student makes a mistake in declaiming he will be corrected openly: will it not be more effective to correct some oration, not to say more enjoyable? We would all prefer to have someone else's mistakes corrected instead of our own. I have much more that I could say on the subject, but I think everyone recognizes the usefulness of this type of exercise. I only wish the reluctance to do this were not so great as the advantage to be gained therefrom.

Once we do adopt this method, it's easy to determine which authors are to be read by beginners. For some have recommended writers of lower quality as seeming easier to understand, others choose those of a more flowery sort, as if better suited to the inclinations of the young. But I say that students should be exposed at once and always to the best writers, albeit those who are most approachable. Thus for boys Livy rather than Sallust,[20] for although the latter is the greater historian, it takes greater proficiency to understand him. Cicero, as it seems to me, is enjoyable for beginners and simple enough; he can be learned from, even loved. After Cicero, just as Livy recommends, authors who most closely resemble him.

Two sorts of writers are to be avoided where boys are concerned. First, whatever your admiration for antiquity, don't let it harden your students through a reading of the Gracchi and Cato[21] and the like. They will be become rough and uninteresting. Not yet understanding the force of such authors, they will grow satisfied with a style that although no doubt excellent for its time is foreign to our own, and, what is worst of all, will imagine that they are somehow similar to these great men.

Second, which is the opposite to this, don't let them become enchanted by the allurements of the modern lascivious style or be taken in by a depraved type of pleasure, falling in love with a sensuality that is more appealing than suitable for boyish natures. Once their judgement has been strengthened and they are well out of danger, I would advise them to read ancient authors (once the squalor of age is cleared away, our present-day cultivation will shine more brightly, especially if the ancients' solid manliness is retained); and also recent authors, in whom there is a great deal of value. It's not that nature has doomed us to be dimwitted; rather, we have changed our style of speaking and indulged ourselves more than we should. Earlier writers surpassed us not in talent but in what they aimed to accomplish.

There will be much of value to select, but we must be careful not to let it be polluted by what it is mixed with. I freely admit, indeed insist, that there are recent and current writers fully deserving of imitation. But it's not up to just anyone to say who they are. It's safer to be mistaken about earlier authors, which is why I postpone the reading of modern writers. Imitation must not outpace judgement.

There's another matter on which the practice of teachers differs. Some, not content just to structure the themes given to the student by setting up the division, press on to supply types of proof and emotional appeals. Others provide just an outline, then after the declamations discuss what each student omitted, developing certain passages as carefully as if they themselves were getting ready to make a speech. Both approaches are useful, and so I won't give preference to either one. Still, if it is necessary to employ only one, it will be more profitable to have demonstrated the correct procedure from the outset than to correct those who have fallen into error. For students only receive correction passively, whereas they must put the division to use in thinking and writing; and they listen more willingly to instruction than correction.

If there are some who are a little feistier, the way things are nowadays they'll become angry with correction and sullenly resist. Of course that's no argument against openly correcting mistakes: the teacher needs to keep in mind the rest of the students who will think that anything not corrected by the teacher is indeed correct. The two approaches should be combined and put to use as the situation demands. Beginners will be given the theme in a form matched to their abilities. Once it's clear that they are sufficiently prepared, we can provide them with prompts that will allow them to proceed on their own without assistance.

Students need to start to trust themselves. We mustn't let the bad habit of following in another's footsteps keep them from knowing how to set out on their own. But once they have a clear sense of what needs to be said, the task of the teacher is all but complete. If they still go astray, then they will have to be led back by their leader. We see birds behaving in a similar manner. They feed weak and vulnerable chicks with food they carry in their own mouths, but when the chicks seem grown, little by little they teach them to emerge from the nest and guide them as they fly about close to home. Only when the chicks' abilities have been tested do they let them take to the open sky, relying on themselves.

There is one practice employed with boys of the age we are now discussing that I think needs to be changed entirely. They should not be learning by heart everything they have written in order to give a recitation on a specified day. Fathers in particular demand this practice, believing that their children are only making progress if they declaim as often as possible, when in fact progress depends chiefly on thoughtful attention. For although I want boys to write and to exert a great deal of effort, I would much rather that they memorize passages selected from orations or histories or another worthwhile genre.

Memory is given a more intense workout learning the words of another rather than our own. Students who master this more difficult task will have no difficulty remembering their own familiar words. Besides, they will grow accustomed to the best writings, and always carry within themselves examples worthy of imitation, and without even realizing it they will speak in the style that has been impressed upon their mind. They will have an abundant supply of excellent vocabulary, arrangement and figurative expressions that will make themselves freely available as if from a treasure house, rather than needing to be tracked down. They will also be able to quote fine sayings, which brings both pleasure and advantage in court. For remarks that have been composed outside the context of the case at hand have greater authority and earn greater respect than they would if we had written them.

Nevertheless, on occasion students should be permitted to recite their own compositions, so that they can enjoy as reward for their labour that most sought-after prize – the praise of the multitude. But this should only take place when they have produced something more polished than usual. That way they will be happy to have received a special reward for their effort and to have earned the opportunity to recite.

It's rightly considered a virtue for a teacher to recognize the different talents of those he has undertaken to educate and to know their natural inclinations. For there is incredible variety in this respect, and as many forms of mind as of body. This can be seen even with orators, who so differ in their styles of speaking that no one quite resembles another, although many have composed their speeches in imitation of their favourite authors. Many also consider it useful to instruct each student in such a way that learning enhances his natural abilities, and in particular to assist talents to develop as they are inclined to do so anyway. Just as a wrestling coach, when he enters a gymnasium full of boys tests the body and mind of them in every way and determines what event each should prepare for, so too the teacher of eloquence, once he has carefully observed whose talent is suited to terse and polished speech, who especially enjoys an aggressive, serious, gentle, rough or urbane style, adapts his instruction so that each can progress in the direction in which he is naturally inclined. Natural ability, on this view, becomes even stronger when supplemented with attention; conversely, the student who is directed away from his inclinations never achieves real competency, and even grows weaker in the areas of his inborn talent, due to neglect.

Such a perspective seems to me only partly true (for it is permissible in pursuit of reason to dissent even from received opinion). To be sure, it is essential to observe the particular nature of each boy's talent, and no one will convince me not to make a corresponding selection of pursuits. One will be more suited to history, another to poetry, another to study of law, with some perhaps to be sent back to the farm. The teacher of rhetoric will discern these things just as an athletics instructor will make one boy a runner, one a boxer, one a wrestler, or whatever else of the events held at the sacred games. Yet, the student who is headed for the forum must prepare not just for one aspect of the profession, but for everything relevant, even if it seems difficult. Education would be completely superfluous if nature alone were sufficient. After all, would we allow someone who had become indulgent and overly confident in his natural talent, as many are, to continue in that direction? Will we not fatten up, or at least disguise with better clothing, the weak and frail speaker? And if some habits must be eliminated, why not acknowledge that others must be introduced? I don't mean to fight against nature. Innate quality should never be abandoned, but it should be improved upon, and what is naturally lacking must be supplied.

The famous teacher Isocrates, whose books attest to his excellence as a speaker, just as his students attest to his excellence as an instructor, assessed Ephorus and Theopompus[22] by saying that one needed reins, the other spurs. Did he mean that the slowness of the one, the precipitous haste of the other required augmentation through instruction, or rather that the natural inclination of each needed to be combined with that of the other?

Still, it's probably best to acknowledge the limits of lesser talents and lead them only where nature beckons anyway. At least they will improve at the only thing they can do. But if we have richer material to work with, such that we might hope to develop a true orator, then no virtue of speaking is to be omitted. For even if such a student is inclined in one direction, as of course he will be, still he will not resist the rest, and with effort will achieve the same level as in the area in which he naturally excels. To return to the example of the athletics trainer: if he plans to train a pancratiast, he won't give instruction merely in punching or kicking or in particular wrestling holds, but will train him in every aspect of the event.

Some will simply be incapable in a given area. Let them

focus on their greatest strength. Two mistakes are to be avoided: first don't make him try what he cannot accomplish; second, don't transfer him from a task at which he excels to one for which he is less well suited. But if the student is like Nicostratus, whom we saw in his old age when we were young, he will likewise benefit from all aspects of instruction, and make himself indomitable, just as Nicostratus[23] was in wrestling and in boxing, for each of which he won the crown at the same competition.

And how much more foresight is required of the one who would teach a future orator. It isn't sufficient to speak only tersely or subtly or roughly, any more than it's sufficient for a singing master to excel only in high or middle or low register, or in particular sections thereof. For, like a harp, eloquence is not perfect unless from lowest to highest all its strings are taut and in tune.

Having said a great deal about the obligations of teachers, I give just one piece of advice to students: love your teachers no less than your studies and consider them parents not, to be sure, of your bodies, but of your minds. This sense of respect will be of great advantage in your studies, for you will listen to them willingly and trust what they are telling you and become eager to be like them, gladly assembling in school, not growing angry when corrected, but rejoicing when praised, earning the teacher's great affection through your enthusiasm.

For just as the duty of teacher is to teach, the duty of students is to present themselves ready to be taught. Otherwise neither is sufficient without the other. Just as a human child is born from two parents, and in vain you would scatter seed unless a previously softened furrow is ready to receive it, just so eloquence cannot come into being unless the giver and receiver are united in common purpose.

During these elementary stages, which, far from being insignificant, are the bases for more advanced studies, when the students have had good instruction and plenty of practice, the time will come for attempting suasoriae and controversiae. Before I explain the method, I need to say a few words about declamation in general, a practice of recent origin yet of the greatest usefulness. It contains pretty much everything we have been discussing so far and comes close to real-life speech-making. As a result, it is so widely practised that many regard it as the only thing necessary for producing eloquence.

Now it is true that there is no virtue in continuous oratory that cannot also be found in this type of speaking. And yet through the fault of instructors the practice has so declined that the wantonness and unsophistication of declaimers are among the primary reasons for the corruption of eloquence. But it is possible to make good use of anything that is in itself beneficial. Therefore, let topics be fashioned which are as close as possible to reality and let declamation, as far as possible, resemble the speeches for which it was invented as preparation.

For we will seek in vain among sponsions and interdicts[24] for magicians and pestilence and oracular utterances and stepmothers even crueller than in tragedy and other more fantastic inventions. What?! you ask. Are we never to allow young declaimers to treat implausible or poetic, as I would call them, themes? Never permit them to revel in the material and throw themselves into their performance? Yes, that would be best, but at least if the themes are grandiose, don't let them be stupid and laughable to those who examine them at all closely, and if some concession is necessary let the declaimer have his fill of them on occasion. But make sure he understands that like cattle bloated with too much green pasture who must be bled before returning to healthful food, he will have to slim down and be purged of the corrosive stuff he has imbibed if he intends to be healthy and strong. Otherwise his empty bluster will be exposed on his first attempt at a real case. But those who regard the whole project of declamation as in every respect different from courtroom cases evidently do not recognize the very reasons for which this exercise was devised. For if it does not prepare the student for the forum, then it is nothing but theatrical display or wild raving.

What is the point of addressing a non-existent judge, of narrating what everybody knows to be false, of providing arguments in a case no one will ever argue? Well these at least are only wastes of effort. But to feel emotion and be driven to anger or grief, what kind of joke is this, unless through mock battles we prepare ourselves for genuine strife and danger? Is there then to be no difference between declamatory practice and courtroom eloquence? None, at least if we practise for the sake of improvement. If only it were possible to add to the current practice the use of real names, for controversiae to be fashioned that are more complex and require longer treatment, if only we could be less fearful of everyday language and more accustomed to adding witticisms. However much we have practised other skills in schools, these things find us novices in the forum.

And even if a declamation is prepared for show, surely we should strive to give at least a little pleasure to our audience. For there are types of speeches that undoubtedly deal with reality, but are also adapted to popular entertainment, for example panegyrics and the whole demonstrative genre. In these it is permitted to speak more elaborately, and before an audience gathered for this express purpose, not just to use but even to flaunt all the artistry that must stay hidden in trials. And so declamation, because it is the image of trials and public deliberations, has to resemble reality, but because it has something of the epideictic about it, must take on a certain polish.

Think of comic actors. They speak not exactly in an everyday manner, for there would be no art in that, yet do not stray far from nature, which would hurt their performance. Instead, they give everyday speech a certain flair.

So too various challenges arise from the fictional nature of themes, especially the fact that many points are left uncertain which we assume as seems best: ages, abilities, children, parents, the resources, laws, customs and other such like of the city in question. Sometimes we even derive arguments from the flaws in the posited themes. But these things will be discussed in the relevant place. Although this work is aimed exclusively at the formation of the orator, I will not ignore issues relevant only to the schools, in case students ask about them.

Now it's necessary to commence the part of the treatise that usually serves as the beginning for those who omit all the prior material. Already there are some ready to block me at the

threshold and mock my efforts. Thinking, as they do, that eloquence does not require instruction of this sort, they are satisfied
with their own natural ability and some mundane school exercises. They follow the example of certain prominent professors,
one of whom, I believe, when asked to define a figure and a
thought, responded that he had no idea, but if they were at all
relevant they were present in his declamation. Another, being
asked whether he followed Theodorus or Apollodorus, said, 'I
follow the Thracians.'[25] He could hardly have been wittier in
avoiding a confession of his own ignorance. These men, considered brilliant due to their inborn ability and frequent memorable
sayings, have many equals in recklessness, few in talent.

And so they boast that they speak on impulse and rely on
their innate strengths. They say that there's no need for proof
or organization where fictional themes are concerned, only for
those remarkable epigrams that fill the auditorium – and are
best sought out in the heat of the moment. And if they do
consider them in advance, they apply no rational method, but
instead stare at the ceiling, spurred on by some vague rum-
bling, like a call to arms, adapting their agitated gestures not
to the delivery of words but to their pursuit.

Some prepare introductions before they have anything to
say, intending to attach something clever to them. Having practised them for a long time both in silence and out loud, they
give up hope of forming a connected whole and abandon what
they have prepared, turning instead to one cliché after another.
The most sensible among them work up not actual cases, but
purple passages, tossing together bits and pieces as they come
to hand, rather than considering the whole body of the speech.
As a result their speeches, fragmented and assembled from mis-
matched parts, cannot possibly cohere, and end up resembling
the notebooks in which schoolboys copy memorable expressions from the declamations of others. True, they sometimes
knock out powerful turns of phrase and other good things, as
they are constantly boasting, but barbarians and slaves can
do the same, and if this is all that's necessary, then the art of
rhetoric counts for nothing.

Now I cannot deny that it's commonly held that untrained

speakers are more forceful, but this is a mistake on the part of those whose poor judgement leads them to believe that what lacks artistry has greater force. They consider it a sign of vigour to smash rather than open, break rather than loosen, drag rather than lead. The same people would praise an untrained gladiator who rushes into combat or a wrestler who applies his whole body against his opponent as 'more courageous', even though the latter is often overthrown by his own strength, while the vehement onslaught of the former is gently turned aside by a flick of his opponent's wrist. There are aspects of this topic that will naturally escape the attention of the inexperienced. For example division, although effective in trials, reduces the appearance of strength; rough stones are bigger than those that have been worked, and scattered items seem more numerous than those that have been organized.

In addition, there are certain resemblances between virtues and vices that allow the abusive speaker to be considered outspoken, the brusque as brave, the long-winded as expressive. The uneducated speaker is more openly and more frequently offensive, although he puts his client, and often even himself, in danger. (Yet even this earns approval, because people gladly hear what they themselves are unwilling to say.) He also takes risks with style, striving so recklessly that in always seeking what is excessive he sometimes hits upon something truly grand. But this is a rare occurrence, and does not outweigh the rest of his vices.

This is why untrained speakers sometimes seem to have a greater fluency. They say anything at all, whereas the learned exercise choice and restraint. The untrained back off from any concern with proving their case, and so they evade the chilly reception given by our corrupted courts to actual investigation and argumentation. They aim only at thrilling the ears of the audience with depraved delights. Epigrammatic expressions, which are all they seek, appear more prominent when everything surrounding them is ugly and abject, as light shines more brilliantly, not in the shade, as Cicero has it,[26] but in the depths of night! So let them be acclaimed as geniuses, as you will, just as long as it is understood that such praise is an insult to a man of real eloquence.

Nonetheless it must be admitted that learning does remove something – the way a file removes rough spots, a whetstone grinds away blunt edges or age takes away something from wine. What it removes is deficiency – and the less of this in polished speech, the better.

These bolder speakers also seek renown for their delivery. They are constantly shouting; they bellow everything, 'with up-lifted hand', as they themselves put it; they run back and forth, huff and puff, throw their arms about and furiously shake their heads. Well, it makes a big impression on the ragged crowd to clap the hands, stamp the feet, strike the thigh, chest, forehead. But the trained speaker, just as he knows how to lower his tone, vary his style and organize his material, also accommodates his delivery to the register of his material. His one goal, constantly in mind, is to be and be seen as a man of restraint.

What the uneducated call force is really violence. Believe it or not, there are not only speakers, but even worse, teachers, who after a short course in rhetoric abandon any method and instead storm about impulsively, calling those with more respect for learning foolish, dry, lukewarm, weak or any other term of abuse that occurs to them.

So allow me to congratulate those who manage to become 'eloquent' without effort, reason or training. I long ago begged off giving instruction and speaking in the forum, because I thought it best to stop while I was still being sought after. Now, in my retirement, I take comfort in my studies and in writing what I consider useful for young men of good sense – and with-out doubt, pleasurable for me.

Cicero
Brutus
305–30

In the Forum

The speaker is Cicero himself.

'The rest of those who were considered leading speakers of the
time held magistracies, and I listened to them on a daily basis
at the meetings of the assemblies. Among them was Gaius
Curio,[27] tribune of the plebs, who in fact was no longer giving
speeches, as he had once been abandoned by the entire assembly; Quintus Metellus Celer, not exactly an orator, but not
inarticulate either; Quintus Varius, Gaius Carbo and Gnaeus
Pomponius[28] were genuinely well spoken and quite at home
on the speakers' platform. Gaius Julius,[29] curule aedile, gave
careful speeches almost every day. I suffered my first blow
of disappointment as an eager auditor when Cotta[30] was banished. I listened to the rest repeatedly and with keen attention,
and although I was writing and reading and taking notes every
day, was not content with mere exercises alone. The following
year Quintus Varius[31] departed for exile, having been condemned by his own law.

'For my part, I turned to the study of civil law with Quintus
Scaevola,[32] son of Publius, who, although he gave formal
instruction to no one, managed to teach eager listeners through
his responses to those who came to consult him. The following
year, during the consulship of Sulla and Pompey,[33] I became
quite familiar with the oratory of Publius Sulpicius,[34] who, as
tribune, spoke in the assembly every day. At the same time,
when Philo,[35] leader of the Academy, together with the leading
Athenians, had fled from the Mithradatic war and come to Rome,

I devoted myself to him, spurred by a real zeal for philosophy. Although the variety and grandness of his subject matter thrilled me, I gave him special attention because it seemed at the time that the entire judicial system had been ruined for good.

'Sulpicius died that year, and in the following year three orators from three different generations were all cruelly put to death, namely Quintus Catulus, Marcus Antonius and Gaius Julius.[36] In the same year I studied at Rome with Molo the Rhodian,[37] who excelled as pleader of cases and as an instructor. Although these matters might seem irrelevant to our proposed line of inquiry, I discuss them so that you, Brutus[38] (for Atticus[39] is familiar with them), can, as you wished, understand my development and see how closely I followed in the footsteps of Quintus Hortensius.[40] For almost three years then the city was free of armed conflict. As a result of the death or retirement or exile of orators (for even the young Marcus Crassus and the two Lentuli[41] were gone), Hortensius conducted the most important cases, and more and more each day Antistius showed his mettle, Piso made frequent speeches, less often Pomponius, rarely Carbo, once or twice Philippus.[42]

'Throughout the same period I devoted myself to studies of every kind. I spent time with Diodotus the Stoic,[43] who died recently at my house, having shared my residence while he lived. He trained me in a number of topics, most especially in dialectic, which can be regarded as a kind of constrained or constricted eloquence. Even you, Brutus, have said that without it, it's impossible to attain genuine eloquence, which the Stoics call expanded dialectic.[44] Although I was devoted to this teacher and his expertise, still I also engaged in oratorical exercise every day. I would often practise declamation – as it's now called – with Marcus Piso or Quintus Pompeius,[45] daily with someone. I would practise a great deal in Latin, more so in Greek, both because the Greek language with its greater supply of adornments prompts a similar tendency when speaking Latin and because I couldn't be corrected or instructed by the best Greek teachers if I didn't declaim in Greek.

'Meanwhile there was a violent struggle to restore the republic, including the cruel deaths of three orators, Scaevola,

Carbo and Antistius;[46] the return of Cotta, Curio, Crassus, the Lentuli and Pompey;[47] laws and courts placed on a firm footing, the republic recovered; but Pomponius, Censorinus and Murena[48] carried off from the roll of orators. That was when I began to take on both public and private cases, not in order to learn in the forum, as many have done, but to enter the forum already having learned as much as I could.

'At the same time, I turned my attention to Molo, who, while Sulla was dictator, had been deputized to approach the senate about the payment due the Rhodians. My first public action, on behalf of Sextus Roscius,[49] received so much praise that no case seemed too great for me to handle. Many cases followed, which I handled with the utmost diligence, burning the midnight oil, so to speak.

'Because you seem to want to know me in my entirety, and not just on the basis of a birthmark or other tokens, I must address some topics that might otherwise seem unnecessary. At that time I was very thin and physically weak, my neck long and slender, my overall condition not far from endangering my life if I strained my lungs through overexertion. My habit of speaking without remission or variation, greatly straining both voice and body, caused a great deal of worry to those to whom I was dear.

'And so with my friends and doctors urging me to give up pleading cases, I decided that I would rather take any risk than abandon my hopes for glory through eloquence. But when I considered that with some relaxation and moderation of my voice and a different manner of speaking I could both avoid danger and speak in a tempered style, I travelled to Asia with just this goal in mind. Having spent two years as an active orator and already achieved some renown in the forum, I set out from Rome.

'Once I arrived at Athens I spent six months with Antiochus,[50] the distinguished and wise leader of the old Academy, and I renewed my study of philosophy, which I had cultivated and improved upon steadily from early adolescence, once again with an outstanding thinker and teacher. Also at Athens I continued my rhetorical exercises with Demetrius the Syrian,[51] an experienced and well-known instructor.

'Afterwards I travelled throughout Asia in the company of leading orators who willingly practised with me. Chief among these was Menippus of Stratonice,[52] in my opinion the most eloquent man in all of Asia at that time; and if being "Attic" means never being boring or inept, then he rightly counts as Attic. Dionysius of Magnesia was regularly in my company, as were Aeschylus of Cnido and Xenocles of Adramyttium,[53] who were considered the chief teachers of rhetoric in Asia at that time.

'Not content with these, I went to Rhodes and attached myself to that same Molo I had studied with at Rome. He was an excellent speaker in real cases, an outstanding writer and very shrewd in noting and correcting vices and in offering guidance and instruction. He set out – if he could only correct one thing – to repress my tendency to gush and swell and, with a certain youthful licence and wilfulness, to overflow, as it were, the banks of speech. And so after two years I found myself not just improved but virtually transformed. My strained voice had relaxed, my language had cooled down, my lungs regained their strength, and my body took on a normal build.

'At that time there were two outstanding orators who inspired me with a desire to imitate them, Cotta and Hortensius. The one was relaxed and mild and easily expressed his ideas in appropriate language. The other was more elaborate, keen and not as you knew him, when his powers were declining, Brutus, but more vigorous in language and delivery. And so I decided my rivalry would be with Hortensius, because I resembled him in the energy of my style and was closer to him in age. And I had noticed that when he and Cotta argued the same cases, for example in defence of Canuleius, and in defence of Dolabella, although Cotta was treated as lead counsel, Hortensius argued the more important sections of the case. For the crush of listeners and noise of the forum required an orator who was bold, impassioned, lively and resonant.

'For one year, then, after I had returned from Asia, I argued prominent cases, while I sought the quaestorship, Cotta the consulate and Hortensius the aedileship. At which point my quaestorship took me to Sicily for a year, Cotta after the consulate proceeded to Gaul and Hortensius was recognized as the top orator. But when in the following year I had returned from Sicily, it was evident that my powers had been perfected, having attained a certain ripeness. I can see that I'm talking about myself too much. My point isn't to get you to recognize my talent and eloquence (far from it!), but to make clear how hard I worked.

'And so after about five years of participating in numerous cases alongside the leading orators, as aedile elect I took the side of the Sicilians[54] in a major contest against Hortensius, who was consul designate. But since this discussion isn't just a list of orators, but an attempt to offer some guidance as well, let me briefly explain what was noteworthy about Hortensius.

'Now after his consulate he eased up on the ambition that had driven him since he was a child – presumably because, seeing no one comparable to himself among the ex-consuls, he failed to consider those who had not been consuls. He decided to enjoy his prosperity, to be happier, as he saw it, and certainly to live in a more relaxed manner. The first, second and third years detracted from him, as if from the colour of an antique painting, not so much that just anyone from among the people could tell, but such that a learned and thoughtful critic could recognize. But as more time passed, every aspect of his eloquence was affected and he especially lost the swiftness and fluency of his language, seeming each day less and less like himself.

'For my part, I did not cease from every type of exercise and to augment whatever capability I had especially through writing. And so as to omit much in this period and from the years following my aedileship, I came in first in the election for praetor with an incredible show of popular support. For thanks to my energy and attentiveness in legal cases as well as my careful and elevated style of oratory I won men over with my new type of eloquence.

'I won't speak about myself. As for the rest, I will say that none of them seemed to have studied literature, which is the font of perfect eloquence, more carefully than the average person; none had embraced philosophy as the mother of all good deeds and sayings, or had studied civil law, a topic absolutely essential for private cases and for the practical wisdom of the orator; none had cultivated awareness of the Roman past, from which, if necessary, the dead can be summoned as the most reliable witnesses; none had acquired the ability to set the judges at ease by wittily mocking the opponent or to lead them gradually from sternness to lightheartedness and even laughter. Not one among them could broaden the scope of discussion and guide the speech from a point of dispute limited in person and time to a general question of universal significance. None could digress a bit from the case at hand for the sake of amusement, none could impel the judge to anger, lead him to tears, or – the greatest task of an orator – direct his mind wherever the issue demanded.

'And so when Hortensius had all but vanished from the scene and I had been elected consul[55] in the sixth year after his consulate (the earliest year I was eligible), he began to summon himself to labour once again, lest being equal to him in political status, I seem superior in anything else. Thus for twelve years after my consulate in the most important cases, when I ranked him ahead of myself, and he ranked me ahead of himself, we worked together in complete harmony; and my consulship, which had at first somewhat hurt his pride, ended up uniting us, thanks to his recognition of my achievements, which he regarded with admiration. Our joint activity had achieved great prominence just before all eloquence suddenly fell silent and speechless, Brutus, out of fear of armed violence. When the Pompeian law[56] decreed only three hours for speakers, we daily argued anew similar or even identical cases. You, too, Brutus, participated in these proceedings, either jointly with us or on your own. Thus although Hortensius' life was too short, he nonetheless rounded out his career as follows: having begun arguing cases ten years before you were born, in his sixty-fourth year, a few days before his death, he joined you in defending your father-in-law Appius. At any rate, our orations will indicate to posterity the type of eloquence each of the two of us employed.

'But if we try to determine why Hortensius had a greater reputation as a young man than when he was older, we'll find two likely reasons. First, his Asiatic style of oratory was better suited to youth than to old age. In fact, there are really two types of Asiatic style, one full of pointed sayings, less grave and serious than polished and balanced, as in the histories of Timaeus,[57] the speeches of Hierocles of Alabanda, known from our youth, and especially those of his brother Menecles,[58] both of whom being outstanding examples of the Asiatic style. The other version of the Asiatic style is less pointed, more hurried, even rushed, all the rage now in Asia, expressing a flow of speech in refined language, as practised by Aeschylus of Cnidos and my contemporary Aeschines of Miletus.[59] Their flowing language prompted admiration, but there was none of the polished symmetry of phrases.

'As I said, both of these styles are more suited to young men, as they lack the gravity appropriate to older speakers. And so Hortensius, capable of both styles, earned accolades when he was young. For he had Menecles' fondness for frequent polished phrases, although, as with Menecles, they were pleasant and charming rather than essential or even useful. At the same time, his oratory could be swift and vibrant without loss of precision or polish. Neither approach met with the approval of older men, indeed I often saw Philippus[60] laughing or even growing angry and disgusted. But young men were in awe, and the people as a whole were deeply impressed.

'The youthful Hortensius thus stood out in the opinion of the common folk and easily held first place. For although his style of speaking commanded little genuine authority, it seemed well suited to his stage of life. In addition, because there was a certain cast to his talent, which he developed through practice, and he kept strict control of his language,[61] he earned the audience's great respect. But when his accumulation of honours and senior status demanded something a little weightier, he stayed the same, although it wasn't appropriate to do so. And because he grew lax in the studies in which he had formerly been so energetic, the symmetry and frequent use of sententious sayings continued, but they were no longer wrapped in the same elegant cloak of language as they had been. This explains why, dear Brutus, the man perhaps pleased you less than he would have pleased you, if you had been able to hear him speak when he was burning with enthusiasm and in full control of his powers.'

Then Brutus replied: 'I understand what you are saying, and I have always regarded Hortensius as a great speaker and I especially approved of his defence of Messalla, which took place when you were away.'[62]

'That's the general opinion,' I went on, 'and the written version, which is said to be just as he delivered it, confirms the verdict. And so he was a leading orator from the consulship of Crassus and Scaevola all the way to that of Paulus and Marcellus,[63] while I had a comparable career from the dictatorship of Sulla[64] also to the time of Paulus and Marcellus. The voice of Hortensius was silenced by his own death, mine by that of the republic.'

'Please, speak words of better omen!' said Brutus.

'Let it be as you wish,' I continued, 'for your sake if not for mine. But the death of that man was fortunate, in that he did not live to see the future he had predicted. For often together we were moved to tears by the impending disasters, as we could see how civil war was arising from private desires, and the possibility of peace had been kept out of public consideration. But the good luck he had always enjoyed seems by death to have rescued him from the wretched situation that has indeed come to pass.

'For our part, Brutus, after the death of that remarkable orator, Hortensius, we are left as guardians of eloquence. Let us then keep her safe with a custody suited to her free status, and reject these unfamiliar and shameless suitors and take precautions to safeguard the chastity of this adult maiden and protect her to the best of our ability from an onslaught of would-be lovers. It saddens me to think that I started on the path of life a little too late, and that before the journey has come to an end, I have stumbled into this dark night of the republic. Yet I am sustained by the consolation that your own kindly letter has provided, in which you urged me to be of strong mind because my accomplishments will speak for me even in my silence and live on after my death, bearing witness to the soundness of my advice concerning the state, whether through its survival, if things turn out well, or through its death.'

Philostratus
Lives of the Sophists
1.486–92 and 514–21

On the Road

I don't know what to call Dio of Prusa,[65] given his all-around excellence. He was what they call a Horn of Amaltheia,[66] filled with the best of the best; resonant of Demosthenes and Plato,[67] but like an octave played on an organ, he produced his own sound with a vigorous simplicity. Also distinctive in his speeches was his compound character. When he rebuked insolent cities he expressed neither abuse nor disgust, but was like one who restrains a horse with a bridle rather than a whip. And when he praised cities[68] that were well ordered, he seemed not to exalt them but to lead them to the view that they would be ruined if they changed their ways. The tone of his presentation was neither vulgar nor ironic, and although he was fierce in critique, he tempered his remarks, sweetening them with gentleness. That he was capable of composing history is evident from his *Getica*. He even travelled among the Getae[69] while he was in exile. The *Euboean Tale* and *Praise of a Parrot*,[70] over which he laboured despite the lightness of the subject matter, shouldn't be dismissed as trivialities, but are sophistic compositions. For it is typical of a sophist to devote serious attention to topics of this sort.

He lived during the time when Apollonius of Tyana[71] and Euphrates the Tyrian[72] were practising philosophy and was on friendly terms with both of them, although in their quarrelling with one another the two men went beyond what is appropriate for philosophers. It's not right to call his journey among the Getae an 'exile', since he hadn't received an actual order of exile;[73] but it wasn't tourism either, since he vanished from sight, stealing away from the eyes and ears of men, busying himself variously in various lands out of fear of the tyrants in the capital city, who were suppressing all philosophy. Planting, digging, drawing water for baths and orchards, and performing other such tasks to earn his keep, he did not neglect his studies, but occupied himself with two books, namely Plato's *Phaedo* and Demosthenes' *Against the Embassy*.

Haunting the soldiers' camps in his customary rags, and observing the soldiers eager for revolution upon the death of Domitian, he could not contain himself at the sight of their disorder, but naked, leaping on to a high altar, he began to speak as follows:

Then much-scheming Odysseus stripped off his rags.[74]

And speaking these things and revealing that he was not a beggar, nor what they thought him to be, but Dio the wise, he energetically denounced the tyrant and convinced the soldiers that it would be better for them to do as the Roman people decided. His persuasive power was enchanting, even to those who knew little of Greek literature. Why, the emperor Trajan,[75] having set him at Rome upon a golden chariot from which rulers were accustomed to lead the triumphal parade, said, turning to Dio, 'I don't understand what you are saying, but I love you as myself.'

The images employed by Dio in his speeches are highly sophistic, and although he used plenty of them, they were always clear and suited to the matter at hand.

[. . .]

The eloquence of Favorinus[76] the philosopher also declared him to be one of the sophists. He was of the western Gauls, from the city of Arles, located on the Rhône river. He was born a hermaphrodite, that is, of both sexes, as was clear from his appearance, for even when old he was beardless, and also from his voice, which was thin, shrill and high-pitched, as nature allots also to eunuchs. Yet he was so hot-blooded when it came to sex that he was prosecuted for adultery by a man of high rank. Despite his differences with the emperor Hadrian,[77] he suffered no harm. Thus he used to intone that his life held three paradoxes: though a Gaul, he lived as a Greek, though a eunuch, he was tried for adultery, though he quarrelled with an emperor, he remained alive. But this is more a credit to Hadrian, who as emperor differed on terms of equality with one he had the power to kill. For a king really is greater if, 'when he is angry with a lesser man',[78] he controls his wrath and 'powerful is the anger of Zeus-nourished kings', provided it is regulated by reason. Those who seek to form the character of rulers would do well to add these sayings to recommendations of the poets.

Appointed high priest, Favorinus argued that, in accordance with local customs regarding such matters, as a philosopher he was exempt from public financial obligations. Seeing that the emperor was intending to vote against him on the grounds that he was not a philosopher, he cut him off by speaking as follows: 'Your majesty, I had a dream which I must report to you. My teacher Dio[79] appeared to me and advised me concerning this case saying that we are born not for ourselves alone but also for our country. I accept this obligation and remain obedient to my teacher.' Now the emperor was acting thus purely for his own amusement, as he would relieve the anxieties of governing by turning his thoughts to sophists and philosophers. But the Athenians took the affair seriously, and their leaders rushed to overturn the bronze statue of Favorinus as if he were a mortal enemy of the emperor. Upon hearing this, Favorinus wasn't angry or resentful at their insolence, saying, 'Socrates would have been better off having his bronze statue overturned by the Athenians than being forced to drink hemlock.'[80]

He was on especially close terms with the sophist Herodes,[81] who regarded him as both teacher and father and wrote 'When will I see you and lick your face?'[82] On his death he bequeathed to Herodes his library, his house in Rome and one Autolecythus. This person was an Indian slave, dark in colour, a jester of sorts for Herodes and Favorinus. At their drinking parties he would entertain them by mixing Attic words into his Indic speech and speaking Greek badly with a stammering tongue.

Favorinus' dispute with Polemo[83] began in Ionia when the Ephesians favoured him, but Smyrna was abuzz over Polemo. It grew more intense in Rome, where the divided support among the leading men and their sons initiated the kind of rivalry that sparks hostility even between men who are wise. But such eagerness for glory is to be forgiven, since by human nature it never grows old. Not to be forgiven are the speeches they directed against each other, for personal abuse is shameful, and even if true, doesn't exempt from disgrace even the person who speaks about such things. As for those who call Favorinus a sophist, his quarrel with a sophist supports their case, for the sort of rivalry just described occurs between those practising the same art.

His style was a little loose, but learned and appealing. It is said that he was fluent when improvising. It's our judgement that he neither planned nor composed the speeches against Proxenus.[84] They were dreamed up by some drunken young man who vomited them out. But the speeches *On One Who Died Too Soon* and *For the Gladiators* and *For the Baths* seem authentic and well composed; even more so his philosophical speeches, of which the one on the Pyrrhonians[85] is the best. For he does not deny their ability to pass judgement in court despite their professed scepticism.

Whenever he spoke in Rome the reception was enthusiastic and even those in the audience whose knowledge of Greek was limited shared in the enjoyment, for he charmed them with the sound of his voice, the communicativeness of his facial expression and the rhythm of his language. He charmed them, too, with his epilogues, which they called an ode but I call showing off, since it was added on to what had already been proven. It is said that he was a student of Dio, but he differed from him as much as did those who were never his students.

[. . .]

I will speak about the sophist Scopelian,[86] but first I must address those who would belittle him, saying he doesn't belong among the circle of sophists, calling him a dithyrambist,[87] unruly and thick-witted. People who speak this way are nitpicking slackers, unimpressed with spontaneous eloquence.

For man is by nature given to envy. The short slander the tall, the ugly disparage the good-looking, the slow and clumsy attack the swift, cowards the brave, the unmusical go after the lyric poets, the unathletic attack those who wrestle: is it any wonder if those who are poor speakers and have the proverbial ox of silence on their tongues,[88] who never conceive of anything grand or approve of others' grand conceptions, tremble in terror at and revile a man whose style was the readiest, boldest and grandest of the Greeks of his time? But as they have not understood him, I will show what sort of man he was and the character of his household.

He was the chief priest of Asia, as were his ancestors, with the position passed from father to son – which is a greater mark of glory than is wealth. He was born a twin, and while both were still in swaddling-clothes, being but five days old, the one was struck by lightning but the other was not maimed in any of his senses although he was lying right next to the one who was struck. The fire of the lightning-bolt was so intense and sulphurous that it killed some of those nearby, while others suffered injury to ears and eyes, still others were shocked in their minds. But Scopelian was not hurt in any way and lived into old age healthy and sound.

I want to explain why I find this so amazing. For once in Lemnos, in the part of the island called The Horn, where the land forms a harbour in the shape of horns, there were eight reapers eating under a large oak tree. A cloud covered the tree, and a bolt flashed out. The tree was struck, and all the reapers died from the shock, losing their lives in the course of their various activities, whether lifting a cup, drinking, kneading bread, eating or whatever each happened to be doing. Their bodies were surrounded with smoke and turned black, like bronze statues that have been darkened by the hot fumes from nearby springs. But Scopelian was protected by the gods, escaping a death that not even the strongest of the farmworkers could avoid. He remained undamaged in his senses and ready of wit and stronger than sleep, not experiencing any sluggishness.

He regularly visited the rhetoric schools in the company of

Nicetes of Smyrna, who was himself an outstanding declaimer but even more impressive in the courts of law. When the city of Clazomenae requested that Scopelian come and declaim, thinking it would boost their reputation if so great a man would offer instruction there, he courteously declined, saying that a nightingale does not sing in a cage. Smyrna, on the other hand, he regarded as a grove suited for his lovely voice, and he thought it best to let it echo there. For while all of Ionia is home to the Muses, Smyrna provides the most perfect setting, like the bridge on a musical instrument.

Many different and disturbing explanations are given as to why his father, who had treated him gently, instead became harsh towards him, but I shall give the one most likely to be true. For after the death of Scopelian's mother, his father was about to bring home a concubine, in violation of the laws. When Scopelian saw this he warned him and tried to stop him, which is never welcome to older men. The woman, for her part, falsely accused him, saying he was in love with her and could not deal with his complete lack of success. As a partner in this slander she had the old man's household cook, named Cytherus, who made up a story, as in a play, speaking to his master as follows: 'O master, your son wants you dead already, and won't even accept a natural death, which surely isn't far off for one your age. Instead he is fashioning a plot, and has tried to hire me to carry it out. He has deadly poisons ready for you and he orders me to put the most effective of them in your food, promising me freedom, land, houses, money and anything I want of your possessions. All of this he promises if I obey, but if I don't, then whips, torture, strong fetters and the yoke of punishment.'

He besieged the master with falsehoods of this sort, and when the latter was dying, not long afterwards, and made his will, the cook was named heir and called 'my son', 'my eyes', 'my entire soul'. We shouldn't be surprised by this, since he deceived an old man in love and perhaps even out of his mind from age and lust – for even young men, when in love, do not keep their wits about them. What is surprising is that despite Scopelian's remarkable talent and success in trials, the cook got the better of him when they went to trial over the will, using Scopelian's money against Scopelian's talent. Drawing on the estate and bribing with extravagant sums the tongues of everyone, not to mention the votes of the jurors, he was victorious on every issue. This was the basis for Scopelian's remark that while the property of Anaxagoras[89] had become a sheep-pasture, his own became a slave-pasture.

Cytherus went on to achieve prominence in public affairs, but as an old man saw his property dwindle. He was so thoroughly despised that he was struck by a man from whom he sought to recover money. He became a suppliant of Scopelian, asking him to set aside his anger and memory of wrongdoing and to take back his father's property, leaving him only a small part of the house (so that he could live in a manner befitting a free man) and two of the fields near the sea. And even to the present a part of the house is called the 'estate of Cytherus'. I have recounted all of these things so that they not remain unknown and to help us understand that human beings are the playthings not only of God, but of one another.

While Scopelian was busy in Smyrna, Ionians, Lydians, Carians, Maeonians, Aeolians and Greeks from Mysia and Phrygia all came there, which is not surprising, since Smyrna is convenient to these peoples, being easy to approach by land or sea. But he also attracted Cappadocians and Assyrians, Egyptians and Phoenicians, the most famous of the Achaeans and all the young men of Athens. To the crowd he seemed easy-going, even careless, since he generally spent the time leading up to his performance conducting public business among the leading Smyrnaeans. In fact, he relied on his brilliant and lofty natural abilities; in addition, he generally didn't do much work during the day, but, being a man who didn't sleep much, he would say, 'O night, you have a greater share of wisdom than the gods!' and treated her as collaborator in his intellectual endeavours. It is said that he would work continuously from dusk until dawn.

He was interested in all kinds of poetry, especially tragedy, seeking to surpass the grandeur of his teacher – for in this aspect of speaking Nicetes was much admired – but he stretched his grandiloquence to such an extent that he composed a *Gigantea* and furnished the Homerids[90] with material for their recitations. Of the sophists he was especially familiar with Gorgias of Leontini,[91] of the orators those who resounded brilliantly.

His charm was natural rather than studied, for sophisticated speech comes naturally to the Ionians. His speeches were full of humour, for he considered excessive seriousness inappropriate and unpleasant. At public meetings he had a relaxed and cheerful countenance, even more so when the debate became acrimonious, relaxing and calming the others with his good-natured appearance. In the courts as well, his character was neither greedy nor abusive. He offered his services for free to those charged with capital crimes, and when speakers became abusive and saw fit to make a display of anger he called them drunk and quarrelsome old crones. He did charge for instruction in declamation, but his fee was in accordance which each person's ability to pay. He presented himself before audiences as neither disdainful nor pompous, not like those who are anxious, but as befits a man competing for glory and confident that he will not be defeated. He would speak in a graceful manner if he was seated, but when he stood up his style became bolder and more vehement. He made preparations neither in private nor in public, but, withdrawing for a brief time, would go through all his points. He had a lovely voice and a pleasant way of speaking and he would strike his thigh to stir up himself and his audience. He was excellent at allusion and ambiguity and especially wonderful on the most elevated themes, in particular those pertaining to the Medes and involving Darius or Xerxes.[92] It seems to me that on these topics he was the best of the sophists in inventing arguments and making them available to his successors. He would display through his delivery the arrogance and fickleness of the barbarians. It was said that on these occasions he would sway more than usual, almost like the Bacchic dancers, and when one of the entourage of Polemo said that he was beating a drum, Scopelian took up the insult and said, 'Indeed I do beat on a drum – it's the shield of Ajax.'[93]

He was often among the ambassadors to the emperor, and

while good luck accompanied him always, his most successful mission had to do with grape-vines. This embassy was not on behalf of the Smyrnaeans alone, as was usually the case, but was sent by all of Asia. Here was the aim of the mission. The emperor had decided that there would be no vines in Asia, since the people there, when under the influence of wine, engaged in civil strife. They were to rip out those that had been planted, and plant no more henceforth. There was need of an embassy to act in the common interest, and of a speaker who, like Orpheus or Thamyris,[94] could charm his listener. They unanimously chose Scopelian, whose embassy was so extraordinarily successful that he returned bringing not just permission to continue planting, but also censure of those who did not do so. How great a reputation he earned from his struggle on behalf of the vines is clear from his own remarks, for the speech is among his most amazing. It is also clear from the aftermath, for gifts were showered on him, such as are considered fit for a king, and he received numerous compliments and speeches of congratulation. Brilliant youths followed him to Ionia, longing to share in his wisdom.

While he was at Athens he was the guest of the father of the sophist Herodes Atticus. His host admired his eloquence even more than the Thessalians admired that of Gorgias. He even ordered that all of the busts of sophists to be found in the corridors of his home be pelted with stones for having corrupted his son. Herodes was a mere youth at the time and still under his father's control. He cared only for extemporaneous speaking, but wasn't confident enough to pursue it, since he hadn't yet made the acquaintance of Scopelian and lacked the energy for that type of performance. Thus he was delighted when Scopelian took up residence in his household. When he heard him speak and handle an issue extemporaneously, he grew wings, as it were, and readied himself by following Scopelian's example. And thinking to please his father he invited him to a practice speech in the style of their visitor. His father was so delighted at the imitation that he gave him fifty talents and Scopelian fifteen. But Herodes, drawing on his own reward, gave Scopelian as much as his father had, addressing him as his

teacher. Hearing this title from Herodes was sweeter to Scopelian than the springs of the river Pactolus.[95]

The good fortune he enjoyed on his embassies can be inferred
from the following as well. The Smyrnaeans were in need of an
ambassador on their behalf on an issue of the utmost importance. But Scopelian had grown old, and was past the age of
travelling, so Polemo was chosen, although he had never gone on
an embassy before. Praying for good luck, Polemo begged that he
be granted the persuasive power of Scopelian, and embraced him
in the presence of the assembly, speaking to him, most astutely,
the following taken from the exploits of Patroclus:

> Give me your armour to buckle around my chest.
> Perhaps they will take me for you.[96]

And Apollonius of Tyana, who far surpasses human nature in his
wisdom, ranks Scopelian among the marvels of humankind.

Glossary

altercation (Latin *altercatio*): the portion of a trial set aside for back-and-forth argument between prosecution and defence

antithesis: a contrast expressed through a balanced pair of phrases or clauses of roughly similar length

apotreptic: term used to describe an argument or speech designed to turn the listener away from a particular course of action (contrast *protreptic*)

barbarism: a linguistic usage that marks the speaker as other than a native user of Greek or Latin

chreia: a short story or anecdote that contains a moral lesson

colon (pl. cola): a subsection of a sentence roughly equivalent to an English clause (cf. comma)

comma (pl. commata): a short, incisive phrase, generally used in clusters of two or more

commonplaces: topics that can be expected to occur in a variety of rhetorical contexts and thus are suitable for preparation in advance of work on a given case

commutation: a rhetorical figure in which two phrases expressing a contrast are placed side by side in a criss-cross pattern, e.g.'live to eat, don't eat to live'

confirmation: the constructive part of a courtroom oration in which the speaker lays out the positive version of his case

conjectural case: a legal case or argument based on inference from facts, rather than facts alone

controversia (pl. controversiae): type of practice speech, or declamation, that requires the student to argue a case in which two laws seem to conflict, or the requirements of the law seem difficult to apply to the particulars of the situation

conversion: a rhetorical figure in which consecutive phrases end in the same word

cutting off (aposiopesis): a rhetorical figure in which the speaker deliberately avoids completing an expression or thought

declamation: a practice speech on a set topic; used for training as well as for entertainment

deliberative (symbouleutic): type of oratory used in discussing public policy; one of the three standard types of oratory as discussed by teachers of rhetoric

delivery: the branch of rhetoric that concerns all aspects of the embodied presentation of a speech, including voice, pacing, gesture, dress and comportment of the orator

denomination (metonymy): rhetorical figure involving the replacement of one term by a related one

dialectic: formal argumentation as practised by philosophers. For Aristotle, rhetoric is a public and less formal 'counterpart' of dialectic.

disconnection (asyndeton): rhetorical figure in which expected conjunctions are omitted from between words or phrases

distribution: a rhetorical figure in which the speaker makes a point of assigning distinct tasks or responsibilities to distinct entities

division: the section of a speech in which the speaker outlines the subsections of the case as he will address them

encomium: a speech of praise; one type of epideictic oratory

enthymeme: according to Aristotle, a type of syllogism adapted for use in public contexts. In particular, whereas syllogisms are to concern things that are necessarily one way or another, enthymemes apply to things that can be one way or another (e.g. topics of deliberation).

epideictic (demonstrative): a speech of praise or blame; one of three standard types of oratory as discussed by teachers of rhetoric

epilogue: see *peroration*

ethos (character): one of three possible bases of persuasion according to Aristotle. Mastery of ethos requires an understanding of human psychology.

exordium: the opening section of a speech

figures of language: rhetorical devices that entail the manipulation of the form of a phrase, through sound effects, word order and the like

figures of thought: rhetorical devices that depend for their effect on a distinctive organization of material or structuring of relationship between speaker and audience

gradation (climax): a rhetorical figure in which the speaker links each phrase to its predecessor through stepwise repetition of words

grammatice: Greek term for the analysis of language and literature. Instructors at this early stage of education are called grammatici.

homoioptoton: the repetition of similar case endings in adjacent words or words in parallel position.

homoioteleuton: Greek term for the repetition of endings in words, also known as near rhyme

hyperbaton: see *transgression*

hyperbole: rhetorical figure that consists of deliberate exaggeration for the sake of effect

impersonation (prosopopoeia): rhetorical figure in which the speaker pretends to give voice to an object or to a person other than himself

intellection (synecdoche): rhetorical figure in which a word signifying a part of something is intended to refer to the entirety or vice versa

intertwining: a series of phrases in which one word is reused at the beginning of each phrase and another word reused at the end of each phrase. A combination of the figures repetition and conversion.

invective: a speech of blame; the negative version of epideictic (or demonstrative) oratory

invention: the division or branch of rhetoric that deals with finding or discovering arguments and approaches to a case

krinomenon: Greek term meaning 'the thing to be decided'; the point of clash or contention between the two sides in a dispute

judicial (dicanic, forensic): type of oratory used in trials; one of the three standard types of oratory as discussed by teachers of rhetoric

Latinity (in Latinitas): correct use of the Latin language, without grammatical error or barbarous vocabulary. There is a corresponding Greek term, *hellenismos*, not cited in this volume.

logos (discourse): one of the three possible bases of persuasion, according to Aristotle. The term covers aspects of linguistic presentation and argumentation not falling under the headings of ethos and pathos.

maxim: a short saying that is understood to express widely accepted wisdom

memory: the division or branch of rhetoric that trains the orator to remember the arguments and remarks he has prepared in advance

metaphor (translatio): transfer of a word or phrase from one referent to another

misuse (catachresis): a version of metaphor in which a similar and closely related term is deliberately used in place of the correct and expected one

narration: the section of a speech in which the orator recapitulates the events that led up to the trial, presenting them in the best possible light for his client

nominatio (onomatopoeia): a word or phrase whose sound alone seems to convey its meaning

ornament, the ornate: terms used to describe language that is made to seem special and appropriate to the occasion; language that is different from everyday conversation or technical discourse

outcry (apostrophe): interruption of a speech to address an absent person or entity

paradigm: an example; in Aristotelian theory a type of proof developed by the speaker

parison: a corresponding structure in a series of phrases, clauses or sentences.

parisosis: use of juxtaposed cola of equal length

paromoiosis: use of juxtaposed cola of equal length and containing words of similar shape

pathos: emotion; one of the three main bases of persuasion, according to Aristotle

period: according to Aristotle, 'an expression that has a beginning and an end in itself and a magnitude that can be taken in at a glance'. In contrast to the strung-out style, periodic construction allows the listener to anticipate the completion of the unit of thought or expression.

periphrasis: expression of an idea in a deliberately roundabout manner

peroration (epilogue): the final section of a speech, especially suited to emotional appeals

personification: see *impersonation*

protreptic: Greek term used to describe an argument or speech designed to turn the listener towards a particular course of action (contrast *apotreptic*)

reduplication: repetition of one or more words for the sake of emphasis

repetition: use of the same word at the beginning of successive phrases

simile: clarification of an idea or expression through explicit comparison

similitude: term for simile used by the author of *Rhetoric to Herennius*

solecism: grammatical error; use of a term that doesn't fit, grammatically or otherwise, with its surroundings

sophist: in fifth century BCE Greece an itinerant teacher of rhetoric and other subjects; under the Roman empire, the term is applied to

speakers who specialize in, but need not be limited to, epideictic
(display) oratory

suasoria (pl. suasoriae): Latin term for practice speech in which the
student pretends to offer advice to a historical or mythological
figure at a turning-point in his life (cf. *controversia*)

subjectio: a rhetorical figure in which the speaker asks and answers
his own questions

substitution: see *denomination*

syllogism: a formal argument in which premises are made explicit
and deductions necessarily follow from them

synecdoche: see *intellection*

transduction: a rhetorical figure in which a word is used several
times in a short passage, often with a slight variation in inflection
or word-ending

transgression (hyperbaton): a rhetorical figure in which a word is
deliberately placed in violation of expected word order

transference: a legal manoeuvre, or issue, in which a defendant seeks
a postponement of a case, a change of prosecutor or a change of
judges

understatement (litotes): a rhetorical device in which an orator
deliberately downplays some achievement or characteristic of him
or his client in order to avoid having him seen as arrogant

visualization: rhetorical technique of detailed, vivid description of a
real or imagined event; designed to transfer the emotional reaction
to the event from the speaker to the audience

Notes

WHY STUDY RHETORIC?

1. *Quintus*: Cicero addresses the treatise to his younger brother Quintus Tullius Cicero (*c*.102–43 BCE), who rose to the rank of praetor and served as governor of Asia.

2. *The very place*: Rome, as centre of an expansive empire.

3. *consulship*: Cicero held the consulship, the highest elected office in the Roman Republic, in 63 BCE.

4. *grammatici*: These were scholars and teachers who specialized in explaining and intepreting language and literature. As the system of instruction at Rome became regularized, *grammatici* directed lower-level studies while rhetoricians (*rhetores*) served more advanced students.

5. *Crassus*: Lucius Licinius Crassus (140–91 BCE), consul 95 BCE, was in Cicero's view one of the leading orators of the generation preceding his own, along with Marcus Antonius, consul 99 BCE. Publius Sulpicius Rufus (tribune of the plebs 88 BCE) and Gaius Aurelius Cotta (consul 75 BCE) were younger nobles, depicted in *On the Orator* as seeking guidance from Crassus and Antonius.

6. *Scaevola*: Quintus Mucius Scaevola (consul 117 BCE), also called the Augur due to his longtime membership of the College of Augurs, was well known as an orator and a legal scholar.

7. *quaestor . . . were in charge*: A quaestor was a financial official who accompanied a governor to a province. The Academy in question was founded by Plato, and still flourished at this time in Athens. Charmadas, Clitomachus and Aeschines were all minor Greek philosophers.

8. *Metrodorus . . . Critolaus*: Metrodorus is probably the philosopher Metrodorus of Stratonicea, to be distinguished from Metrodorus of Scepsis, who was famous for his memory-system.

Carneades (214/13–129/8 BCE) led the philosophical movement known as the New Academy. His views were often discussed in Cicero's philosophical treatises. Panaetius of Rhodes (c.185–109 BCE) was an important Stoic philosopher whose approach had great influence at Rome, including on the works of Cicero. Critolaus was a leading Peripatetic philosopher, in other words a follower of the school of thought initiated by Aristotle. Diodorus of Tyre was his successor as head of the Peripatetic school at Athens. Carneades and Critolaus were both part of a famous philosophical delegation to Rome in 156/5 BCE. Crassus refers here to representatives of three of the four main philosophical movements of the period.

9. *Plato ... Gorgias*: Plato (c.429–347 BCE), famous Athenian philosopher. In his dialogue *Gorgias* he presents Socrates as engaging in a debate with the orator Gorgias and others over the meaning and value of rhetoric.

10. *Democritus*: Democritus was a Greek philosopher active in the latter half of the fifth century BCE. Only fragments remain of his writings, in which he developed an atomic theory of the universe.

11. *Theophrastus*: Theophrastus was the successor of Aristotle as leader of the Peripatetic movement. He wrote extensively on topics in ethics, logic and natural science.

12. *Chrysippus*: Chrysippus of Soli (c.280–207 BCE) was a prolific and vigorous defender of Stoic philosophy.

WHAT IS RHETORIC?

1. *counterpart of dialectic*: Aristotle suggests that rhetoric is the version of dialectic, or formal argumentation, that is to be deployed in public venues. The term 'dialectic' was generally reserved for argumentation in a philosophical context.

2. *court of the Areopagus*: The Areopagus was a hill at Athens dedicated to the war-god Ares. The court that met there heard cases of murder and arson and held varying degrees of political influence during the period of the Athenian democracy.

3. *syllogism*: A formal argument structured in terms of explicit premises and conclusions. As part of his effort to give rhetoric a philosophical legitimacy, Aristotle here suggests that there is a type of syllogism called 'enthymeme' that is specific to the contexts of public speaking.

4. *Topics*: Aristotle's treatise of this title considers the construction of logical syllogisms.

5. *sophistry ... moral intent, not ability*: Aristotle's point is that sophistry is the intentionally immoral use of arguments. It is, in effect, a subdivision of dialectic. The term rhetoric, in his view, applies whether arguments are sound or fallacious, or used to good or bad ends.

6. *Isocrates*: Isocrates (436–338 BCE) was an Athenian writer and teacher. No handbook of rhetoric by him survives.

7. *Ennian variant, 'the marrow of persuasion'*: Ennius, *Annals* 304.

8. *Rhetorica, which he himself does not approve*: Quintilian may refer to Cicero's later embarrassment about the technical austerity of his early treatise *On Invention*. No work of Cicero with the title *Rhetorica* survives.

9. *Antonius ... Manius Aquillius*: Quintilian refers to Marcus Antonius, consul 99 BCE, who was also an interlocutor in Cicero's dialogue *On the Orator*. Manius Aquillius, consul 129 BCE, was charged with corruption but acquitted.

10. *Cato ... Sulpicius Gallus*: Servius Sulpicius Galba, consul 144 BCE, was prosecuted by Marcus Porcius Cato (Cato the Elder) and others for his slaughter of the Lusitanians, who had come to him seeking peace. Gaius Sulpicius Gallus, consul 166 BCE, was respected as a soldier, politician, ambassador and scholar.

11. *Phryne was released no thanks to the speech of Hyperides*: The Athenian *hetaira* (female companion of elite men) Phryne was charged with impiety and successfully defended by the orator Hyperides around 350 BCE.

12. *Theodectes*: Greek rhetorician, orator and tragic poet, fourth century BCE.

13. *Apollodorus*: Rhetorician, first century BCE. His students included the future emperor Augustus.

14. *Aristotle ... means of persuasion in speech*: Quintilian seems to have added the expression 'in speech' to Aristotle's definition; but it is certainly implied by Aristotle's focus on arguments and language.

15. *Hermagoras*: Greek rhetorician of the first century BCE.

16. *Iatrocles*: Unknown, as is Patrocles, a name that occurs in this place in some manuscripts.

17. *Eudorus*: Unknown.

18. *Critolaus*: Peripatetic philosopher, second century BCE. We have little information about his pupil Ariston. The Peripatetics

were philosophers who continued the tradition of Aristotle and
Theophrastus.

19. *Stoics*: Stoicism, founded by Zeno of Citium (*c.* 335–*c.* 263
    BCE), was one of the major schools of ancient philosophy.
    Among other things, the Stoics were famous for their emphasis
    on precise definitions.

20. *Theodorus of Gadara*: Greek rhetorician, late first century
    BCE. His students included the future emperor Tiberius.

21. *Celsus*: Aulus Cornelius Celsus, first century CE, wrote trea-
    tises on a wide variety of arts and sciences. His work on rhetoric
    does not survive, but his treatise on medicine does.

22. *Athenaeus*: Unknown.

23. *spoken by Socrates*: The citations are from Plato, *Gorgias*
    462c–465e.

24. *'the manner in which you conduct public affairs'*: Plato, *Gor-
    gias* 500c.

25. *'therefore the rhetorician . . . do what is just'*: Plato, *Gorgias*
    460c.

26. *'whoever truly intends . . . what is just'*: Plato, *Gorgias* 508c.

27. *those who died for their country*: The reference is to Plato's
    Menexenus.

28. *political science*: Cicero, *On Invention* 1.6.

29. *Isocrates*: Isocrates described the kind of teaching he provided as
    philosophia, using a word whose meaning was still unresolved.

30. *Chrysippus*: Chrysippus of Soli (*c.*280–207 BCE) was a prolific
    and vigorous defender of Stoic philosophy.

31. *Cleanthes*: Chrysippus' predecessor as leader of the Stoic
    movement.

32. *Areus*: Possibly Areus Didymus, Stoic philosopher and teacher
    of the emperor Augustus.

33. *Albucius*: Gaius Albucius Silus, an Italian orator mentioned by
    Seneca the Elder.

THE SYSTEM OF RHETORIC

1. *Books 1, 2 and 3*: The passages translated here are from Aristotle, *Rhetoric* 1.2.2–14, 1.2.22–1.3.1, 1.3.1–1.4.3, 1.4.7–13, 1.9.
   1–2, 1.9.33–7, 1.9.40–41, 1.10.1–11, 2.1.1–9, 2.12.1–2.14.4,
   2.20.1–9, 2.22.1–12, 3.1.1–10, 3.9.1–10. For a useful discussion of the logical relationship among the different parts of
   Aristotle's *Rhetoric*, see C. Rapp, 'Aristotle's Rhetoric', *The*

        Stanford Encyclopedia of Philosophy, ed. Edward N. Zalta (spring 2010 edition), available at: https://plato.stanford.edu/archives/spr2010/entries/aristotle-rhetoric/.

2. *through speech itself*: The general means of persuasion referred to here are often abbreviated as ethos, pathos and logos.

3. *Analytics*: Two Aristotelian treatises by this name survive, the so-called *Prior* and *Posterior Analytics*.

4. *Topics*: A treatise by Aristotle. Syllogism and induction are discussed in *Topics* 1.1 and 1.12 respectively.

5. *Methodics*: This work by Aristotle does not survive.

6. *spectator*: The audiences at an epideictic or display speech are not expected to make an official judgement, as they are at a trial or political deliberation; thus Aristotle considers them spectators there for the show.

7. *Achilles ... Patroclus*: Achilles, the chief Greek hero in Homer's *Iliad*, succeeded in recovering the corpse of Patroclus and taking vengeance only by killing the Trojan hero Hector. In returning to the fight against the Trojans, Achilles chose a course of action that his divine mother had foretold would lead to his early death.

8. *as Pittacus said in regard to Amphiaraus*: Pittacus was one of the legendary seven sages, known for their pungent sayings. Amphiaraus is a figure from Greek mythology. His wife Eriphyle, corrupted by the promise of a magnificent necklace, encouraged him to join the ill-fated expedition of the Seven against Thebes.

9. *precept of Chilon*: The Spartan wise man Chilon is credited with the saying 'nothing in excess'.

10. *Aesop and the Libyan tales*: Many fables and witticisms, not all of them concerning animals, were attributed to the legendary Aesop: see discussion by L. Kurke, *Aesopic Conversations* (Princeton: Princeton University Press, 2010); also Aesop, *The Complete Fables* (Harmondsworth: Penguin, 1998). Aristotle's student Chamaileon is said to have made a collection of Libyan fables.

11. *Darius ... Xerxes*: Darius I (*c*.550–486 BCE) was king of Persia. His troops' invasion of mainland Greece was halted by their defeat at the Battle of Marathon. His son Xerxes I (518–465 BCE) renewed the invasion, but withdrew his forces after the Greeks' naval victory at the Battle of Salamis.

12. *Stesichorus concerning Phalaris*: Stesichorus was a Greek lyric poet, first half of the sixth century BCE. Phalaris was the

notorious tyrant of Acragas in Sicily. He built an empire that included Himera, also in Sicily.

13. *'the ignorant are better at enchanting the crowd'*: Aristotle cites Euripides, *Hippolytus* 989.

14. *Salamis ... and so forth*: The Greeks, led by the Athenians, defeated the Persians at sea at Salamis (480 BCE) and on land at Marathon (490 BCE). In Greek mythology, the Heracleidae were the sons of Heracles, who continued to be persecuted by his nemesis Eurystheus after their father's death. The Athenians in historical times boasted of their support of the Heracleidae, and even held hero-cult for them.

15. *Aeginetans and Potidaeans*: The island of Aegina was forcibly incorporated into the Athenian empire in 458/7 BCE, despite having cooperated with the Athenians in the struggle against the Persian invasion. In 431 BCE the Athenians expelled the residents of Aegina, alleging that they were Spartan collaborators (see Thucydides 2.27). Potidaea, which had also resisted the Persians, revolted against the Athenian empire and was destroyed in 430 BCE.

16. *Achilles ... Hector ... Cycnus*: All are familiar figures from Greek mythology: Achilles the greatest of the Greek warriors at Troy, Hector the chief defender of Troy, and Cycnus, whom Achilles killed by suffocation since his body was impenetrable.

17. *Three things must be considered ... speech*: Aristotle's list of the subdivisions of rhetoric, in essence, invention, style and arrangement, is shorter than that of most other rhetoricians, who include memory and delivery.

18. *rhapsody*: Rhapsodes were solo performers of poems composed by others. Aristotle implies that delivery is only an issue when someone other than the original author presents a speech or poem.

19. *Glaucon of Teos*: A Glaucon is mentioned at Plato, *Ion* 530, and Aristotle, *Poetics* 1461b1, but nothing else is known.

20. *Delivery*: The topic of performance of a speech is treated more fully by later rhetoricians, such as Quintilian (this volume).

21. *Thrasymachus in his Eleoi*: The *Eleoi*, or *Laments*, of Thrasymachus are also mentioned by Plato, *Phaedrus* 267c.

22. *Gorgias*: Gorgias of Leontini, in Sicily, was one of most influential speakers and teachers of the late fifth century BCE. He is also the title character of Plato's *Gorgias*. Surviving fragments and testimony suggest that his rhetorical style was distinctive for its use of balanced clauses, assonance and other figures of language.

23. *Poetics*: A separate treatise by Aristotle. The surviving section deals with tragedy.

24. *dithyrambs . . . antistrophes*: A dithyramb was a type of poetry that originated as a cultic hymn to the god Dionysus. An antistrophe is a poetic stanza that matches the metre of a preceding stanza, or strophe.

25. *Of the inquiry of Herodotus of Thurii herewith the exposition*: Aristotle cites the opening of Herodotus' massive history of the Persian Wars, dating to the late fifth century BCE. He seems to suggest that Herodotus in general, and not necessarily this phrase, is characterized by the 'strung-out' style.

26. *Sophocles . . . in the Peloponnese*: Aristotle mistakenly assigns the opening words of Euripides' *Meleager* to Sophocles. The quoted passage goes on to make clear that land of Pelops is across the gulf from Calydon.

27. *Democritus . . . most of all*: Melanippides was a Greek lyric poet, renowned as a composer of dithyrambs. Democritus of Chios is not otherwise known, but the verses quoted from him parody similar verses from Hesiod, *Works and Days* 265–6.

28. *Often have I marvelled . . . competitions*: Aristotle cites the opening of Isocrates' *Panegyricus*. Isocrates' style is strongly marked by the use of parallelism and antithesis. Subsequent examples are also drawn from or based on Isocrates' speech.

29. *At home they sold you, here they bought you*: The source of the quotation is unknown. Pitholaos and Lycophron assassinated the tyrant Alexander of Pherae.

30. *awaiting their gifts, berating their guests*: The Greek, taken from Homer, *Iliad* 9.526 is more accurately translated as 'they were ready for gifts and verbal persuasion'. I have varied it to capture the internal rhyme, which is a significant feature of the Greek verse. Subsequent quotations in this section are also altered to achieve the sound effects that characterize the Greek.

31. *Theodectes*: Rhetorician, orator and tragic poet, fourth century BCE.

32. *Epicharmus*: Sicilian comic poet of the early fifth century BCE.

INVENTION OR DISCOVERY
OF ARGUMENTS

1. *Others have specified four central issues*: For example, Hermagoras of Temnos, a Greek rhetorician of the first century BCE, and thus probably a contemporary of the author of the *Rhetoric to Herennius*.

2. *factual*: The Latin term translated by this word, *coniecturalis*, refers more specifically to the inference of one fact (e.g. what happened?) from other facts (e.g. evidence).

3. *For example*: The selection, like many in the *Rhetoric to Herennius*, seems to have been invented by the anonymous author or one of his sources for purposes of illustration. The characters and situation are drawn from Greek mythology of the sort that would have been familiar to readers.

4. *augur*: Augurs were Roman religious officials charged with ensuring the correctness of ritual procedures. In the late republic augurs were elected by one of the Roman assemblies.

5. *When Lucius Saturninus . . . such an outlay*: The example is based on recent events in Roman history. Evidently Saturninus' law would have required the treasury to subsidize the price of grain, with the individual purchaser required to spend no more than five-sixths as, a historically low price. Lucius Appuleius Saturninus was tribune of the plebs in 103 BCE and again in 100 BCE, when he was killed in rioting. Caepio is probably the Quintus Servilius Caepio who went on to become praetor in 91 BCE. The urban quaestor was, as the anecdote suggests, a financial official.

6. *the bridges*: These were paths to allow voters at the assemblies to proceed to the ballot boxes in an orderly manner.

7. *but not the latter*: The example given seems to suggest that for this author 'transference' could also entail a redefinition or transfer of the charge.

8. *praetor*: An elected official, here serving as the presiding magistrate in a court of law.

9. *Malleolus*: An otherwise unknown individual who, according to Livy, *Periochae* 68, was the first to undergo such punishment for matricide.

10. *A certain mime verbally attacked the poet Accius*: The Romans differentiated between mimes, who performed informal sketch comedies that included speech and action, and pantomimes, who communicated exclusively through bodily movement set to music. Lucius Accius (170–c.86 BCE) was a Roman dramatist and scholar.

11. *Caepio . . . loss of his army*: Quintus Servilius Caepio (consul 106 BCE, proconsul 105 BCE) was deemed responsible for the Roman loss to the Cimbrians in the Battle of Arausio (modern Orange). As a result, he lost his command and was expelled from the senate.

12. *ignorance . . . had been set free*: Had the surviving brother known that the slave was in fact a free man, he would have been

expected to pursue him legally rather than taking immediate vengeance.

13. *Orestes ... responsibility to his mother*: In Greek mythology Orestes killed his mother Clytemnestra because she had killed her husband, Orestes' father Agamemnon.

14. *Publius Sulpicius*: Publius Sulpicius Rufus (tribune of the plebs 88 BCE) was killed during the proscriptions of Sulla. He appears as a minor character in Cicero's treatise *On the Orator*.

15. *surrounded by the Gauls*: The example seems to refer loosely to an episode from the Romans' war against the Cimbrians in 107 BCE. The Romans used the word Gauls to refer to a wide range of ancient peoples.

ARRANGEMENT

1. *Book*: The passages translated are from Cicero, *On Invention* 1.19–20, 1.25, 1.27, 1.28, 1.29, 1.31, 1.34, 1.78, 1.79, 1.98–99, 1.100–109. Omitted passages cover many of the guidelines about invention of arguments and summoning of emotions treated elsewhere in this volume.

2. *commonplaces*: Cicero seems to assume that his readers will have at hand a set of stock observations concerning these issues, which can be brought to bear regardless of the specifics of the case.

3. *Apollonius*: Probably Apollonius Molon, also known as Apollonius of Rhodes, a teacher of Cicero and Julius Caesar.

STYLE

1. *the genres of style*: The present selection is preceded by the author's discussion of a general categorization of style into high, middle and low. For him high (or serious) style consists of a 'smooth and polished arrangement of impressive language', the middle employs 'language of a lower register, but not low or colloquial', while the reduced or low style uses a 'common but correct way of speaking' (*Rhetoric to Herennius* 4.11). The examples he devises as illustrations of the three styles also display a richer use of figures of speech and figures of thought in the more elevated genres. Although it is doubtful that a strict taxonomy of styles was applied in practice, it is clear that writers

and speakers drew more or less heavily on stylistic devices in different sections of their speeches.

2. *our treatise on grammar*: The treatise referred to here is unknown.

3. *frequent juxtapositions of vowels*: The placement of a word ending in a vowel just before a word beginning with a vowel is sometimes called hiatus.

4. *O Titus Tatius tyrant truly triply tormented*: The verse is generally assumed to be from Ennius, *Annals*.

5. *who hadn't heard how he'd hidden his horse**: Occasionally throughout this section I have composed English examples that illustrate the point being made by the author but do not precisely translate the Latin. Such examples are marked with an asterisk. In this instance the alliteration of h-sounds recalls the repeated qu- of the Latin example, which is drawn from an unknown early Latin comedy.

6. *When the reason ... what he reasons*: Quotation from an unknown Latin playwright.

7. *weepingly, whiningly, woefully, pray for me*: Quotation probably from Ennius, *Annals*.

8. *In a previous book ... Lucius Aelius*: Quotation from Roman historian Lucius Coelius Antipater (late second century BCE), who dedicated his work to Lucius Aelius Stilo.

9. *distinction*: What the author calls 'distinction' is very similar to what Cicero and others refer to as 'ornamented speech'.

10. *figures of language*: There seems to be a short gap in the transmitted Latin text, which moves immediately to a list of figures that are obviously figures of language.

11. *a source of honour*: This and subsequent quotations that are left unannotated are most likely composed by the author of the treatise himself.

12. *as follows*: In the Latin examples the repeated word sometimes shows subtle variation in inflection or in vowel quantity (long versus short). This seems to contribute to what the author describes as the harmonious effect of transduction.

13. *He loves women, hates children, fears vixen**: The Latin phrase is *hominem laudem egentem virtutis, abundantem felicitatis*, which translates, without sound effect, as 'Am I to praise a man devoid of virtue but abounding in good luck?'

14. *Here the words ... endings*: The author differentiates between words whose similar endings are due to similar grammatical form and those whose similarities have another basis.

15. *a slave before he became a Slav**: The Latin puns on the words *venīt* (to be sold as a slave) and *venit* (to come).

16. *The song of the swan distracted the swain**: The Latin puns on *avium* (birds) and *āvium* (wilderness). Latin differentiated the pronunciation of long and short vowels.

17. *prefer the Cūria to Curia*: The Cūria was the Roman senate-house; *Curia* the name of a woman.

18. *friends ... fiends**: The Latin puns on *lenones* (pimps) and *leones* (lions).

19. *case*: In Latin as in Greek, the grammatical function of a substantive is expressed through a case ending. In the English translations, the change in grammatical function is indicated through prepositions, word order or a possessive ending.

20. *Gaius Gracchus*: Presumably Gaius Sempronius Gracchus (tribune of the plebs 123 and 122 BCE), reformist politician killed in political violence in 121 BCE.

21. *You must eat to live, not live to eat*: Ancient sources attribute the saying to Socrates.

22. *I avoid writing poetry ... the kind I can*: The saying has been attributed to Aristarchus, the ancient Greek scholar and editor of Homer.

23. *A poem ... a silent poem*: The saying is often attributed to the Greek lyric poet Simonides (sixth century BCE).

24. *additional examples*: These seem to have disappeared from the manuscript tradition.

25. *asyndeton*: For a number of figures in this section I include in parentheses the more familiar Greek names.

26. *the Gracchi*: Brothers Tiberius Sempronius Gracchus (tribune of the plebs 133 BCE) and Gaius Sempronius Gracchus (tribune of the plebs 123 and 122 BCE) were grandsons of Publius Cornelius Scipio Africanus (sometimes known as Africanus the Elder) (consul 205 BCE), who played a critical role in bringing Rome's Second Punic War, against Hannibal and the Carthaginians, to a successful conclusion.

27. *Capitoline ... Tarpeian Rock*: The Capitoline hill was the traditional citadel of Rome and site of an important temple to Jupiter, Juno and Minerva. The Tarpeian Rock was an outcropping of the hill.

28. *sarisae ... mataris*: Lances and pike, characteristic weapons of the Macedonians and Gauls respectively.

29. *virtue – yours*: 'Your virtue' would be the more natural expression.

30. *Fortune prevailed ... single one*: Translation following the Latin order would be something like 'Unreliable against you most of all did fortune prevail. Every single one chance removed the means of living well', which is incomprehensible in English, but not in Latin due to the use of word inflections that indicate grammatical relationships.

31. *chests ... lungs*: In the Latin example, the word *pulmones* (lungs) is plural in form, even though the Romans conceived of a person's paired lungs as a singular entity.

32. *Permutation*: The figure resembles what other writers call allegory.

33. *Drusus*: Marcus Livius Drusus (tribune of the plebs 91 BCE). Like the brothers Gracchi he advocated land reforms and was assassinated.

34. *Agamemnon ... Atreus*: In Greek mythology Agamemnon was the supreme leader of the Greek forces at Troy. His father, Atreus, was notorious for feeding the children of Thyestes to their unknowing father.

35. *Aeneas ... Hippolytus*: Aeneas was a legendary Trojan hero who escaped the destruction of his city and piously brought his father with him. In Greek mythology Hippolytus, who had taken a vow of sexual chastity, died because of a false accusation made by his stepmother Phaedra.

36. *The duty ... defend himself twice*: The example is either cited or more likely adapted from a speech by Lucius Licinius Crassus (consul 95 BCE, chief speaker in Cicero's *On the Orator*) in defence of a Vestal Virgin charged with inchastity. Lucius Cassius Longinus Ravilla (consul 127 BCE, censor 125 BCE) was official investigator in the case.

37. *Decius ... midst of the enemy*: Decius' act is considered an example of *devotio*, a religious procedure whereby a commander seeks to sacrifice himself in exchange for the success of his troops. Such an act was attributed both to Publius Decius Mus in 340 BCE and to his son of the same name in 295 BCE.

38. *palaestra*: Technically, palaestra refers to a wrestling-ground, especially one that has been enclosed. The palaestra at Olympia was quite large: according to the *Oxford Classical Dictionary*, 217½ ft by 219 ft, large enough to hold an event of the sort described here.

39. *cithara*: The cithara or lyre was a stringed instrument often used to accompany vocal performance. The example asks us to imagine a deficient performance at a musical competition.

40. *chlamys*: A cape of a sort the Romans would have associated with Greeks.

41. *castrated priest from Phrygia*: For the Romans the so-called *galli*, or male worshippers of the goddess Cybele, were exemplary of exotic Asiatic customs. Phrygia is a region of Asia Minor (modern Turkey).

42. *Samian ware*: Inexpensive everyday dishware.

43. *Lucius Brutus*: Lucius Junius Brutus, legendary liberator of Rome from the tyrannical Tarquins and first consul, in 509 BCE.

44. *see so much*: The Latin word translated here as 'see' (*cernis*) can also mean to receive a legacy.

45. *Saturninus ... Gracchi are still unavenged*: Lucius Appuleius Saturninus was tribune of the plebs in 103 BCE and again in 100 BCE, during which year he was killed in rioting. The Gracchi were reformist tribunes of a generation prior who both died in political violence.

46. *Recently consul ... for the seventh time*: The passage provides a concise summary of the career of Gaius Marius (*c.*157–86 BCE) without mentioning him by name.

47. *Gracchus*: The passage describes the assassination of Tiberius Sempronius Gracchus, tribune of the plebs, in 133 BCE. The leader of the assassins was Publius Cornelius Scipio Nasica Serapio, who at the time was pontifex maximus, or chief priest, of Rome.

MEMORY

1. *artificial*: By artificial the author means 'developed through skill or art', not 'false' or 'fake' as the English term sometimes implies.

2. *Decimus*: This name is derived from *decem*, the Latin word for 'ten'.

3. *testicles of a ram*: The Latin word *testiculi* is meant to serve as a reminder of witnesses (*testes*).

4. *Domitius*: No Domitius is mentioned in the verse. Rather, the words *domum itionem* (homecoming) are meant to be remembered through their similarity in sound to the name Domitius.

5. *Marcii Reges*: This was a family at Rome. The example suggests that one might remember the word *reges*, meaning king, by thinking of the family with the same name.

6. *Aesop and Cimber*: Clodius Aesopus was a prominent actor in the first half of the first century BCE. Cimber is otherwise unknown.

7.   *Atridae parant*: The Latin words mean 'the sons of Atreus pre-
     pare'. In Greek mythology Agamemnon and Menelaus were the
     sons of Atreus.

8.   *without his having to seek it*: Throughout this section on mem-
     ory, the author seems to recognize that the active process of
     finding or inventing images strengthens recollection.

9.   *Hortensius*: Quintus Hortensius Hortalus (114–49 BCE, consul
     69 BCE), the most prominent orator of the late Roman Repub-
     lic, with the exception of Cicero.

10. *five speeches of the second action against Verres*: About one
     hundred pages in a modern edition.

11. *Charmadas ... Metrodorus of Scepsis*: Charmadas was a
     Greek philosopher (second century BCE) and follower of Car-
     neades. Metrodorus of Scepsis (late second and early first
     century BCE) was a Greek intellectual closely affiliated with
     King Mithradates of Pontus.

12. *Fabius the famous Delayer*: Quintilian refers to the Roman
     general Quintus Fabius Maximus Verrucosus Cunctator, who
     during the second Punic War sought to wear down the enemy
     forces by leading them on without engaging in pitched battle.

13. *Cicero, Verrius or Aurelius*: These Roman names recall the
     Latin words for chick-pea, swine and gold, respectively.

14. *Scaevola, in a game of twelve rows*: Probably P. Mucius
     Scaevola, consul 133 BCE, who is mentioned as an adept of
     'twelve rows' and of ball-playing at Cicero, *On the Orator*
     1.217. The game of twelve rows involved throwing dice and
     moving pieces on a board.

15. *either*: I.e., remember what's he written or speak well
     extemporaneously.

16. *Themistocles ... Cyrus*: Themistocles (*c.*524–459 BCE) was the
     leader of the Athenians against the invading Persians. Mithra-
     dates VI Eupator Dionysus (r. 120–63 BCE) was king of Pontus
     in Asia Minor and a powerful opponent of Roman expansion in
     the East. Marcus Licinius Crassus (115–53 BCE) was an impor-
     tant politician and military leader during the later years of the
     Roman Republic, part of the so-called First Triumvirate
     together with Pompey the Great and Julius Caesar. Cyrus is pre-
     sumably Cyrus the Great, Persian king (sixth century BCE).

17. *Theodectes*: Greek poet, orator and rhetorician of the fourth
     century BCE.

DELIVERY

1. *Calvus . . . Vatinius*: Gaius Licinius Calvus (82–*c*.47 BCE) was a Roman orator, politician, poet and younger contemporary of Cicero. In 54 BCE he prosecuted Publius Vatinius for bribery, but the latter was successfully defended by Cicero.

2. *Speeches against Verres*: Gaius Verres was successfully denounced by Cicero (70 BCE) for his mistreatment of the residents of Sicily while governor there. Six Ciceronian speeches against Verres survive, but only one was actually delivered, so successful was Cicero's rhetorical onslaught.

3. *Cossutianus Capito*: Roman senator tried for extortion in 57 CE. See Tacitus, *Annals* 13.33 and 16.21.

4. *Demosthenes . . . Meidias . . . occasion of the crime*: The Greek orator Demosthenes registered a judicial complaint against fellow Athenian Meidias for publicly slapping him at a religious festival (351–350 BCE). The speech, known as *Against Meidias*, is extant.

5. *Messalla . . . defendant herself*: Quintilian mentions this case at 4.2.106, 10.1.22, but the date and details are obscure. See E. Malcovati, *Oratorum Romanorum Fragmenta*, 4th edn (Turin: Paravia, 1976), p. 531.

6. *Aeschines . . . making a defence*: The reference is to Aeschines, *Against Ctesiphon* 207.

7. *Cicero . . . elder Scaurus . . . the younger*: Marcus Aemilius Scaurus (praetor 56 BCE) was successfully defended by Cicero against charges of extortion in his province of Sardinia. Nothing more is known about the legal troubles of his son of the same name.

8. *For Milo*: Quintilian quotes Cicero, *For Milo* 102. Cicero unsuccessfully defended Titus Annius Milo (praetor 54 BCE) on the charge of murdering his political rival Publius Clodius Pulcher. The surviving speech was not the one Cicero delivered at the trial, which was repeatedly disrupted by violence.

9. *In vain . . . My useless plans!*: Cicero, *For Milo* 94.

10. *bloody toga of Julius Caesar*: Gaius Julius Caesar (100–44 BCE), the famous general, politician and dictator, was assassinated in Rome in 44 BCE. His funeral, discussed by several ancient sources (Plutarch, *Caesar* 68 and *Brutus* 20, Suetonius, *Deified Julius* 84), was an occasion for rallying his supporters against his assassins.

11. *defence of Lucius Murena against very distinguished accusers*: Cicero, as consul in 63 BCE, defended Lucius Licinius Murena,

the consul-elect for the following year, against charges of bribery during his campaign. The 'distinguished accusers' of Murena included the jurist Servius Sulpicius Rufus and the senator Marcus Porcius Cato (Cato the Younger).

12. *the Caepasii*: As Cicero discusses in his speech *For Cluentius* 56–9, the brothers Caepasii were energetic but ineffective orators. One of them delivered such an embarrassing speech that his client left the courtroom before it was over, leaving the speaker in an even more embarrassing situation when he got to the part of his script that told him and the audience to 'look closely' at the defendant – who of course was out of the line of sight.

13. *Cassius*: Orator during the early years of the Roman principate, renowned for his caustic wit.

14. *Saturninus in defence of Rabirius*: In his surviving speech in defence of Rabirius, Cicero indicated that opposing counsel had introduced a portrait of the tribune of the plebs Saturninus, who with his wife was killed in political violence. Cicero suggests that possession of such a portrait could lead to banishment.

15. *defence of Varenus*: The speech does not survive.

16. *Passienus ... Ahenobarbus*: Gaius Sallustius Passienus Crispus (consul 27 and 44 CE), a prominent orator and politician during the early years of the principate, was married to the emperor Augustus' great niece Domitia. Her brother, Gnaeus Domitius Ahenobarbus (consul 32 CE), was the father of the future emperor Nero.

17. *applaud*: Many of the surviving plays of Plautus and Terence end just this way.

18. *altercation*: Altercation was a section of the legal process set aside for back-and-forth sparring between representatives of the prosecution and defence. As Quintilian suggests, it required special training and handling.

19. *Lycians and Carians*: Quintilian refers to some of the Greek-speaking communities of Asia Minor.

20. *Speakers from Lycia and Caria all but sang their perorations*: Cicero, *Orator* 57 actually speaks of orators from Phrygia (also in Asia Minor) and Caria

21. *'hint of song' in oratory*: See Cicero, *Orator* 57.

22. *in a manly manner*: See Cicero, *Orator* 59.

23. *Cleon*: Athenian general and orator during the early years of the Peloponnesian War between Athens and Sparta. He was killed in battle in 422 BCE. The historian Thucydides assigns

a number of important speeches to Cleon in his history of
the war.

24. *'no smacking of the forehead, no striking of the thigh'*: Quoted
from Cicero, *Brutus* 278.

25. *rare and of no long duration*: Cited from Cicero, *Orator* 59.

26. *what Domitius Afer called Manlius Sura's 'hyperactivity'*:
Gnaeus Domitius Afer (consul 39 CE) achieved notoriety as a
prosecutor, or *delator*, under the emperor Tiberius. The Manlius Sura to whom Afer referred is unknown.

27. *Flavus Verginius*: First century CE rhetorician, exiled by the
emperor Nero (Tacitus, *Annals* 15.71).

28. *as Cicero indicates*: Cicero, *On the Orator* 3.220.

29. *Cicero faulted in Titius*: *Brutus* 225.

30. *Julius made fun of in the elder Curio*: Quintilian refers to Gaius
Julius Caesar Strabo Vopiscus (curule aedile 90 BCE) and Gaius
Scribonius Curio (consul 76 BCE).

31. *Sicinius ... Curio ... Octavius*: Gnaeus Sicinius (perhaps the
Sicinius who was tribune of the plebs 76 BCE), Gaius Scribonius
Curio (consul 76 BCE), and Gnaeus Octavius (also consul 76
BCE).

32. *storm of eloquence*: Homer, *Iliad* 3.217.

33. *as I have explained above*: At Quintilian, *Oratorical Instruction* 11.3.142, not included here.

RHETORIC AND COGNITION

1. *Antonius*: Marcus Antonius, consul 99 BCE, and one of the
main speakers in the dialogue *On the Orator*.

2. *Men of old*: Crassus doesn't specify who he has in mind, but the
account of universal, harmonious integration closely resembles
that of the Stoics, which Cicero describes in detail in Book 2 of
On the Nature of the Gods, available in the Penguin volume
Cicero on Living and Dying Well (Harmondsworth, 2011).

3. *a true saying of Plato*: There is no clear source for this saying in
the surviving writings of Plato.

4. *Catulus*: Quintus Lutatius Catulus (consul 102 BCE) is depicted
by Cicero as a lover of Greek learning.

5. *Myro, Polyclitus and Lysippus*: Greek sculptors of the mid-
fifth, late fifth and early fourth centuries BCE, respectively.

6. *Zeuxis, Aglaophon and Apelles*: Greek painters of the fifth and
fourth centuries BCE.

7. *Ennius, Pacuvius and Accius*: Quintus Ennius (239–169 BCE), Marcus Pacuvius (220–*c*.130 BCE) and Lucius Accius (170–*c*.86 BCE) all wrote Greek-style tragic dramas in Latin.

8. *Aeschylus, Sophocles and Euripides*: Aeschylus (*c*.525/4–456/5 BCE), Sophocles (*c*.496–406 BCE) and Euripides (*c*.480–*c*.406 BCE) were the three most famous tragic playwrights of ancient Athens.

9. *Isocrates ... Demosthenes*: Crassus lists five pre-eminent speech-writers from the late fifth to the late fourth century BCE: Isocrates (436–338 BCE), Lysias (*c*.459–*c*.380 BCE), Hyperides (389–322 BCE), Aeschines (*c*.397–*c*.322 BCE) and Demosthenes (384–322 BCE).

10. *Africanus ... Carbo*: Crassus lists outstanding Roman orators of the previous century, including Publius Cornelius Scipio Aemilianus Africanus (185–129 BCE), Scipio's close friend Gaius Laelius (184–*c*.124 BCE), Servius Sulpicius Galba (consul 144 BCE) and Gaius Papirius Carbo (*c*.163–119 BCE), a political opponent of Crassus who committed suicide after a conviction in a case prosecuted by Crassus.

11. *Catulus*: Quintus Lutatius Catulus (consul 102 BCE).

12. *Caesar*: Gaius Julius Caesar Strabo Vopiscus (*c*.130–87 BCE). Caesar and Catulus both died during civic strife.

13. *Sulpicius and Cotta*: Publius Sulpicius Rufus (*c*.124–88 BCE), who, like Caesar and Catulus, died as a result of political turmoil, and Gaius Aurelius Cotta (*c*.124–*c*.74 BCE, consul 75 BCE).

14. *Isocrates ... Ephorus ... Theopompus*: Isocrates (436–338 BCE) was famous as both a writer and a teacher. Ephorus (*c*. 405–330 BCE) and Theopompus (378/7–*c*.320 BCE) were Greek historians whose works are mostly lost to us but had a significant impact on other ancient writers. Crassus' choice of examples shows that he regards rhetoric as relevant to other genres besides oratory, as indeed it was.

15. *The ornate*: For a fuller treatment of this concept see the section of this volume called 'Rhetorical Ornament'.

16. *'There stood ... each contestant'*: Quintilian quotes without attribution Virgil, *Aeneid* 5.426.

17. *on the shore ... propped up on his pathetic female companion*: Quintilian quotes Cicero, *Against Verres* 2.5.86.

18. *sumptuous banquet*: The quoted passage is from a speech of Cicero that does not survive, probably on behalf of Quintus Gallius.

19. *Chill horror ... congeals from fear*: Virgil, *Aeneid* 3.29–30.

20. *Trembling mothers . . . to their breasts*: Virgil, *Aeneid* 7.518.
21. *like a dark cloud of ravenous wolves*: Virgil, *Aeneid* 2.355–6.
22. *like a bird . . . fish-filled reefs*: Virgil, *Aeneid* 4.254–5.
23. *as when Apollo . . . maternal Delos*: Virgil, *Aeneid* 4.143–4.
24. *as the soil . . . cut away*: The examples seem to have been invented by Quintilian for purposes of illustration.
25. *Rocks and deserts . . . the sound of song*: Cicero, *For Archias* 19.
26. *As when the chariots . . . restraint*: Virgil, *Georgics* 1.512–14.
27. *As they say of Greek musicians . . . the law*: Cicero, *For Murena* 29.
28. *For just as storms . . . no apparent reason*: Cicero, *For Murena* 36.
29. *speech against Clodius*: Publius Clodius Pulcher (*c*.93–52 BCE) was a fierce political enemy of Cicero. The speech in question does not survive.
30. *Celsus*: Aulus Cornelius Celsus, first century CE, wrote treatises on a wide variety of arts and sciences. His work on rhetoric does not survive, but his treatise on medicine does.
31. *Our villain . . . flashing with cruelty*: The quotation is from Cicero, *Against Verres* 2.5.161.
32. *what Clodius . . . praetorship*: See Cicero, *For Milo* 32.
33. *what you didn't see . . . your minds*: There is no known source for this quotation.
34. *Lead, I follow . . . block my view*: The quotations are from a lost section of Seneca the Elder's treatise on *Controversies*.

RHETORICAL ORNAMENT

1. *Eloquence, you see, is one of the greatest virtues*: Crassus here follows Stoic doctrine, with modifications.
2. *Lycurgus, Pittacus and Solon*: Cicero has Crassus list three legendary Greek lawgivers. Lycurgus of Sparta, Pittacus of Mitylene and Solon of Athens. Pittacus and Solon were also traditionally included among the Seven Sages of the Greek world.
3. *Coruncanius, Fabricius, Cato and Scipio*: Here as elsewhere in his writings Cicero identifies figures from the Roman past as comparable to the legendary leaders of Greece. These include Tiberius Coruncanius (consul 280 BCE), Gaius Fabricius Luscinus (consul 282 and 278 BCE), Marcus Porcius Cato (consul 195 BCE), also known as Cato the Elder or Cato the Censor, and almost certainly Publius Cornelius Scipio Aemilianus Africanus (consul 147 and 134 BCE).

4. *Pythagoras, Democritus and Anaxagoras*: Three well-known Greek philosophers, considered pre-Socratics for pre-dating Socrates and especially Plato. Pythagoras lived in the second half of the sixth century BCE, Democritus in the latter part of the fifth century BCE, and Anaxagoras from about 500 to 428 BCE. Although it is probably true that none of the three 'governed' a community, the followers of Pythagoras played an important role in the political life of south Italian communities.

5. *Phoenix in Homer . . . and a doer of deeds*: See Homer, *Iliad* 9.438–43, part of an episode in which Phoenix and others seek to induce Achilles to reconcile with the Greek leader, Agamemnon.

6. *as you, Caesar, will have to do in the coming year*: At the dramatic date of the dialogue, Caesar had been elected as curule aedile, a position that included responsibility for public works. Crassus may be drawing an analogy between the organization of material resources and the construction of a speech.

7. *although as censor . . . their impudence strengthened*: The character Crassus refers in somewhat evasive terms to the historical Crassus' closure of the Latin schools of declamation in 92 BCE. The explanation given here, that he thought the teachers were not very good, is unlikely to be the whole story.

8. *Roscius*: Quintus Roscius, the most famous stage actor of the first half of the first century BCE. Cicero represented him in a private lawsuit from which his speech, *For Roscius the Actor*, survives.

9. *The wise man . . . prey*: This verse and the next from an unknown Roman tragedy, perhaps the *Hecuba* of Ennius, which would have dealt with the destruction of Troy, the city of Priam.

10. *O Father . . . Priam*: This and the preceding quotation are from Ennius, *Andromacha*.

11. *topics*: These are general themes that arise in many oratorical contexts and thus can be prepared ahead of time. The use of the Latin term *locus* (place) in this context should not be confused with the use of the same word for the backgrounds selected as part of the memory-system described in the *Rhetoric to Herennius*.

12. *two schools of philosophy I discussed earlier*: Crassus seems to refer to philosophers who believed in the knowability of truth (so-called dogmatics) versus those who denied the possibility of secure human knowledge (sceptics). More specifically, he may have in mind the Old Academy and the New Academy.

13. *small part of their city*: Crassus treats the Peripatetics, i.e. Aristotle and his successors, as part of the Old Academy more generally. Before its association with philosophy, the Academy was the site of a grove near Athens sacred to the goddess Athena.

14. *Philo*: Philo of Larissa (159/8–84/3 BCE), leader of the Academy at Athens before relocating to Rome. He was a teacher of Quintus Lutatius Catulus, who appears elsewhere in *On the Orator*, and of Cicero himself.

15. *Hippocrates of Cos*: A physician to whom many writings are attributed, although little is known about his life. He probably lived in the fifth century BCE, and is the source of the famous 'Hippocratic Oath' taken by medical professionals.

16. *Euclid and Archimedes, Damon and Aristoxenus, or Aristophanes and Callimachus*: Crassus lists some of the most famous scholars of Greek antiquity: the mathematicians Euclid (perhaps third century BCE) and Archimedes (third century BCE), the musicologists Damon (fifth century BCE) and Aristoxenus (fourth century BCE), the literary scholar Aristophanes of Byzantium (c.257–180 BCE) and the poet-scholar Callimachus (third century BCE).

17. *Sextus Aelius . . . Manius Manilius*: Crassus refers to two earlier Romans, both of whom he describes as distinguished legal experts elsewhere in *On the Orator*: Sextus Aelius Paetus Catus (consul 198 BCE) and Manius Manilius (consul 149 BCE).

18. *Publius Crassus . . . Tiberius Coruncanius . . . Scipio*: Publius Crassus (consul 205 BCE), Tiberius Coruncanius (consul 280 BCE) and Publius Cornelius Scipio Nasica Corculum (censor 159 BCE).

19. *pontifex maximus*: The chief priest of Rome, head of the college of pontiffs that made determinations about ritual propriety.

20. *Cato*: Marcus Porcius Cato (consul 195 BCE), also known as Cato the Elder. There is good reason to believe that Cato was more knowledgeable about Greek literature and culture than many ancient sources would seem to imply: see A. E. Astin, *Cato the Censor* (Oxford: Clarendon Press, 1978), pp. 157–81.

21. *Thales the Milesian*: A natural philosopher from the sixth century BCE. The Seven Sages were generally regarded as Thales, Bias of Priene, Cleobulus of Rhodes, Pittacus of Mitylene, Solon of Athens, Chilon of Sparta and Periander of Corinth.

22. *Peisistratus*: Sixth-century BCE tyrant of Athens. During his rule and that of his successors Athens emerged as a powerful city-state. Peisistratus was said to have commissioned full

copies of Homer's *Iliad* and *Odyssey*, to be deposited in archives at Athens.

23. *Pericles*: Pericles (*c*.495–429 BCE) was perhaps the most influential leader of democratic Athens. He favoured monumental building projects in the heart of the city, initiated a reform of requirements for citizenship and articulated the military strategy followed by the Athenians in the early years of the Peloponnesian War against Sparta and her allies.

24. *Anaxagoras of Clazomenae*: A natural scientist who was convicted of impiety and expelled from Athens in 433 BCE.

25. *Critias or Alcibiades*: Critias (*c*.460–403 BCE) was an orator, playwright and politician. He died fighting as one of the Thirty Tyrants, an oligarchic group that briefly governed Athens after its defeat by Sparta. Alcibiades (451/5–404/3 BCE) was an unusually controversial Athenian general and politician. Critias and Alcibiades are both depicted as students of Socrates in the dialogues of Plato.

26. *Dio the Syracusan*: Would-be ruler of Sicily (*c*.408–353 BCE), his political agenda was said to have been strongly influenced by his studies with the philosopher Plato.

27. *Isocrates . . . Timotheus . . . Conon*: Isocrates (436–338 BCE) was an important writer and thinker with many famous pupils, including the Athenian general Timotheus, whose father Conon was also a military leader.

28. *Lysis the Pythagorean . . . Epaminondas of Thebes*: Lysis was a fifth-century BCE follower of Pythagoras from southern Italy. Epaminondas was a highly successful Theban general (fourth century BCE) who led his city's forces in struggles against Sparta and Athens.

29. *Xenophon teacher of Agesilaus*: Xenophon (*c*.430–355 BCE) was a well-known Athenian writer, soldier and follower of Socrates. Agesilaus (*c*.445–359 BCE) was king of Sparta, leader in its continuing military struggles, especially against Persia and Thebes.

30. *Philolaus . . . Archytas of Tarentum*: Philolaus (*c*.470–390 BCE) was a southern Italian follower of Pythagoras. Archytas (died *c*.350 BCE) was also a Pythagorean philosopher, as well as being elected general at Tarentum repeatedly.

31. *Pythagoras . . . called 'great'*: Pythagoras was an important philosopher who lived in the second half of the sixth century BCE. His followers were influential in southern Italy and Sicily for many years. The areas of Sicily and the Italian peninsula that

were colonized by the Greeks as early as the eighth century BCE achieved great wealth and were sometimes clustered together under the name Magna Graecia, or Great Greece.

32. *For Philoctetes ... shameful to let Isocrates speak*: The anecdote is not preserved in the surviving treatises attributed to Aristotle. The remark from Philoctetes may be drawn from Euripides' play of that name, as David Mankin (ed.), Cicero, O *De Oratore, Book III* (Cambridge: Cambridge University Press, 2011), p. 229, suggests.

33. *wise king Philip ... his son*: Philip is Philip II (382–336 BCE), king of Macedon, and his son is Alexander the Great (356–323 BCE), whose conquests extended as far as India.

34. *Caelius*: Either Caelius, and thus probably the Roman historian Lucius Coelius Antipater, whose works included a history of the Second Punic War between Rome and Carthage; or, as in the manuscripts, Laelius, thus Gaius Laelius (184–*c*.124 BCE), the close friend of Scipio and also the grandfather of Crassus' wife.

35. *progeny, scion, prognosticate or appellation*: The terms are rough equivalents of the Latin *proles, suboles, effari, nuncupare*.

36. *I reckoned not ... I opined*: The Latin expressions are *non rebar* and *opinabar*.

37. *The sea shudders ... is boiling*: The quoted lines are from a tragedy by the Latin author Pacuvius (220–*c*.130 BCE), in a scene describing the destruction of much of the Greek fleet on its return from Troy. See discussion by Mankin (ed.), Cicero, *De Oratore, Book III*, p. 244.

38. *he cloaks himself ... with deceit*: Verse quoted from an unknown Latin drama.

39. *if the weapon flees his hand*: Cited from the Twelve Tables of early Roman law.

40. *'foot' on a boat*: The Latin word *pes* refers to the rope that binds the bottom of a sail to the deck of a ship.

41. *the massive archways of heaven*: Citation from an unknown play of Ennius.

42. *yet a sphere is nothing like an archway*: It's not clear what Crassus finds objectionable about the metaphor.

43. *Live, Ulysses ... with your eyes*: Citation from an unknown Latin drama.

44. *Syrtis ... whirlpool*: The Syrtes were notoriously dangerous sand banks off the coast of Libya. Charybdis was a whirlpool in the Straits of Messina, sometimes depicted in mythology as a water-belching monster.

45. *Africanus ... Glaucia*: Presumably Publius Cornelius Scipio
     Aemilianus Africanus, also known as Scipio Africanus the
     Younger, who led the Roman forces in the third and final war
     against Carthage; and Gaius Servilius Glaucia (praetor 100
     BCE).

46. *decline*: The Latin word used here, *abnuas* or *abnutas*, indi-
     cates general disapproval, which is rather weak in context, as
     Crassus points out. The cited verses are thought to be from a
     play by Ennius.

47. *I will not suffer ... yoke of authority*: Both quotations are from
     unknown Latin dramas.

48. *rugged Africa ... tumult*: The verse is Ennius, *Annals* 309.

49. *the sea with smashingrock waves*: A phrase possibly drawn
     from Ennius, *Annals*.

50. *the sea softens*: The passage is from a lost play by the Roman
     dramatist Pacuvius.

51. *cease, Rome, your enemies*: It is unclear whether this and the
     following quotation are from specific works or expressions
     invented for this context.

52. *the Roman ... in his heart*: The verses are Ennius, *Annals*
     560–61.

53. *Rudine*: Ennius, *Annals* 525. The Latin expression uses plural
     forms throughout, even though the passage is understood to
     refer only to an individual speaker, namely the poet Ennius
     himself.

54. *father-in-law*: The author in question is the early Roman sati-
     rist Gaius Lucilius (*c.*180–103/2 BCE). The father-in-law of
     Crassus is Quintus Mucius Scaevola Augur (*c.*165–87 BCE).

55. *Albucius*: Titus Albucius (praetor 105 BCE), a Roman politician
     and philhellene who brought an unsuccessful prosecution
     against Scaevola.

56. *Isocrates ... Naucrates*: Isocrates: see note 27 above. Naucrates
     the Erythraean was a less prominent fourth century BCE
     intellectual.

57. *And, much to our amazement ... most beautiful*: The entire
     passage resembles Balbus' presentation of Stoic physical doc-
     trine in Book 2 of Cicero, *On the Nature of the Gods*, which
     emphasizes the beauty and functionality of nature. The descrip-
     tion of the relationship of the earth to the other planets also
     corresponds to the theories of the Greek astronomer Eudoxus.

58. *your Aristotle, Catulus*: Aristotle is of course the famous Greek
     philosopher. Catulus, one of the characters in *On the Orator*, is

Quintus Catulus (consul 102 BCE), often depicted as a lover of Greek learning.

59. *iamb and trochee*: Generally speaking, an iamb consists of a short syllable followed by a long, a trochee is the reverse. But Cicero here uses the term *trochaeus* to refer to a run of three short syllables.

60. *heroic metre*: That is, the dactylic hexameter, standard metre of heroic epic in both Greek and Latin. A dactyl is a metrical foot consisting of a long syllable followed by two short.

61. *then give it up ... push down on it*: The Latin words are *desinite, incipite, comprimite*.

62. *'when they had crushed' ... 'the clatter of hooves'*: The Latin words are *domuerant, sonipedes*.

63. *'how to seek, where to find, when to run'*: The English roughly translates a passage Cicero quotes from Ennius: 'quid petam praesidi, aut exsequar? quove nunc?'

64. *Fannius ... threats*: The identity of this Fannius is uncertain. The English roughly translates the Latin *si Quirites, minas illius*.

65. *Theophrastus*: Greek philosopher and scientist, successor of Aristotle.

66. *dithyramb*: Dithyramb was originally a type of Greek cultic poetry. As it developed, it abandoned the strict correspondence between stanzas that generally characterized lyric metres.

67. *Antonius*: Marcus Antonius (consul 99 BCE), one of the two main speakers in *On the Orator*.

68. *Antipater of Sidon*: A Greek poet contemporary with Catulus and Crassus.

69. *Numa*: Numa was the second king of Rome, often regarded as having created the musical culture of the city, along with various rituals.

70. *Salian priests*: A troupe of priests who periodically sang and danced their way around the city of Rome. Their ritual was said to have been founded by Numa, who was their first leader.

71. *But there's a difference ... words you use*: Compare the discussion in the *Rhetoric to Herennius* in the section 'Style', above. Cicero has Crassus present an informal list of figures rather than detailed definition with examples. As often within the rhetorical tradition, the names of figures as presented by one rhetorician do not necessarily match those used by another. Yet by and large, the actual figures remain the same.

72. *the precepts of Caesar*: Crassus refers to the instructions on wit provided earlier in *On the Orator* by Gaius Julius Caesar Strabo Vopiscus (curule aedile 90 BCE).

73. *Cotta*: Gaius Aurelius Cotta (consul 75 BCE).

74. *Demosthenes*: Pre-eminent Athenian orator, fourth century BCE.

75. *Aeschines*: Athenian orator, fourth century BCE, and rival of Demosthenes.

76. *the famous speech against Ctesiphon*: Athenian orator and politician, he proposed that Demosthenes be awarded a crown for his services to the city. Aeschines prosecuted him for this action, while Demosthenes defended him in his own speech, *On the Crown*.

77. *Where in my misery ... despondent*: Crassus quotes from a famous speech by Gaius Sempronius Gracchus (tribune of the plebs 123 and 122 BCE), purportedly delivered the day he was killed. He refers to the earlier death of his brother Tiberius Sempronius Gracchus, also in political violence.

78. *He urges me ... my jaws*: Verses quoted from either Ennius' *Thyestes* or Accius' *Atreus*. Thyestes was fed morsels of his murdered sons by his evil brother Atreus.

79. *You dared to separate from yourself*: From the *Teucer* of Pacuvius.

80. *Does no one take note? Tie him up!*: Quoted from Accius' *Atreus*.

81. *Atreus*: Accius wrote a play called *Atreus*; but the Latin may also mean 'just about anything said by Atreus' (i.e., the character, who would have appeared in Ennius' *Thyestes* as well).

82. *Where now am I ... daughters of Pelias*: Lines spoken by the title character in Ennius' *Medea*. Medea has had Pelias murdered.

83. *O father ... deprived of life*: From Ennius' *Andromacha*. The title character laments the destruction of Troy.

84. *I am besieged ... these threats*: The verses are taken from Ennius' *Alcmeo*. The title character has killed his mother Eriphyle.

85. *Again Thyestes ... cruel heart*: The verses are quoted from Accius' *Atreus*.

86. *But when she carried ... delicately*: The source of the quotation is unknown.

87. *At the time ... Polydorus*: The verses are quoted from a Roman drama, possibly Pacuvius' *Iliona*.

88. *Theophrastus quotes Tauriscus*: Theophrastus: see note 65 above. Tauriscus is unknown.

89. *Gracchus ... Catulus*: The Gracchus in question is Gaius Sempronius Gracchus (tribune of the plebs 123, 122 BCE). The slave who reported the story had at some point been freed and become a client (free dependant) of Catulus. Many slaves were war captives who had been well educated prior to enslavement. Catulus is Quintus Catulus (consul 102 BCE).

90. *Hortensius*: Quintus Hortensius Hortalus (114–49 BCE, consul 69 BCE), most prominent orator of the late Roman Republic, with the exception of Cicero.

91. *my consulship*: Crassus was consul in 95 BCE.

92. *king of Bithynia*: Bithynia was a small independent kingdom in Asia Minor. Its king, as a non-Roman, could have sought the assistance of a Roman politician in advancing his diplomatic interests.

93. *Cotta ... Sulpicius*: Gaius Aurelius Cotta (*c.*124–*c.*74 BCE, consul 75 BCE) and Publius Sulpicius Rufus (tribune of the plebs 88 BCE) appear as representatives of a generation between Crassus and Hortensius.

THE LIFE OF THE ORATOR

1. *declamations in character or on deliberative themes*: Such declamations are sometimes classified as *Suasoriae*, as in the treatise of the same name by Seneca the Elder. They ask the student to give advice to a historical or mythical figure at some crisis in his life.

2. *Quintus Hortensius*: Quintus Hortensius Hortalus (114–49 BCE, consul 69 BCE), most prominent orator of the late Roman Republic, with the exception of Cicero.

3. *Timotheus*: Greek lyre player and composer of dithyrambs (*c.* 450–360 BCE).

4. *Phidias*: Athenian sculptor (latter part of fifth century BCE). His statue of Zeus (Roman Jupiter) at Olympia was considered one of the most remarkable sculptures of the ancient world.

5. *Phoenix*: The tutor of Achilles, he accompanied him to the war at Troy according to Homer's *Iliad*.

6. '*I want creativity to express itself in the young*': Cicero, *On the Orator* 2.88.

7.   *shrink from the blade*: The phrase echoes Virgil, *Georgics* 2.369.

8.   *whether it's believable ... Egeria*: The themes ask the student to reflect on the likelihood of famous incidents from Roman history. Marcus Valerius Corvus was military tribune in 349 BCE. When he faced an enormous Gallic warrior in single combat, a raven is said to have attacked the enemy's face, making it possible for Valerius to defeat him. Various legends clustered around Publius Cornelius Scipio Africanus (236–183 BCE), who led the Roman victory in the Second Punic War. Romulus, the first king of Rome, was supposedly nursed (together with his twin Remus) by a she-wolf, and Numa, the second king of Rome, was said to have held consultations with the local water-nymph Egeria.

9.   *Livy*: Titus Livius (59 BCE–17 CE), Roman historian, author of a 142-volume work on the history of Rome from its legendary origins to his own lifetime. Livy explicitly withholds judgement about the veracity of many stories concerning the early periods of Roman history.

10. *the third section of rhetoric ... own place*: Quintilian discusses the topic in *Oratorical Instruction*, Book 3, chapter 7.

11. *Cicero ... Speech in Defence of Murena*. In 63 BCE Cicero defended the newly elected consul Lucius Licinius Murena against charges of electoral misconduct. During the speech he contrasts Murena's contributions to the Roman state with that of the highly legalistic prosecution team.

12. *why is Cupid ... arrows and a torch*: The question forms the basis for Elegy 2.12 by the Augustan-era poet Sextus Propertius.

13. *controversiae*: Controversiae are exercises that deal with a problematical application of a law or conflict between laws. Numerous examples survive in Seneca the Elder's treatise called *Controversiae*.

14. *suasoriae*: These are exercises in which the student must advise a character from history or legend at a moment of crisis, or persuade an imaginary audience to follow a particular course of action. Numerous examples survive in Seneca the Elder's treatise called *Suasoriae*.

15. *Publius Clodius*: Presumably Publius Clodius Pulcher (*c*.93–52 BCE). He had himself transferred from the patrician to the plebeian wing of his clan in order to run for the position of tribune of the plebs. He was an inveterate enemy of Cicero.

16. *the Manilian law, on which we have Cicero's speech*: The Manilian Law of 66 BCE gave Pompey command of the Roman forces against King Mithradates VI Eupator of Pontus. Cicero argued strongly in its favour in a speech called *On the Manilian Law* or *On the Command of Pompey*.

17. *Demetrius of Phalerum*: Athenian orator, scholar and politician (*c*.350–*c*.280 BCE). He was appointed by the Macedonians as, in effect, regent of Athens.

18. *Cicero is the one ... being the most famous*: The early Latin schools of declamation, which were suppressed by Crassus (consul 95 BCE), are discussed in Cicero, *On the Orator* 3. 93–4.

19. *chunk by chunk*: Roman students often encountered texts written continuously without punctuation. The preliminary reading mentioned here may have included the addition of punctuation on the part of the student. See T. Habinek, *The Colometry of Latin Prose* (Berkeley: University of California Press, 1985).

20. *Livy rather than Sallust*: Livy: see note 9 above. The surviving works of Sallust (86–*c*.35 BCE) include monographic studies of the Conspiracy of Catiline and the War with Jugurtha.

21. *Gracchi and Cato*: Tiberius Sempronius Gracchus (tribune of the plebs 133 BCE), Gaius Sempronius Gracchus (tribune of the plebs 123 and 122 BCE) and Marcus Porcius Cato (consul 195 BCE) left a number of speeches that were still available to readers of Quintilian's day.

22. *Isocrates ... Ephorus ... Theopompus*: Isocrates (436–338 BCE) was an Athenian intellectual who had many prominent students including the historians Ephorus and Theopompus.

23. *Nicostratus*: Famous athlete of the middle of the first century CE. The victories referred to here took place in 37 CE.

24. *sponsions and interdicts*: Technical features of Roman law. A sponsion is a formal pledge made on behalf of another; an interdict is a remedy imposed by the praetor in cases where the law offers no specific guidelines.

25. *Theodorus or Apollodorus, said, 'I follow the Thracians'*: Theodorus and Apollodorus were leaders of opposing schools of rhetoric. The unnamed wit acts as though they were leaders of athletic teams or representatives of particular sports (the word translated here as 'Thracians' is *parmularius*, which refers to a type of shield used by so-called Thracian gladiators).

26. *not in the shade, as Cicero has it*: The reference is to Cicero, *On the Orator* 3.101.

27. *Gaius Curio*: Gaius Scribonius Curio (consul 76 BCE), occasionally a political opponent of Cicero.

28. *Quintus Metellus Celer ... Quintus Varius, Gaius Carbo and Gnaeus Pomponius*: Cicero lists of number of less well-known figures who were active in his youth, i.e. Quintus Caecilius Metellus Celer (consul 60 BCE), Quintus Varius (tribune of the plebs 91 BCE), Gaius Papirius Carbo (tribune of the plebs 90 BCE), who was killed by supporters of Marius in 82 BCE, and Gnaeus Pomponius (tribune of the plebs 90 BCE).

29. *Gaius Julius*: Gaius Julius Caesar Strabo Vopiscus was curule aedile in 90 BCE. He has a speaking part in Cicero's dialogue *On the Orator*.

30. *Cotta*: Gaius Aurelius Cotta (*c*.124–*c*.74 BCE, consul 75 BCE) was exiled in 90 BCE by a commission charged with identifying Romans who had aided the Italians during the Social War. He appears as a character in Cicero's *On the Orator*.

31. *Quintus Varius*: Tribune of the plebs in 91 BCE, established the commission that exiled Cotta. It ended up exiling him as well.

32. *Quintus Scaevola*: Quintus Mucius Scaevola, the augur (consul 177 BCE). He has an important speaking role in Cicero, *On the Orator*.

33. *Sulla and Pompey*: Lucius Cornelius Sulla Felix (*c*.138–78 BCE) was a Roman military and political leader known for his brutal treatment of political opponents. Quintus Pompeius Rufus, was consul along with Sulla in 88 BCE.

34. *Publius Sulpicius*: Publius Sulpicius Rufus was tribune of the plebs in 88 BCE and a political ally of Gaius Marius (*c*.157–86 BCE). He also figures in Cicero's treatise *On the Orator* as an eager student of the chief speaker, Crassus.

35. *Philo*: Philo of Larissa (159/8–84/3 BCE), leader of the Academy at Athens before fleeing to Rome.

36. *Quintus Catulus, Marcus Antonius and Gaius Julius*: Quintus Lutatius Catulus (consul 102 BCE) and Gaius Julius Caesar Strabo Vopiscus (curule aedile 90 BCE) both appear in Cicero's *On the Orator*. Marcus Antonius (consul 99 BCE) was one of the two main speakers in the same work.

37. *Molo the Rhodian*: A famous professor of Greek rhetoric who also served as ambassador from Rhodes to Rome. Besides Cicero, Julius Caesar also studied with him. Also known as Apollonius Molon.

38. *Brutus*: Cicero turns to one of the interlocutors in the represented dialogue and the namesake of the treatise, Marcus Junius
Brutus (85–42 BCE). The date of composition of the *Brutus* is
46 BCE, during the dictatorship of Julius Caesar. Cicero seems
uncertain of Brutus' political commitments, a situation that
will change dramatically with Brutus' leadership in the assassination of Caesar in 44 BCE.

39. *Atticus*: Titus Pomponius Atticus (110–32 BCE), close friend,
adviser and correspondent of Cicero. He is the subject of a biography by Cornelius Nepos, who was his contemporary.

40. *Quintus Hortensius*: Quintus Hortensius Hortalus (114–49
BCE, consul 69 BCE) was Cicero's older contemporary and rival
for oratorical pre-eminence at Rome.

41. *young Marcus Crassus . . . two Lentuli*: Marcus Licinius Crassus (consul 70 and 55 BCE) had fled to Spain in 87 BCE to avoid
proscription. The whereabouts of Gnaeus Cornelius Lentulus
Clodianus (consul 72 BCE) and Publius Cornelius Lentulus Sura
(consul 71 BCE) are unknown. Clodianus is perhaps best known
for being defeated by the forces of Spartacus.

42. *Antistius . . . Philippus*: Cicero adopts an elegiac tone in commemorating the many talented speakers of his lifetime. Included
here are Publius Antistius (tribune of the plebs 88 BCE), Marcus
Pupius Piso Frugi Calpurnianus (consul 61 BCE), Gnaeus Pomponius (tribune of the plebs 90 BCE), Gaius Papirius Carbo
(tribune of the plebs 90 BCE) and Lucius Marcius Philippus
(consul 91 BCE).

43. *Diodotus the Stoic*: Little is known of him except for his relationship to Cicero. It was fairly common for leading Romans of the late
republic to have Greek intellectuals as part of their large house-
holds: see E. Rawson, *Intellectual Life in the Late Roman Republic*
(Baltimore and London: Johns Hopkins University Press, 1985).

44. *the Stoics call expanded dialectic*: In a famous image, the Stoic
Zeno likened dialectic to a closed fist, rhetoric to the same hand
unclenched.

45. *Marcus Piso or Quintus Pompeius*: Presumably Marcus Pupius
Piso Frugi Calpurnianus (consul 61 BCE) and Quintus Pompeius Rufus (praetor 63 BCE, the year of Cicero's consulship).

46. *Scaevola, Carbo and Antistius*: Quintus Mucius Scaevola (consul 95 BCE), Gaius Papirius Carbo (tribune of the plebs 90 BCE)
and Publius Antistius (tribune of the plebs 88 BCE) were all
killed during the struggles between Marius and Sulla.

47. *Cotta, Curio, Crassus, the Lentuli and Pompey*: Gaius Aure-
    lius Cotta (*c.*124–*c.*74 BCE, consul 75 BCE) had been exiled in
    90 BCE. Gaius Scribonius Curio (consul 76 BCE) had served
    in the war against Mithradates. Marcus Licinius Crassus (con-
    sul 70 and 55 BCE) had fled to Spain in 87 BCE to avoid
    proscription. Gnaeus Pompeius Magnus (106–48 BCE) returned
    to Rome in 81 BCE after defeating the supporters of Mar-
    ius, who had fled to Sicily and Africa. Gnaeus Cornelius
    Lentulus Clodianus (consul 72 BCE) and Publius Cornelius
    Lentulus Sura (consul 71 BCE) may have been with him on
    campaign.

48. *Pomponius, Censorinus and Murena*: Gnaeus Pomponius (trib-
    une of the plebs 90 BCE); probably Gaius Marcius Censorinus,
    an opponent of Sulla; probably Lucius Licinius Murena, general
    in the war against Mithradates and father of the consul of the
    same name (62 BCE).

49. *on behalf of Sextus Roscius*: Cicero's first public case was his
    defence of Sextus Roscius of Ameria against a charge of
    parricide.

50. *Antiochus*: Antiochus of Ascalon (*c.*125–*c.*68 BCE), Greek phi-
    losopher who sought to revive the traditional teachings of the
    Academy against more recent sceptical philosophers.

51. *Demetrius the Syrian*: Unknown.

52. *Menippus of Stratonice*: Greek orator from Stratoniceia in
    Caria.

53. *Dionysius of Magnesia . . . Aeschylus of Cnido and Xenocles of
    Adramyttium*: Dionysius of Magnesia and Aeschylus of Cnido
    are known only from the *Brutus*; Xenocles of Adramyttium is
    said to have made a speech before the Roman senate on behalf
    of Asia during the conflict with Mithradates (Strabo, *Geog-
    raphy* 13.1.66).

54. *the side of the Sicilians*: Cicero refers to his prosecution of
    Verres for extortion and abuse of power as governor of Sicily.

55. *been elected consul*: Cicero held the consulate in 63 BCE.

56. *Pompeian law*: A law of 52 BCE designed to restrict the length
    of trials.

57. *Timaeus*: Greek historian from Sicily (*c.*350–260 BCE).

58. *Hierocles . . . his brother Menecles*: Cicero refers to these two
    admired orators from Alabanda in Caria, Asia Minor, at *On
    the Orator* 2.95 and *Orator* 231.

59. *Aeschines of Miletus*: Aeschines of Miletus reported by other
    ancient sources to be a 'rhetor' and 'political writer'.

60. *Philippus*: Presumably Lucius Marcius Philippus (consul 91 BCE).

61. *strict control of his language*: The Latin text here is muddled. It's possible that Cicero is saying that Hortensius used a disciplined periodic style in his speeches.

62. *defence of Messalla ... when you were away*: Marcus Valerius Messalla Rufus (c.104/3–26 BCE, consul 53 BCE) was acquitted in 51 BCE on a corruption charge at a trial in which he was defended by his uncle Hortensius. See Cicero, *Letters to Atticus* 5.12. Cicero was serving as governor of Cilicia at the time.

63. *from the consulship ... Marcellus*: I.e. from 95 BCE to 50 BCE.

64. *dictatorship of Sulla*: 81 BCE.

65. *Dio of Prusa*: Also known as Dio Chrysostom or Dio Cocceianus (c.40/50–after 110 CE), a rhetorician and preacher of Stoic doctrine who was banished under the emperor Domitian, but returned to Rome and became an associate of the emperor Trajan. His hometown, Prusa (modern Bursa), was in northwest Asia Minor (modern Turkey). Almost eighty speeches attributed to Dio survive from antiquity. On his life and work see S. Swain (ed.), *Dio Chrysostom: Politics, Letters and Philosophy* (Oxford: Oxford University Press, 2000).

66. *Horn of Amaltheia*: In Greek mythology, Amaltheia was a goat-goddess who provided nourishment for Zeus during his infancy on the island of Crete. Her horn, when broken off, was filled with food of various sorts. It is the origin of the modern notion of a Horn of Plenty, or cornucopia.

67. *Demosthenes and Plato*: Demosthenes (384–322 BCE) was the most prominent Greek orator; Plato (c.429–347 BCE) one of the chief philosophers of the ancient world.

68. *praised cities*: Speeches in praise of cities were a common type of epideictic oration, especially under the Roman Empire when Greek cities sought to maintain a sense of local identity and distinction.

69. *Getica ... Getae*: Getae was a name used by Greek and Roman writers to refer to various groups of non-Greek people residing in modern Bulgaria and Romania. Dio's *Getica*, or *Getic Affairs*, may have been an ethnographic account of the region.

70. *Euboean Tale and Praise of a Parrot*: Dio's *Euboean Tale* survives, his *Praise of a Parrot* does not.

71. *Apollonius of Tyana*: A travelling philosopher and holy man who lived during the first century CE. Philostratus' writings include a laudatory biography of the man.

72. *Euphrates the Tyrian*: Stoic philosopher of the first century CE. The Roman author Pliny the Younger was an admirer, as indicated by his Letter 1.10.

73. *It's not right . . . order of exile*: Dio's exact status during his years away from Rome is unclear, as is the reason for his departure.

74. *Then much-scheming Odysseus stripped off his rags*: As Homer, *Odyssey* 22.1, said of Odysseus as he prepares to take vengeance on the men who have been pursuing his wife in his absence.

75. *Trajan*: Marcus Ulpius Traianus (53–117 CE), Roman emperor, 98–117 CE.

76. *Favorinus*: Sophist from Gaul (modern France) who became intellectually and socially prominent at Rome (c.85–155 CE).

77. *Hadrian*: Publius Aelius Hadrianus (76–138 CE), Roman emperor, 117–138 CE. Although emperor of Rome, he demonstrated a strong interest in contemporary Greek culture.

78. *when he is . . . a lesser man*: Quotation from Homer, *Iliad* 1.80.

79. *My teacher Dio*: Dio of Prusa, subject of the preceding biography.

80. *forced to drink hemlock*: The Athenian authorities forced the philosophical gadfly Socrates (469–399 BCE) to drink hemlock for the crimes of which he was convicted. The episode provides the context for several works of classical literature, including Plato's *Apology of Socrates*, *Crito* and *Phaedo*.

81. *Herodes*: Tiberius Claudius Atticus Herodes (101–77 CE) was an Athenian sophist and Roman consul (143 CE). He is also the subject of a biography by Philostratus, not included here.

82. *When will I see you and lick your face*: Possibly a reference to a verse from the comic playwright Aristophanes.

83. *Polemo*: Marcus Antonius Polemo (c.88–144 CE), another sophist and subject of a biography by Philostratus, not included here.

84. *the speeches against Proxenus*: None of the speeches of Favorinus mentioned here survive.

85. *Pyrrhonians*: A school of philosophy that took its name from Pyrrho of Elis (c.365–275 BCE). The Pyrrhonians to whom Philostratus refers, and whom Favorinus defended, deny the possibility of secure human knowledge and are thus treated as early Sceptics.

86. *Scopelian*: Philostratus is almost our only source of information about this teacher, who must have flourished in the late first and early second centuries CE.

87. *dithyrambist*: Dithyramb was a genre of poetry that originated in the cult of Dionysus. As used here, the term seems to
imply a self-indulgent, highly emotional type of language and
performance.
88. *proverbial ox of silence*: See Theognis 651, Aeschylus, *Agamemnon* 36, Philostratus, *Life of Apollonius* 11. The origin
and exact significance of the proverb are uncertain.
89. *Anaxagoras*: A fifth-century BCE philosopher, like Scopelian a
native of Clazomenae. He lost his property in Athens when he
was exiled from that city.
90. *Gigantea ... Homerids*: A *Gigantea* would most likely be a
poem on the exploits of the mythical Giants; Homerids were
professional reciters of epic poetry.
91. *Gorgias of Leontini*: One of most influential speakers and
teachers in Sicily of the late fifth century BCE. He specialized in
a literary style full of balanced phrases and sound effects.
92. *Darius Xerxes*: Presumably Darius I (c.550–486 BCE) and
Xerxes I (518–465 BCE), kings of Persia who directed invasions
of Greece. Among the many themes for declamation were trans-
formative events from earlier periods of history.
93. *shield of Ajax*: Scopelian seems to suggest that if he is in fact
dancing and playing, it is the dancing and playing characteristic
of military training. Ajax was an important Greek hero at the
time of the Trojan War.
94. *Orpheus or Thamyris*: In Greek mythology Orpheus was a
singer so compelling that he could cause rocks and trees to
move to his music, and Thamyris a human musician who sought
to rival the Muses.
95. *Pactolus*: This river in Asia Minor was reputed to carry gold
dust in its waters.
96. *Give me your armour ... take me for you*: Scopelian quotes
Homer, *Iliad* 16.40–41, in which Patroclus seeks to don the
armour of Achilles.

THE ILIAD

Homer

'Look at me. I am the son of a great man. A goddess was my
mother. Yet death and inexorable destiny are waiting for me'

One of the foremost achievements in Western literature, Homer's
Iliad tells the story of the darkest episode in the Trojan War. At
its centre is Achilles, the greatest warrior-champion of the Greeks,
and his refusal to fight after being humiliated by his leader
Agamemnon. But when the Trojan Hector kills Achilles' close
friend Patroclus, he storms back into battle to take revenge –
although knowing this will ensure his own early death. Interwoven
with this tragic sequence of events are powerfully moving descriptions of the ebb and flow of battle, of the domestic world inside
Troy's besieged city of Ilium and of the conflict between the gods
on Olympus as they argue over the fate of mortals.

Originally translated by E. V. Rieu
Revised and updated by Peter Jones with D. C. H. Rieu
Edited with an introduction and notes by Peter Jones

ISBN: 978 0 14 044 794 1

THE ODYSSEY

Homer

'I long to reach my home and see the day of my return. It is my
never-failing wish'

The epic tale of Odysseus and his ten-year journey home after the
Trojan War forms one of the earliest and greatest works of Western
literature. Confronted by natural and supernatural threats – ship-
wrecks, battles, monsters and the implacable enmity of the sea-god
Poseidon – Odysseus must test his bravery and native cunning to
the full if he is to reach his homeland safely and overcome the
obstacles that, even there, await him.

E. V. Rieu's translation of *The Odyssey* was the very first Penguin
Classic to be published, and has itself achieved classic status. For
this edition, Rieu's text has been sensitively revised and a new
introduction added to complement his orignial introduction.

Translated by E. V. Rieu
Revised translation by D. C. H. Rieu
with an introduction by Peter Jones

ISBN: 978 0 14 044 911 2

THE HISTORIES

Herodotus

'No one is fool enough to choose war instead of peace – in peace
sons bury fathers, but in war fathers bury sons'

One of the masterpieces of classical literature, *The Histories*
describes how a small and quarrelsome band of Greek city states
united to repel the might of the Persian empire. But while this epic
struggle forms the core of his work, Herodotus' natural curiosity
frequently gives rise to colourful digressions – a description of the
natural wonders of Egypt; an account of European lake dwellers;
and far-fetched tales of dog-headed men and gold-digging ants.
With its kaleidoscopic blend of fact and legend, *The Histories*
offers a compelling Greek view of the world in the fifth century
BCE.

Translated by Aubrey de Sélincourt
Revised with an introduction and notes by John Marincola

ISBN: 978 0 14 044 908 2

THE THEBAN PLAYS

Sophocles

'O Light! May I never look on you again,
Revealed as I am, sinful in my begetting,
Sinful in my marriage, sinful in shedding of blood'

The legends surrounding the royal house of Thebes inspired
Sophocles (496 –406 BCE) to create a powerful trilogy about
mankind's struggle against fate. *King Oedipus* tells of a man who
brings pestilence to Thebes for crimes he does not realize he has
committed and who then inflicts a brutal punishment upon himself.
With profound insights into the human condition, it is a devestating
portrayal of a ruler brought down by his own oath. *Oedipus at
Colonus* provides a fitting conclusion to the life of the aged and
blinded king, while *Antigone* depicts the fall of the next generation, through the conflict between a young woman ruled by her
conscience and a king too confident of his own authority.

Translated with an introduction by E. F. Watling

ISBN: 978 0 14 044 003 4

REPUBLIC

Plato

'We set about founding the best city we could because we could
be confident that if it was good we would find justice in it'

Republic, Plato's masterwork, was first enjoyed 2,400 years ago
and remains one of the most widely read books in the world: as
a foundational work of Western philosophy, and for the richness
of its ideas and virtuosity of its writing. Presented as a dialogue
between Plato's teacher Socrates and various interlocutors, it is
an exhortation to philosophy, inviting its readers to reflect on the
choices to be made if we are to live the best life available to us.
This complex, dynamic work creates a picture of an ideal society
governed not by the desire for money, power or fame, but by
philosophy, wisdom and justice.

Translated with an introduction and notes by
Christopher Rowe

ISBN: 978 0 14 144 243 3

THE LAST DAYS OF SOCRATES

Plato

'Consider just this, and give your mind to this alone: whether or
not what I say is just'

Plato's account of Socrates' trial and death (399 BCE) is one of
the most significant moments in Western literature and philosophy.
In these four works Plato illustrates Socrates' fundamental belief
in the necessity for us to 'examine ourselves and others', portraying the man himself living and dying by his philosophy. In
Euthyphro, Socrates debates the nature of 'piety'; in *Apology*, he
defends himself in court against the charge of impiety; in *Crito*,
now in prison and awaiting execution, he considers whether escape
can be justified; finally, in *Phaedo*, he reflects on the ethics of
suicide, describes his intellectual history, and mounts a series of
arguments for supposing that we continue to exist as intelligent
beings after death. Then, after a magnificent description of the
earth and its regions, he drinks the hemlock and dies.

Translated with an introduction and notes by
Christopher Rowe

ISBN: 978 0 14 045 549 6

THE ANALECTS

Confucius

'The Master said, "If a man sets his heart on benevolence, he will
be free from evil"'

The *Analects* are a collection of Confucius's sayings brought
together by his pupils shortly after his death in 497 BCE. Together
they express a philosophy, or a moral code, by which Confucius,
one of the most humane thinkers of all time, believed everyone
should live. Upholding the ideals of wisdom, self-knowledge, courage and love of one's fellow man, he argued that the pursuit of
virtue should be every individual's supreme goal. And, while following the Way, or the truth, might not result in immediate or
material gain, Confucius showed that it could nevertheless bring
its own powerful and lasting spiritual rewards.

Translated with an introduction and notes by D. C. Lau

ISBN: 978 0 14 044 348 6

ON THE GOOD LIFE

Cicero

'Good men are always happy'

For the great Roman orator and statesman Cicero (106–43 BCE), 'the good life' was at once a life of contentment and one of moral virtue – and the two were inescapably intertwined. This volume brings together a wide range of his reflections on the importance of moral integrity in the search for happiness. In essays that are articulate, meditative and inspirational, Cicero presents his views on the significance of friendship and duty to state and family, and outlines a clear system of practical ethics that is both simple and universal. These works offer a timeless reflection on the human condition, and a fascinating insight into the mind of one of the greatest thinkers of ancient Rome.

Translated with an introduction by Michael Grant

ISBN: 978 0 14 044 244 1

THE AENEID

Virgil

'Some of us looked in awed wonder at that massive horse ...
which was to be our destruction'

Aeneas the True – son of Venus and of a mortal father – escapes
from Troy after it is sacked by the conquering Greeks. He undergoes many trials and adventures on a long sea journey, from a
doomed love affair in Carthage with the tragic Queen Dido to a
sojourn in the underworld. All the way, the hero is tormented by
the meddling of the vengeful Juno, Queen of the Gods and a bitter
enemy of Troy, but his mother and other gods protect Aeneas from
despair and remind him of his ultimate destiny – to found the
great city of Rome. Reflecting the Roman peoples' great interest
in the 'myth' of their origins, Virgil (70–19 BCE) made the story
of Aeneas glow with a new light in his majestic epic.

Translated with an introduction by W. F. Jackson Knight

ISBN: 978 0 14 044 932 7